The Globalization of Theatre 1870–1930

Between 1895 and 1922, the Anglo-American actor and manager Maurice E. Bandmann (1872–1922) created a theatrical circuit that extended from Gibraltar to Tokyo and included regular tours to the West Indies and South America. With headquarters in Calcutta and Cairo and companies listed on the Indian stock exchange, his operations represent a significant shift towards the globalization of theatre. This study focuses on seven key areas: family networks, the business of theatrical touring, the politics of locality, repertoire and publics, an ethnography of itinerant acting, legal disputes and the provision of theatrical infrastructure. It draws on global and transnational history, network theory and analysis as well as in-depth archival research to provide a new approach to studying theatre in the age of empire.

CHRISTOPHER B. BALME holds the chair in theatre studies at the Ludwig Maximilian University of Munich. His books include *The Theatrical Public Sphere*, published by Cambridge (2014), and he is a senior co-editor of the six-volume *Cultural History of Theatre* (2017). He is also principal investigator of the ERC project 'Developing Theatre'.

Cambridge Studies in Modern Theatre

Series editors

Maria Delgado, *Queen Mary University of London*
Simon Williams, *University of California, Santa Barbara*

The new Cambridge Studies in Modern Theatre series explores, through the discussion of theatre, what it has meant to be modern over the last two centuries. Encompassing a global range of theatrical exchange, cultural productivity and historiography, it encourages contributions that probe both the aesthetic and sociopolitical dimensions of performance. Studies will cover not only plays, but operas, musicals, dance, circus and public ceremonies and rites and incorporate new inflections in Theatre Studies that recognise the importance of space, architecture and time. Building on the first wave of books published under David Bradby's editorship, the series will generate a dialogue as to what constitutes a global theatrical culture within modernity and how local cultures help constitute that global context. It also seeks to explore how theatre operates as an active agent in the political and social world, by bringing communities together and formulating agendas, both in the cultural and social field.

Founding editor

David Bradby

Advisory board

Maggie Gale, *University of Manchester*
Carl Lavery, *University of Glasgow*
Erin Mee, *New York University*
Mark Ravenhill
David Savran, *City University of New York*
Joanne Tompkins, *University of Queensland*
Patricia Ybarra, *Brown University*
Ted Ziter, *New York University*

Books published

Brian Crow and Chris Banfield, *An Introduction to Post-Colonial Theatre*
Maria DiCenzo, *The Politics of Alternative Theatre in Britain, 1968–1990: The Case of 7:84 (Scotland)*
Jo Riley, *Chinese Theatre and the Actor in Performance*
Jonathan Kalb, *The Theatre of Heiner Müller*
Claude Schumacher, ed., *Staging the Holocaust: The Shoah in Drama and Performance*

The Globalization of Theatre 1870–1930

The Theatrical Networks of Maurice E. Bandmann

Christopher B. Balme

Ludwig Maximilian University of Munich

CAMBRIDGE
UNIVERSITY PRESS

CAMBRIDGE
UNIVERSITY PRESS

University Printing House, Cambridge CB2 8BS, United Kingdom

One Liberty Plaza, 20th Floor, New York, NY 10006, USA

477 Williamstown Road, Port Melbourne, VIC 3207, Australia

314–321, 3rd Floor, Plot 3, Splendor Forum, Jasola District Centre,
New Delhi – 110025, India

79 Anson Road, #06-04/06, Singapore 079906

Cambridge University Press is part of the University of Cambridge.

It furthers the University's mission by disseminating knowledge in the
pursuit of education, learning, and research at the highest international
levels of excellence.

www.cambridge.org
Information on this title: www.cambridge.org/9781108487894
DOI: 10.1017/9781108768252

First published 2020

Printed in the United Kingdom by TJ International Ltd, Padstow Cornwall

A catalogue record for this publication is available from the British Library.

Library of Congress Cataloging-in-Publication data

Names: Balme, Christopher B., author.
Title: The globalization of theatre 1870-1930 : the theatrical networks of
Maurice E. Bandmann / Christopher B. Balme.
Description: Cambridge ; New York, NY : Cambridge University Press, 2020. |
Series: Cambridge studies in modern theatre | Includes bibliographical
references and index.
Identifiers: LCCN 2019025501 | ISBN 9781108487894 (hardback) | ISBN
9781108487894 (ebook)
Subjects: LCSH: Bandmann, Maurice E. (Maurice Edward), 1872-1922. |
Theatrical managers – United States – Biography. | Actors – United
States – Biography. | Traveling theater – History. | Theater and
globalization. | Actors – Social networks. | Actor-network theory.
Classification: LCC PN2287.B1644 B35 2020 | DDC 792.02/3092 [B] – dc23
LC record available at https://lccn.loc.gov/2019025501

ISBN 978-1-108-48789-4 Hardback

Contents

Figures

Tables

Acknowledgements

This book was written as part of a larger research project entitled 'Global Theatre Histories: Modernization, Public Spheres and Transnational Theatrical Networks 1860–1960'. It was funded by the DFG (the German Research Society) under the auspices of the Reinhart Koselleck funding scheme devoted to 'high risk' research. It enabled me to assemble a small research team and work on a number of doctoral and postdoctoral projects over a six-year period. There were few strings attached, and in retrospect the Reinhart Koselleck programme remains a remarkable funding initiative in today's highly bureaucratized research environment. In other words, the DFG took a punt, and although the writing of this book took almost twice as long as envisaged, I hope the result shows that the bet paid off. My first word of thanks is to the DFG, without whose assistance this global research endeavour would not have been possible. Equally important, however, were the members of the research team, all of whom have now published their theses and much else besides: Anirban Ghosh (Kolkata/Delhi), Gero Tögl (Graz), Melê Yamomo (Amsterdam), Rashna Nicholson (Mumbai/Hong Kong) and Nic Leonhardt (Munich) were and continue to be stimulating interlocutors on questions of global and transnational theatre. Each member contributed to this book in different ways: through local knowledge, archival exchanges and theoretical discussions. Around this core team we gathered many other students and colleagues at different times, who contributed in myriad ways to the ideas and material found in this book: Tracy C. Davis, Laurence Senelick, Richard Waterhouse, Stephen Hughes, Ayumi Fujioka, Stanca Scholz-Cionca, Hugh Rayner (India Books, Bath), Helena Cowell, Veronica Kelly, Lisa Warrington, Rustom Bharucha, Abha Narain Lambah, Tobias Becker, Priyanka Chatterjee, Darius and Anjali Nicholson, Bishnupriya Dutt and, finally, Vanessa Lopez, without whose splendid archive and generous help this book would be a much lesser work.

A number of research assistants made important contributions over the years, especially Julia Huber, David-Benjamin Berger, Aydin Alinejadsomeeh and Miriam Bornhak.

A fellowship at the Centre for Interweaving Performance Cultures in Berlin provided both writing time and a stimulating environment to discuss some of the ideas arising in this project. My thanks also go to Martin Puchner (Harvard), who invited me to present my research at the Mellon Summer School in 2013 devoted to 'world theatre'. The final writing phase took place under the auspices of a Leverhulme visiting professorship at the Royal Central School of Speech and Drama in London: my sincere thanks to Tony Fisher and Maria Delgado for making this possible. My thanks also go to colleagues at Exeter, Manchester and Portsmouth who were subjected to various chapters: your patience is appreciated. A special word of thanks goes to Nic Leonhardt, who has been a constant fellow traveller in transnational theatre history, friend and colleague for more years than I care to remember. Finally, my sincere gratitude and affection to Micha and Henry, who have been competing with Maurice E. Bandmann for my attention for almost ten years now. It is almost over.

Notes on Currency

The Bandmann Circuit operated across many countries and currencies. Most expenses (rentals, transportation costs, actors' salaries) were paid in local currencies. Following are some of the most common exchange rates for the period 1900–1922.

The conversion is to sterling, whose value changed over the period in question. According to the currency converter of the National Archives, London, the purchasing power of £100 (measured against the same amount in the year 2017) fluctuated in the two decades between 1900 and 1920:

1900	1915	1920	1925
£7,817	£5,899	£2,905	£4,105 (return to the Gold Standard in 1925)

India (1900–1913): 15 rupees = £1
Straits Settlements (1920): $1 = £2s 4d
Egypt (1920): 100 piastres (pt) = £1

Sources: *Statistical Abstract Relating to British India from 1903–04 to 1912–13* (London: His Majesty's Stationary Office, 1915), p. ii; www.nationalarchives.gov.uk/currency-converter/; *The Directory & Chronicle for China, Japan, Corea, Indo-China, Straits Settlements, Malay States, Siam, Netherlands India, Borneo, the Philippines, and etc.* (Hong Kong, 1920), p. 462.

Introduction

When the Anglo-American theatre manager and actor Maurice E. Bandmann died of enteric fever at the Colonial Hospital in Gibraltar on 9 March 1922, shortly before his fiftieth birthday, the event was reported across the English-speaking world from Madras to Singapore and from Cairo to Hong Kong, with many newspapers carrying lengthy obituaries. *The Times of India* called him 'the pioneer of musical comedy in this part of the world', having 'brought to the East some forty or fifty companies'.[1] *The Straits Times* in Singapore claimed that 'he inaugurated the system that will remain as a monument to his memory in theatrical circles'.[2] *The Era*, London's theatrical trade paper, emphasized 'the fine plays and well-equipped companies he presented [which] became famous in all parts of the world, many stars appearing under his management, and the Bandman Opera Company, with all the latest musical comedy successes, was exceedingly popular everywhere in the East'.[3] As these statements indicate, Maurice Bandmann was at the time considered a key figure in what will be called in this book the globalization of theatre. For over two decades, Bandmann was a household name in the theatre world, a guarantor of quality itinerant theatrical entertainment and especially of musical comedy, performed by the legendary Bandmann Opera Company. The Bandmann Circuit, as it was known, extended from Gibraltar to Tokyo and included more than two dozen towns and cities across the Asian continent as well as

---

[1] 'Death of Mr Bandman: An Eastern Impresario', *The Times of India*, 11 March 1922, 12. After 1916, Bandmann's name was usually written with one 'n', and this spelling will be retained where used in quotations and cited sources.
[2] 'The Late Mr. M. E. Bandman: India's Greatest Amusement Provider', *The Straits Times*, 23 March 1922, 11.
[3] 'Death of Maurice E. Bandman', *The Era*, 22 March 1922, 8.

occasional forays to the West Indies and even South America. In terms
of sheer reach and territory covered, Bandmann was a global theatrical
entrepreneur, who, while certainly concentrating on English-speaking
settlements, also performed regularly in Japan to Japanese audiences,
before Chinese in Shanghai and Peking and in numerous cities where
audiences were linguistically mixed.

Yet the 'monument to his memory' remained short-lived, scarcely
surviving beyond the closure of his companies. Despite his global
reach and ubiquitous presence in the theatrical world of late colonialism, today he is largely forgotten, his name at best a footnote in the
annals of musical comedy or Indian and Japanese theatre history.
Although historiographical amnesia is common in theatre over the
years and linked among other things to the ephemeral nature of theatrical performance, the Bandmann case is a special one because of
the spatial and temporal extent of his presence. While theatrical touring outside the United Kingdom at the height of the age of empire
was common, Bandmann developed it on a scale that was unprecedented. Western-style theatre reached places it had never been before
and with a regularity that was new. This was transnational, flexible,
highly mobile, tightly organized commercial theatre dependent on
and responsive to culturally diverse and geographically dispersed
publics.

Maurice Edward Bandmann was born in New York in 1872 as the
second child of two prominent actor-managers, Daniel E. Bandmann
and Millicent Bandmann-Palmer. After completing his schooling at a
classical German *Gymnasium* in Wiesbaden, Bandmann entered the acting profession, touring with both his father in the United States and his
mother in the United Kingdom. Although he quickly became an accomplished actor, he became known in theatrical circles in the 1890s as the
youngest actor-manager in the business. It is his managerial career that
marks a new phase in the organization of theatrical touring. Within a few
years, he controlled four separate troupes in Britain and in 1897 joined
forces with Malcolm Wallace to form the English Comedy Company to
tour Gibraltar, Tangiers, Malta and Egypt, the first stage in building the
circuit that was to extend east all the way to Japan and then westwards
across the Atlantic to the West Indies.

After a first and somewhat unsuccessful foray into India in 1901,
which coincided with the death of Queen Victoria and hence a temporary lack of interest in musical comedy, Bandmann took a light opera
company to the West Indies. In 1902, he embarked on a tour to South
America extending from Brazil to Peru, with a return route that included
Halifax, Nova Scotia. In 1905, Bandmann resumed operations in India

and made Calcutta his headquarters; here he rapidly established a 'circuit', which by his own account took in 'Gibraltar, Malta, Egypt, India, Burmah, with the Malay States, the Straits Settlements, China, Japan, Java and Philippine Islands'.[4] A calendar he issued to prospective theatres along the route in 1906 already figured him as a 'global player' positioned between ships, trains and different theatrical genres, his hand resting nonchalantly on a globe (see cover jacket). Bandmann built, owned, managed or leased numerous theatres along his circuit, thus extending commercial control over all aspects of theatre production and reception.

A stranger to modesty and an expert in self-advertisement, for over twenty years Bandmann and his name stood for high-quality theatrical entertainment aimed at European and local audiences alike. As a Singapore paper noted in 1906, 'the name of Bandmann is a sort of guinea stamp among itinerant theatrical circles'.[5] In 1900 he floated the Mediterranean and the East Entertainment Syndicate, his first joint-stock company. This was followed in 1914 by the Bandman Varieties Ltd, and some years later by the Bandman Eastern Circuit Ltd (he dropped the second, Germanic-looking 'n' from his name because of the war), which controlled his many interests, including cinema distribution. These were public companies listed on the Indian stock exchange.[6] Upon his premature death in 1922, his personal fortune was assessed at around £33,000, the equivalent of just under £1 million in today's currency, a modest fortune perhaps by impresario standards, but a fortune nonetheless. Despite his death, Bandman Varieties and the Bandman Eastern Circuit companies continued to operate in India well into the 1930s.

This book will focus on Bandmann's transnational theatrical networks and how they emerged, functioned and ultimately dissolved in the context of early globalization. These networks were based on theatrical touring, perhaps the most under-researched of the various manifestations of transnational, even global, theatre in the period under scrutiny. The focus of this book is threefold. Firstly, this volume covers the relational structures created by theatrical circuits operating around the turn of the century that were transitioning from the almost moribund actor-manager model to complex, syndicated systems of theatrical entrepreneurship such as the theatrical circuit established

[4] *Weekly Sun* (Singapore), 30 September 1911, 12.
[5] *Eastern Daily Mail and Straits Morning Advertiser*, 16 February 1906, 2.
[6] See 'Variety Theatres. Big Scheme for "All-Red Circuit"', *The Straits Times*, 10 March 1914, 2.

by Bandmann. Secondly, the book examines how theatre responded to and participated in the processes known as the first phase of globalization – roughly the period extending from the opening of the Suez Canal in 1869 to the outbreak of the First World War in 1914. Aided by technological developments such as steamships, railways and telegraphic communication, this period saw an almost unprecedented expansion of peoples, empires and economic activity that led quite literally to global connectivity, with many parallels to current conceptions of globalization. It also saw an unprecedented expansion of theatre-building, the provision of theatrical infrastructure in which Bandmann was heavily involved. The third area concerns how spectators and performers responded to and were involved in this kind of theatrical globalization under conditions of mobility. For the former group the question is how did highly heterogeneous publics respond to the theatrical repertoire on offer? For the latter we need to ask how theatrical labour was organized under conditions of extreme duress – situations of propinquity lasting between eighteen months and two years – which sometimes resulted in legal action by employees and management.

These heterogeneous factors will be framed within the coordinates of network theory, a primarily sociological approach which is now beginning to be adapted for historical research. It offers a way to comprehend and analyse a complex of phenomena that combined affective (familial) interaction, commerce, theatrical repertoire, continual mobility, the politics of locality and legal disputes. Each of these elements comprises nodes in the network of performers on the move. If we apply the usual criteria for justifying arts-based research – the innovation and creativity of the artist and works – then Bandmann's companies provide little to interest the humanities scholar: his repertoire was derivative, essentially touring versions of London hits. The originality and uniqueness of the Bandmann enterprise was the network itself – its complex pattern of interconnected elements that had to mesh to succeed. The remarkable achievement is the sheer extent and complexity of a network that extended geographically from London to Japan and was held together by shipping timetables, a constant stream of telegrams, contracts, shifting jurisdictions and an indefatigable manager at the centre.

Theatrical Networks

The material presented in this book is almost entirely absent from theatre histories, lexica and archives. Why is this? And perhaps more importantly, how can one examine this material in such a way that its dynamics and interconnections become visible? I propose that network theory can offer a fruitful avenue for historiographical recuperation. There are, of course, as many network theories as there are networks: social, technological, biological, political and economic, to name only some. What connects most of these quite disparate concepts and theories is a common emphasis on relational structures. By definition, relational structures are changing configurations of agents and nodes that constitute relay points around which communication and interaction take place. Relational structures are dependent on the actions of other agents in the network. Some forms of network analysis attempt to plot these interconnections visually to demonstrate degrees of connectivity and tend to privilege aggregated data demonstrating multiple connections and correlations. Such connections take precedence over monocausal factors such as class, sex, clan membership or individual agency. This has been termed the 'anticategorical imperative', an approach which rejects attempts to explain human behaviour or social processes 'solely in terms of the categorical attributes of actors, whether individual or collective'.[7] This book will draw on two main strands of network theory and methodology: historical network analysis and actor-network theory (often playfully abbreviated as ANT).[8]

Historical network analysis adapts social network theory and applies it to historical phenomena. The former draws on both mathematical and economic approaches that have led in turn to the emergence of a branch of sociology which employs network theory as an analytical tool to explain economic behaviour. Sociologists such as Mark Granovetter have argued that networks can be divided into strong (homophilic) and weak (heterophilic) types. Strong networks such as extended families evince a high degree of homophily, a tendency to gravitate to people similar to ourselves. Granovetter's and many subsequent studies have, however, demonstrated that, generally speaking, heterophilic (or weak) ties are the more beneficial because a predominance of homophilic ties would lead to a highly fragmented world. In a society with relatively few weak ties, 'new ideas will spread slowly, scientific endeavours will be handicapped, and subgroups separated by race, ethnicity, geography, or other characteristics will have difficulty reaching a modus vivendi'.[9] In contrast, heterophilic networks, because of their reliance on weak ties, can much more easily form connections with other networks, a precondition for innovation and adaptation.

---

[7] Mustafa Emirbayer and Jeff Goodwin, 'Network Analysis, Culture, and the Problem of Agency', *American Journal of Sociology* 99(6) (May 1994): 1411–54, here 1414.
[8] See Charles Wetherell, 'Historical Social Network Analysis', *International Review of Social History* 43 (December 1998): 125–44.
[9] Mark Granovetter, 'The Strength of Weak Ties: A Network Theory Revisited', *Sociological Theory* 1 (1983): 201–33, here 202.

Almost all network theories work with concepts of nodes, edges and hubs (or their terminological equivalents). Nodes are entities (people, events, places, etc.) that stand in a relation of connectedness to other nodes. These connective relations are known as 'edges'. Hubs are usually understood as nodes with a particularly high degree of connectedness: they have an unusually large number of edges. Because edges can differ greatly in their intensity and degree of importance for a network, they are differentiated according to three main categories of centrality: *degree* centrality refers to the number of edges radiating from a specific node; *betweenness* centrality designates the importance of a specific node in a network (usually the number of connections it enables); while *closeness* centrality refers to the proximity of a node to other nodes (this might influence a person's access to information). According to Freeman, a high degree of betweenness centrality is necessary to control communication, which is of key importance, for example, to both a mother of a family and a theatrical entrepreneur.[10]

In his book *The Square and the Tower: Networks and Power, from the Freemasons to Facebook*, historian Niall Ferguson gives historical network analysis a new urgency. He offers an incisive review of network theory, both mathematical and sociological, before arriving at an oversimplified (as he states) distinction between hierarchies and networks.[11] His argument is the following: very broadly, historians have been overly focused on hierarchical structures because these leave behind the kinds of archives that historians like to study, whereas networks generally do not. Networks, on the other hand, tend to be more creative than hierarchies; we should expect a network-driven disruption of hierarchies that cannot reform themselves. Ferguson is aware that hierarchies are just a particular form of network with the special feature that they form nodes and edges in vertical rather than horizontal structures that index power and control. If we are looking for innovation, then we should be looking at the points of contact between diverse networks. His broad historical argument is that hierarchies are the dominant mode of governmentality between 1790 and 1970, the so-called corporate age. Recent times – since the 1970s – have seen a reassertion of network structures.

Aided by a growing selection of software, network analysis has become famous for its ability to visualize large amounts of data in order

---

[10] For this distinction explained in mathematical terms, see Linton C. Freeman, 'A Set of Measures of Centrality Based on Betweenness', *Sociometry* 40 (1977): 35–41; and 'Centrality in Social Networks: Conceptual Clarification', *Social Networks* 1 (1978/79): 215–39, here 226.

[11] Niall Ferguson, *The Square and the Tower: Networks and Power, from the Freemasons to Facebook* (New York: Penguin, 2018), xx.

to demonstrate the various connections that exist between nodes: not only their relations to one another but also the degree or intensity of the relations.[12] Numerous studies have demonstrated the potential of visualizations to represent 'centrality' as previously defined. Historical network analysis enables us to plot ties, relations and connections. The argument put forward here is that the Bandmann Circuit was a complex network predicated on weak ties. We can see that the circuit, if we view it as a network and not just as a succession of ports of call, had multifarious edges (Fig. I.1). It intersected not just with the performers in the troupe but with venues, copyright holders, the stock market, colonial and municipal officials, and business partners. The elucidation of these varied and often complex connections is a central task of this book.

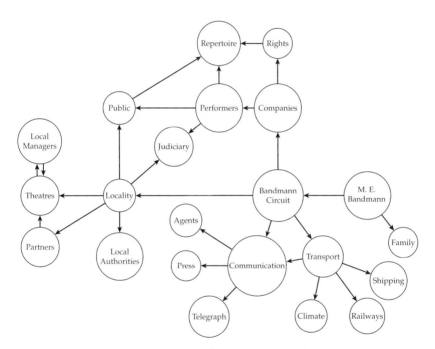

Figure I.1 A visualization of the Bandmann Circuit emphasizing its betweenness centrality.

12 The origins of network visualization lie probably in J. L. Moreno's famous 'sociograms' of school children who were asked the simple question 'Who would you like to sit next to?' The results demonstrated a highly uneven distribution of affections between obvious class favourites and a few isolated loners. See www.martingrandjean.ch/social-network-analysis-visualization-morenos-sociograms-revisited/ (last accessed 1 April 2019).

Historical network analysis has, however, some shortcomings. It does not model diachronic change well, nor is it particularly sensitive to interpretive ambiguity. The latter feature is one of the strengths of actor-network theory. Actor-network theory, or ANT, is a particular variant of social network analysis that emerged in the 1970s in the field of the sociology of science, or what is now known as science studies. It is linked to a group of French sociologists, the best known of whom is Bruno Latour, but also includes Michel Callon and the English sociologist John Law. Broadly and abstractly speaking, and at the risk of some simplification, ANT looks at interconnected networks of exchange known as actor networks. Actor networks consist in turn of interrelated nodes and actants in which human beings are as much relational effects as initiating, all-controlling subjects.[13] The revolutionary and controversial move of ANT has been to make non-social entities – microbes and scallops, to cite two famous examples – into actors. From objects being acted upon by conventional social actors (i.e. human beings), they were re-conceptualized as part of a network in which, under certain circumstances, they are seen to have considerable agency. The multiple perspectives and descriptive imperatives of ANT can help us rethink the complex relationships between theatrical trading, imperial formations and an understanding of what it meant to circulate and perform theatre in the first age of globalization.

Theatre and performance studies have engaged energetically with ANT in recent years as opposed to historical network analysis, which has largely been ignored. This is probably because, as Laura Smith-Doerr and Walter Powell argue, actor-network theory 'stresses the process of translation, in which problems are redefined, supporters mobilized, and ideas and practices transformed in *the process of interpretation*' (my emphasis).[14] Marlis Schweitzer and Leo Cabranes-Grant have both demonstrated how actor-network theory can be productively employed for theatre history. In her book *Transatlantic Broadway: The Infrastructural Politics of Global Performance*, Schweitzer examines 'the transnational performances of ocean liners, piers, telegraph cables, telegrams, typewriters, office spaces, newspapers, and postcards' and

---

[13] The term 'actant' is a terminological residue of Greimasian semiotics that exerted a considerable influence on Latour and his group in the early period of research in the 1970s. It refers to any forces that exert agency within a network, ranging from natural forces to individuals and collective bodies.

[14] Laurel Smith-Doerr and Walter W. Powell, 'Networks and Economic Life', in Neil Smelser and Richard Swedberg, eds., *The Handbook of Economic Sociology* (Princeton: Princeton University Press; Russell Sage Foundation, 2005), 379–402, here 42.

asks how these objects, 'as participants in a series of complicated networks, transformed the machinery of US theatre as well as the everyday practices of those who produced and consumed it'.[15] Cabranes-Grant has demonstrated persuasively how ANT can be harnessed to explain 'ethnographically' historical intercultural encounters – in this case in early modern Mexico. Both Schweitzer and Cabranes-Grant recognize that Latour's interest in the performative aspect of actor networks, where agents modify a relation in the act of connection, is especially productive for theatre and performance studies. For Cabranes-Grant, Latour's actor-network theory is attractive 'because it portrays the social as poiesis, a series of labors. ANT provides a methodology of transitions, a critical discourse in which cultural structures are manifestations of flow: not closure.'[16]

Methodologically, actor-network theory can be considered a form of ethnography where techniques and practices of fieldwork and participant observation are applied to contemporary society and its many fields. Latour states that ANT is 'simply another way of being faithful to the insights of ethnomethodology'.[17] Darryl Cressman refers to ANT's 'ethnographic bent: micro-level studies of the labs and boardrooms tracing how actors exert influence over the trajectory of scientific and technical innovation'.[18] Since ethnography tends to focus on the present, the question poses itself how theatre historians can extend such insights gathered from present-day laboratories and boardrooms and make them useful for their concerns. And does not ANT have tautological implications for theatre, not the least of which is the term 'actor', but more so because theatre is intrinsically 'social' on account of its conditions of collaborative production and collective reception? If we simply revisit the usual objects of theatre research – plays, performances, performers, audiences and occasionally theatre buildings – then there is a real danger that we simply reformulate old insights with new metaphors. A more productive application of actor-network theory would require a

---

[15] Marlis Schweitzer, *Transatlantic Broadway: The Infrastructural Politics of Global Performance* (Basingstoke: Palgrave Macmillan, 2015), 4.
[16] Leo Cabranes-Grant, *From Scenarios to Networks: Performing the Intercultural in Colonial Mexico* (Evanston: Northwestern University Press, 2016), 25. For a cogent discussion of actor-network theory in relation to theatre history, see also Gero Tögl, *The Bayreuth Enterprise 1848–1914* (Würzburg: Königshausen & Neumann, 2017).
[17] Bruno Latour, 'On Recalling ANT', in John Law and J. Hassard, eds., *Actor-Network Theory and After* (Oxford: Blackwell, 1999), 15–26, here 19.
[18] Darryl Cressman. 'A Brief Overview of Actor-Network Theory: Punctualization, Heterogeneous Engineering & Translation', here 7. www.sfu.ca/content/dam/sfu/cmns/research/centres/cprost/recentpapers/2009/0901.pdf (last accessed 1 April 2019).

recalibration of epistemological assumptions regarding why we do not know anything about Maurice E. Bandmann and his global activities. If the *person* did not register in the theatre historical archive, then perhaps his circuit might. An ANT perspective would force us to concern ourselves more with the network than with the biographical person of Maurice Edward Bandmann. As Schweitzer states, an actor-network approach leads to a concern with objects and processes such as shipping and railway networks. To her list we could add newspapers, advance agents, the colonial judiciary, storms and tropical heat.[19] Actants would include texts, companies of performers, contracts and even courts, all of which acted upon each other in 'webs of relations'.[20]

Although one has not needed network theory to study Shakespeare, for example, the same cannot be said, I argue, for Maurice Bandmann's now forgotten 'circuit' and indeed the whole branch of itinerant theatrical activity, which is also largely overlooked and often not even recorded in our theatre archives.[21] While we can certainly map the activities of Bandmann and his many colleagues onto commonly understood historical processes such as commodification, imperial expansion and colonial power structures, in this book they will be viewed from the perspective of connectivity.[22] In the chapter entitled 'First Move: Localizing the Global' of his book *Reassembling the Social*, Latour emphasizes the importance of examining connectivity itself:

We have to lay continuous connections leading from one local interaction to the other places, times, and agencies through which a local site is made to do something. This means that we have to follow the path indicated by the process of delegation or translation.[23]

---

[19] On the networked newspaper in this period, see G. M. Winder, 'Imagining Geography and Citizenship in the Networked Newspaper: "La Nación" Reports the Assassination at Sarajevo, 1914', *Historical Social Research/Historische Sozialforschung*, Special Issue, 35(1) (2010): 140–66.

[20] John Law, 'Actor Network Theory and Material Semiotics', in Bryan S. Turner, ed., *The New Blackwell Companion to Social Theory* (Oxford: Blackwell, 2009), 141–58, here 141.

[21] There is, for example, no entry on Bandmann in the standard four-volume reference work *Who Was Who in the Theatre: 1912–1976. A Biographical Dictionary of Actors, Actresses, Directors, Playwrights, and Producers of the English-Speaking Theatre* (Detroit: Gale Research, 1978). There is also currently no Wikipedia entry on him.

[22] Other theatre entrepreneurial networks are better known, such as J. C. Williamson in Australia and I. W. Schlesinger's African Theatre Trust in South Africa. Nevertheless, the method I propose here could be used to analyse them as well.

[23] Bruno Latour, *Reassembling the Social: An Introduction to Actor-Network-Theory* (Oxford: Oxford University Press, 2005), 173.

'Translation' is a technical term in ANT vocabulary and refers to a relation that 'induces two mediators into coexisting'.[24] Mediators in turn transform and modify the elements they carry (as opposed to intermediaries, which do not). ANT is in this sense a theory that tries to analyse in precise terms the manifold dynamics of how various entities relate to one another in different degrees of intensity and transformative agency.

Following this perspective, we need to conceptualize itinerant theatre such as the Bandmann Circuit as a set of interconnected nodes that together constitute the relay points or 'edges' for these associations. We can try and map these nodes and their forms of agency; this means that 'connections, vehicles and attachments are brought into the foreground'.[25] We must try and conceptualize this network of associations across time and space spanning thousands of miles, interacting in more than two dozen locales, each regulated by a different legal system, cultural mores, audience tastes and compositions.

Actor-network theory is not just something that is 'applied' to a preexisting object of research; research itself constitutes an actor network in its own right. Prior to the accessibility of digital technology, it could be argued, the Bandmann Circuit did not exist historiographically. The type of research to be described in this book has only been made possible with the digital revolution and the advent of digitalized newspapers, books and other resources, which enable peripatetic artists to be tracked. This technology ultimately prescribes what is discoverable and knowable and thus is also a key 'actor'.

In order to examine Bandmann's circuit (and the many others like it), it is necessary to investigate the different nodes that were required for it to function at all. Besides the managerial role of Bandmann himself, which was obviously crucial but ultimately not essential (his circuit continued to function, albeit in an attenuated form, after his death), it is more productive to try and grasp if not the totality at least the multiaxial nature of the system and its various nodes. These can be represented as in Fig. I.1. In this conceptualization of a theatrical network, it is not exclusively the person Maurice E. Bandmann who forms the central node, but rather the circuit itself, although he certainly saw himself in this role. The biographical person Bandmann is only one fulcrum exerting pressure on the rest of the network.

---

[24] Ibid., 108.
[25] Ibid., 220.

Of central importance for any actor network are what Latour terms 'mediators', as mentioned earlier. These are transporters of meaning that 'transform, translate, distort and modify the meaning or the elements they are supposed to carry'.[26] In this sense they should be distinguished from 'intermediaries', where there is no such distortion and modification. In Latour's terminology, an intermediary is a 'black box' where input equals output and no modification takes place.[27] In both cases, the function of a mediator can be human or non-human: a scientific panel of experts can be an intermediary, or a machine such as a computer can be a mediator. Concepts such as 'mediators' carry major epistemological implications. A conventional way of looking at touring theatre such as the Bandmann Circuit would be to regard the passage of productions along it and measure their degree of modification and 'distortion' from the originating source – the original Gaiety production in London – to their versions in Bombay or Calcutta or Yokohama. Our object of interest would be, then, the local production of meaning, whether colonial or indigenous or some mixture of the two.

A less conventional and more networked way of looking at touring practices would examine certain mediators in terms of the connectivity the Bandmann Circuit exerted on the social fabric of the many communities it interacted with on a regular basis. This is clearly a difficult question to answer in the light of a complete dearth of research into Bandmann's activities. Following ANT terminology, it would be necessary to understand a term such as 'social fabric' quite literally as a kind of texture of interwoven connections and associations. The diagram of the Bandmann Circuit gives an indication of the different weaves or nodes in this fabric. I propose, therefore, to discuss familiar topics of theatre history – repertoire, theatre buildings, publics and actors – but also some less familiar ones such as enterprise capitalism, incorporated companies and litigation, from the perspective of 'mediation' in the ANT sense of the term. In each case, I suggest, such mediators or mediation processes can be seen to 'translate, distort and modify meaning', not in a pejorative sense but as factors that cast light on the social dynamics of touring theatre in the first age of globalization.

[26] Ibid., 39.
[27] Ibid.

Transnational Theatre in the First Age of Globalization

Many historians regard the period between 1870 and 1914 as a 'first phase of globalization' in as much as it evinces many parallels with current uses of the term, even though the word 'globalization' does not appear until the 1960s.[28] The watershed for this reading of world history is, according to Michael Geyer and Charles Bright, the worldwide 'processes of unsettlement' emerging in the mid- to late nineteenth century, which saw an accelerating 'mobilization of peoples, things, ideas, and images and their diffusion in space and time' and the efforts of both local rulers and global regimes (empires) to 'settle' them.[29] The tensions ensuing from these dynamic processes form a central focus of the discipline of global history. Concomitant with these tensions are technological advancements such as the laying of telegraph lines, the introduction of fast steamships and the growing networks of colonial and administrative centres, as well as the rapid spread of newspapers, which all combined to create the prerequisites for globalization in almost the present sense: a compression of time and space, movement towards standardization and a growing sensation of being part of an interconnected world.

The importance of technological innovations for theatrical touring was already evident to contemporaries. In his preface to Daniel Bandmann's account of his three-and-a-half-year world tour in the 1880s, Barnard Gisby highlights the effects of technological innovation on travel and theatre:

---

[28] Niall Ferguson, for example, draws this comparison: 'a hundred years ago, globalization was celebrated in not dissimilar ways (the earth is flat) as goods, capital and labour flowed freely from England to the ends of the earth ... In 1914 the first age of globalization ended with a spectacular bang.' Niall Ferguson, *The War of the World: Twentieth-Century Conflict and the Descent of the West* (New York: Penguin Press, 2006), 643. One should add that capital and labour flows did not just issue from England but were much more multidirectional. England was, however, by far the largest foreign investor of the time. See in the same vein John Darwin: 'By the 1870s, it becomes possible to speak of a global economy in which improvements in transport and communication by telegraph had encouraged the integration of markets and the convergence of prices in ordinary foodstuffs – perhaps the best indicator that the world was becoming a single economic space.' *Unfinished Empire: The Global Expansion of Britain* (London: Penguin Press, 2012), esp. 179.

[29] Michael Geyer and Charles Bright, 'World History in a Global Age', *American Historical Review* 100 (October 1995): 1034–60, here 1053.

Science has wrought marvels.... Steam and electricity ... have revolutionized conceptions and thoughts in relation to the world, encircling it with a network of appliances that makes communication and travel between the most distant places possible, so that with a not very considerable amount of money and a few months of leisure the most ordinary mortal may become a rival of Captain Cook.[30]

But beyond these 'appliances', Gisby develops an idea of globalization *avant la lettre* when he argues that modern science, through its discoveries, explorations, inventions, and adaptations of natural forces, 'has ... made man conscious of the limitations of the world as a whole ... that humanity lives and moves and has its being in a very small place; that the orb which is its home is "cribbed, cabined, and confined" – an atom-world in the immensities of space and the eons of eternity'.[31] This is essentially an early formulation of the familiar globalization topos of the shrinking world that reappears with each technological shift.

Parallel with these demographic and technological changes, theatre too began to internationalize or 'globalize'. This pattern was repeated throughout many of the former and existing colonial empires, particularly in South East Asia and Latin America. In addition to the construction of permanent theatre spaces, the same period saw a massive expansion of theatrical touring, which began to be organized on an industrial scale and brought European-style theatre to all of those parts of the globe that could be reached by steamship or rail or a combination of both. Telegraph networks, countless local newspapers and syndicated news agencies provided the communications infrastructure enabling the touring companies to find their audiences. The same networks that brought European troupes to Asia and South America also enabled movement in other directions as Japanese troupes came to the United States and Europe, Chinese opera moved around the Pacific rim[32] and Parsi theatre spread throughout the Indian subcontinent and into South East Asia, where it generated local variants (*bangsawan* in Malay regions and *komedi stambul* and *likay* in the Dutch East Indies).[33] Manila became

---

[30] Preface to Daniel E. Bandmann, *An Actor's Tour; or, Seventy Thousand Miles with Shakespeare* (Boston: Upham and Co., 1885), v.

[31] Ibid., vi. The phrase 'cribbed, cabined, and confined' is a common misquotation from *Macbeth* III, iv: 'But now I am cabined, cribbed, confined, bound in.'

[32] See Daphne Pi-Wei Lei, *Operatic China: Staging Chinese Identity across the Pacific* (New York: Palgrave Macmillan, 2006).

[33] On Parsi theatre, see Somanatha Gupta, *The Parsi Theatre: Its Origins and Development*, trans. Kathryn Hansen (Calcutta: Seagull Books, 2005). For the other South Asian forms, see Matthew Isaac Cohen, *The Komedie Stamboel: Popular Theater in Colonial Indonesia, 1891–1903* (Athens, OH: Ohio University Press and KITLV Press, 2006); and *Performing Otherness: Java and Bali on International Stages, 1905–1952* (Basingstoke: Palgrave Macmillan, 2010).

a hub for opera and European music in the second half of the nineteenth century, providing highly trained singers and musicians for the burgeoning Western-style music culture around the Pacific Rim.[34]

The rapid spread of theatre in this period was largely the work of theatrical managers, entrepreneurs and agents, who established networks for dissemination of the theatrical traffic. Of these players, Bandmann was the most prominent because he developed theatrical touring on a hitherto unimagined scale. Although he drew most of his productions from London, the centre of his operations was not the British capital, however, but rather India, where he had his headquarters in Calcutta, and during the First World War, in Cairo. His operations represent a significant shift towards the globalization of theatre. The period immediately pre-dating the First World War saw a major change in theatrical touring, which reflected the economic structures of capitalism in the age of empire. Prior to this time, it was, of course, quite normal practice to tour theatre. Its organizational form was based, however, on the actor-manager, an almost premodern business model in as much as at the close of the nineteenth century it did not differ greatly from the touring English or Italian troupes of the late sixteenth and early seventeenth centuries. It was characterized by strong familial ties, often a husband and wife as the lead performers and business managers in personal union, supported by about a dozen performers. The geographical reach was mostly limited to particular regions, with companies seldom leaving the borders of the United Kingdom. Bandmann's theatre, on the other hand, was organized along the principles of joint-stock companies with limited liability. Its range was not regional or national but instead global and conditioned by continual mobility.

Theatre under Conditions of Mobility

Touring theatre is predicated on mobility, which by definition poses challenges both to those producing and those receiving it as well as for theatre historians trying to study it. Mobility follows logically from the processes of 'unsettlement', characteristic of nineteenth-century globalization. The dominant epistemological paradigm in theatre studies has been to privilege locality in its depth and boundedness, assuming a stable, albeit by no means homogeneous, cultural matrix: Shakespeare's London or Molière's Paris connote a symmetrical relationship between place, performance and performers. It is clear that the

---

[34] See MeLê Yamomo, *Theatre and Music in Manila and the Asia Pacific, 1869–1946: Sounding Modernities* (London: Palgrave Macmillan, 2018).

theatrical landscape traversed by Bandmann and his companies was anything but culturally homogeneous; it was characterized by extreme cultural mobility.

Theatre historian Nic Leonhardt has argued that this period saw the emergence of a new 'theatrical geography' and a reconfiguration of the global 'theatrescape'. The latter term she adapts from Arjun Appadurai's famous global 'scapes', with which he conceptualizes the flow of ideas, media, finance and people across national boundaries as symptoms of the globalization of the 1990s.[35] Concretely, theatre-scapes in the context of early globalization correspond to Appadurai's 'mediascapes' and refer to the 'relational dynamics of a worldwide distribution of theatre as well as the global or transnational cultural mobility of theatrical performers, artists and managers since the mid-nineteenth century'.[36] Leonhardt also draws on Stephen Greenblatt's much-cited 'manifesto' on cultural mobility, with its five principles: lit-eralness, attention to hidden as well as conspicuous movement, contact zones, the tension between individual agency and structural restraint, and the sensation of rootedness.[37] At the centre of these new theatre-scapes are the diverse publics with whom ultimately cultural mobility needed to engage.

Central to the present analysis are the third and fifth 'pillars' of Greenblatt's manifesto: the former concerns 'contact zones' and 'mobilisers', while the latter addresses the sensation of 'rootedness'. Contact zones are places, locales or relay stations where cultural goods are exchanged. They constitute interfaces where groups of people with different religious, ethnic and social backgrounds meet and interact. Vital to the sustainability of contact zones are so-called mobilizers that pass through them. These are agents and intermediaries who facilitate contact and catalyse the exchange of cultural goods. Diplomats provide one example of mobilizers; merchants, who profit from contact zones

---

[35] Arjun Appadurai, *Modernity at Large: Cultural Dimensions of Globalization* (Minneapolis: University of Minnesota Press, 1996).

[36] Nic Leonhardt, "'From the Land of the White Elephant through the Gay Cities of Europe and America": Re-routing the World Tour of the Boosra Mahin Siamese Theatre Troupe (1900)', *Theatre Research International* 40(2) (2015): 140–55, here 142–3. The concept of theatrescapes also forms the basis of a digital mapping project developed by Leonhardt at LMU Munich which utilizes geo- and chronoreferenc-ing. See http://theatrescapes.gwi.uni-muenchen.de/#home (last accessed 1 April 2019). The site provides a searchable, interactive database of over 1,000 theatres built in the nineteenth and early twentieth centuries.

[37] Stephen Greenblatt, *Cultural Mobility: A Manifesto* (Cambridge: Cambridge University Press, 2010), 250–2.

economically, are another. Itinerant troupes, with their entourage of actors, musicians, make-up artists and technicians as well as the local theatre owners, agents and journalists, also fulfilled such 'mobilising functions'. The fifth pillar of Greenblatt's mobility manifesto stresses the importance of rootedness. He argues that mobility studies are subject to a paradox: 'it is impossible to understand mobility without also understanding the glacial weight of what appears bounded and static'. Moreover, culturally mobile platforms often, in a somewhat contradictory manner, 'produce results that are strikingly enmeshed in particular times and places and local cultures'.[38] The dialectical relationship between mobility and stasis that underpins the concept of cultural mobility is also at the heart of itinerant theatre and its publics.

Volume Outline

Each chapter in the book examines a node in the theatrical network and how it contributed to ensuring the efficacy of the whole. The first chapter will situate Maurice E. Bandmann's activities in the context of his family network. He was the child of two itinerant and prominent actors, Daniel E. Bandmann and Millicent Bandmann-Palmer, while his older sister, Lily Bandmann, also became an actor and spent her professional life touring the British provinces with her husband, William Maclaren. Both his parents and his sister adhered to the actor-manager model. Theatrical families were often informal unions, peripatetic and sometimes dysfunctional, ending often in separation, divorce and highly publicized litigation. Theatrical families in this sense often defied prevailing moral standards. Following the 'actors' in the double sense of performers and nodes of a network, theatrical families of the Bandmann kind were both affective as well as economic networks, held together at least initially by bonds of emotional attraction and, later, economic dependency. What distinguishes the theatrical family network from other models of the time is the extreme mobility required of it. Both Maurice and his sister, Lily, were born on tour, and both spent most of their lives on the road. Both married within the profession and combined symbiotically theatrical and marital activity.

The family as an economic unit also points towards Chapter 2, where the economic and organizational aspects will be examined. One of the main arguments of this book is that Maurice E. Bandmann shifted to a new, 'modern' managerial model, compared to that practised by his

---

[38] Ibid., 252.

parents and sister who plied their theatrical trade on the old model. Theatrical production under conditions of liberal capitalism, risk-management, investment, and incorporated, limited liability companies was the norm in a period and culture where state support for the theatre was known only as peculiar continental habit. The special nature of Bandmann's operations was its vast extent, operating in at least three empires and a score of countries. The transnational nature of the circuit meant that he needed to coordinate various questions of commercial and copyright law, local partnerships, communication with the press, corporate identity, logistics and the leasing, and on occasions even construction, of theatres. To operate his business, Bandmann required intermediaries and mediators of different kinds; these included advance agents, local newspapers and theatre owners. Of these intermediaries, business partnerships were perhaps the most important, as they connected the peripatetic entrepreneur with the culture of the locale, which became a distinguishing characteristic of the Bandmann network. The partnerships Bandmann entered into in Bombay, Calcutta and Cairo, where his operations were physically based, were particularly important. In order to build the Royal Opera House in Bombay, he formed a partnership with a Parsi coal merchant and entrepreneur, Jehangir Framji Karaka. In Calcutta, where he co-owned two large theatres – the Empire and the Theatre Royal – Bandmann formed a partnership with an Armenian-born property investor, Arratoon Stephen. Later he alternately joined forces and competed with Calcutta-based Parsi merchant Jamshedji Framji Madan (1857–1923), who was also expanding his operations with theatrical performances and was to establish the foundations of a local film industry. In Cairo he entered into a partnership with the Italian 'Chevalier' Augusto Dalbagni (1874–1951), who had been an Egyptian resident since the 1890s and had established himself as an impresario.

Chapter 3 examines the politics of locality for Bandmann's itinerant operations. The Bandmann Circuit comprised roughly two dozen towns and cities that the companies visited on a regular basis. If the commercial operations were on one level largely de-spatialized (the companies played largely the same repertoire wherever they performed), each locality required specific knowledge; the infrastructure was highly disparate, and the local politics varied in the extreme. This chapter investigates some of these localities, selected both for their cultural specificities and their micropolitics.

As mentioned earlier, localizing the global in terms of network theory requires a perspective that sees locality not just in splendid isolation but also as a set of interconnected nodes combining both entrepreneurial and political dynamics. From this perspective, the port of call Singapore is important both as one colonial city among many and also as an entrepôt enabling the distribution of opium exports. Bombay and Calcutta as well as Alexandria and Cairo could be seen in these terms, broadly understood. Both the Indian cities were important in their own right as major cities with relatively large theatre-going populations, but they were also important as stopping-off points for extended tours throughout the Indian subcontinent. Coming from the West, Bombay was usually the first port of call where the repertoire and new performers were tested. Its response was invariably reported in the press both inland and further along the circuit. In Japan, Yokohama had the same function.

Bandmann's engagement with the colonial project took place mainly at the micropolitical local level. The term 'micropolitics' is borrowed from organizational sociology, where it referred initially to the political dynamics of institutional change within organizations.[39] Today, historians apply the term to any manner of political dealings outside the established fields of political activity which are predicated on the use of personal relationships and networks. In several chapters it will be demonstrated how Bandmann cultivated relationships with business people, colonial officials and others in order to advance his theatrical business. This micropolitical level of dealings with local entrepreneurs, the press and colonial institutions is made explicit not just in Chapter 3 but in others too, especially Chapter 2 ('Mobile Enterprises'); Chapter 6, which focuses on theatre and the law in the context of colonial regimes; and Chapter 7, on infrastructure. The term will be glossed in more detail in Chapter 3. Because micropolitics often revolve around personal relationships, network analysis provides an accurate method for mapping these structures of power and influence.

Bandmann also utilized a particular theatrical form of micropolitical networking – namely the organization of performances or ceremonies where guests representing positions of influence were accorded special prominence or even integrated into the performance. These could be either gala performances, often for a charitable cause, or (more spectacularly) foundation stone–laying ceremonies to mark the construction of Bandmann's new theatres. These events, which were invariably reported in the local and even international press in great detail,

---

[39] Tom Burns, 'Micropolitics: Mechanisms of Institutional Change', *Administrative Science Quarterly* 6 (1961): 257–81.

demonstrate networking *through performance*, where the normally invisible nodes and edges are made manifest. Two examples will be analysed in detail: in Chapter 3, a gala performance at the Kursaal Theatre in Cairo in 1919, where the guests included personages and groups ranging from General Allenby to a delegation of Greek sailors; in Chapter 7, the widely reported foundation-stone ceremony of the Royal Opera House in Bombay in 1911. Such evenemential performance networks were designed to both signal and strengthen support for the theatrical enterprise.

Chapter 4 examines the specifics of repertoire and the publics it targeted. The Bandmann repertoire was highly varied and specialized, with each troupe representing a different genre: musical comedy, comedy, drama, variety shows. These catered in turn to pre-existing patterns of taste, derived mainly from British theatre-going practices. At the height of his activities, Bandmann had several companies moving around the globe in a chain of changing genres and repertoires. Although in reality the operation was not quite as seamless as he envisaged, the rotation system was in fact implemented. The Bandmann Opera Company 'never breaks up', as he explained it; performers were simply rotated in and out, often joining the company in Colombo or Bombay. This was a significant innovation compared to most stock companies, which were assembled and disbanded for a specific tour.[40] The repertoire of a company could consist of up to two dozen different works, half of which might be performed in one locale over the course of a two-week run. A fourteen-week season in Calcutta, with its population of over a million, was the longest period that a Bandmann company remained in one place. A normal sojourn in most cities comprised a week to ten days at most.

Repertoire will be examined from several perspectives. As a question of genre, it is necessary to revisit some of the largely forgotten works of the late Victorian and Edwardian period: melodramas such as *Sign of the Cross*, *Trilby* or *The Manxman*, and (importantly) the musical comedies derived from the George Edwardes stable, which provided ample opportunities to highlight often scantily clad 'girls' or exotic ladies in overtly Orientalist works such as *The Geisha* or *The Mousmé*, both performed in Japan to enthusiastic Japanese audiences. Repertoire was a question of intellectual property, as its composition was determined as much by access to and control of copyright as by questions of taste.

---

[40] 'Mr. Maurice Bandmann. His Enterprises in the East: Shakespeare in India'. *The Referee*, 28 May 1911, 6.

Most importantly perhaps, repertoire had to be calibrated to the tastes of culturally heterogeneous and spatially dispersed publics, extending from Gibraltar to Yokohama, the West Indies and South America. Although the repertoire was drawn from Edwardian theatre culture, the performances were frequented by Europeans and non-Europeans alike – indeed, patronization by the latter guaranteed the commercial success of the whole enterprise.

Bandmann's performers were both literally and metaphorically 'transported' (Chapter 5). Studying the work of actors and performers in an actor network has a somewhat tautological ring, yet they composed the centre of the rotation system, the most visible of the bodies being moved around the circuit.[41] If actor-network theory has become (in)famous for theorizing the agency of objects as well as or even instead of human beings, it can also be used to reposition the human performer as an agent in a network. Sometimes these performers were quite literarily 'objectified' as subjects of erotic desire; at other times they exerted considerable agency by litigating against their employer, Maurice E. Bandmann, who also litigated against his performers, as we will see in Chapter 6. Performers were both essential and unreliable: they fell ill, argued, jumped ship, married on tour and demanded pay increases.

The act of touring highlights performers both as individuals and as collectives. The experience of being on the move for up to eighteen months, on occasions even longer, and travelling through diverse climate zones and currency regimes constituted the norm. The performers can be understood as 'mediators' in ANT terminology – that is as transporters of meaning that modify, even distort, the meaning or the elements they are supposed to carry. This certainly holds true for the leading, virtuosic actors such as Henry Dallas, Harry Cole, Florence Beech and Georgie Corlass, who created loyal followings along the circuit and guaranteed full houses as much as the plays or operas on offer. In collective terms, we need to see the larger company, which included musicians, musical directors and stagehands as a form of theatrical labour. The touring system required extraordinary versatility on the part of the performers in both the dramatic and operatic comedies. Theatrical touring also created and fostered intimate relations, as especially the younger chorus girls were seen as marriageable commodities who attracted a largely male audience and who regularly deserted the company to marry (usually) wealthy colonials. Bandmann's companies provided a constant supply of young women in the notoriously male-centred colonial communities.

---

[41] The term 'actor' will be used throughout this book in a gender-neutral manner to refer to both men and women. The term 'actress' will be used only when citing source material.

Chapter 6 will examine the law and litigation. There are many connections one could trace in Bandmann's case: his interaction with the judicial system as he became embroiled in a series of legal disputes with partners and performers, his contacts with colonial bureaucracy, and the importance of modern communication systems to facilitate the movement of people and intellectual property around the globe. Bandmann's career is punctuated throughout by court cases, and in particular litigation. These disputes were often reported at great length in the press (and frequently reprinted) and provide insights not only into theatrical contract law but often performance practices. They also included questions of copyright, its infringement and enforcement during a period when copyright on dramatic works was attaining international reach.

The performance of law across time and space can be seen as a necessary agent in the circulation of theatre on the move. Exercising the law in colonial contexts meant by definition that law was 'multi-jurisdictional', often having to accommodate cultural as well as spatial differences.[42] English magistrates in Calcutta would pass judgement on English actors in India over their breach of contract with Bengali-Jewish managers by interpreting Indian law against English legal precedents. The 'common places' of the law, theorized and examined by Patricia Ewick and Susan S. Silbey, are extended here to what could be termed legal heterotopias, as the disputes invariably took place outside the 'common places' of law, and a court in Cairo might rule on questions of infidelity committed on tour in Northern India.[43] The concern in this chapter will be less with the 'niceties' of legal rulings than with the light the trials themselves shed on the circulation process and the follow-on effects of the theatrical networks. Broadly speaking, public trials both stabilized and destabilized the networks. Bandmann's propensity to litigate against his own performers, even though often unsuccessfully, suggests that such court cases served as a disciplinary measure to ensure compliance. The potential for destabilization was equally pronounced, as negative rulings (and there were many) could rewrite the loosely codified practices of theatrical touring.

Bandmann's concern with infrastructure and cinema is the subject of Chapter 7. Perhaps the clearest sign of deepening locality was investment in theatre buildings. In the early phase of his touring operations, Bandmann was hampered by inadequate performance spaces. Often they were just town halls rather than purpose-built theatre houses.

---

[42] Lauren Benton, 'Law and Empire in Global Perspective: Introduction', *American Historical Review* 117 (2012): 1092–1100, here 1093.
[43] Patricia Ewick and Susan S. Silbey, *The Common Place of Law: Stories from Everyday Life, Language and Legal Discourse* (Chicago: University of Chicago Press, 1998), 17.

Investing capital in a building rather than just leasing the theatre as a warehouse became a characteristic of Bandmann's activities. In most of the major ports of call, he publicly espoused the need for high-quality theatre buildings. In 1908, he built the Empire Theatre in Calcutta and, three years later, the Royal Opera House in Bombay. The latter, after a chequered history of refurbishment as a cinema and then closure, has been totally renovated and restored to its original condition as a working theatre. The former was refurbished as a cinema and renamed the Roxy, still operating today under that name. The functional shift from theatre to cinema had already been prefigured by Bandmann himself. His last infrastructural investment was the renovation of a cinema in Gibraltar: its opening in February 1922 came only days before his death.

The final chapter, Chapter 8, will discuss Bandmann's legacy both in terms of communicative memory over time and the fields in which his companies had an effect beyond the performances themselves. Large-scale theatrical touring of the Bandmann companies did not long survive his death. Whether this demise was occasioned by the loss of the charismatic entrepreneur or by wider economic forces that would have made this process inevitable is a question that needs to be weighed up. The most obvious legacy can be seen in the theatres he built in Bombay and Calcutta, although the Bandmann connection is largely unknown in the latter city. An analysis of his traces on the Internet can give a provisional, if continually shifting, snapshot of his current historiographical status. A final section will summarize the historiographical journey behind this book, combining as it does family genealogy, formal archival research and countless hours scanning digitalized newspapers that continually throw up new traces. From ubiquity to oblivion is but one step in theatre history; the task now is to slowly reclaim what has been lost.

1   Family Networks

It is still not possible to write a satisfactory biography of Maurice E. Bandmann – and may never be. He left behind no personal papers that have survived and very few letters. This dearth of conventional biographical material is the result of a peripatetic existence. His life both as a child and as an adult was spent on the road, touring first with his parents and then with his own companies. In order to grasp his later success as the pre-eminent theatrical impresario in the Far East, it is necessary to explore the transition from an actor-manager model of theatrical production to a new way of producing and distributing theatre. This transition was both familial (his parents and sister were all established actor-managers) and organizational (Maurice ran several companies, not just one).

At least since the peregrinations of the Commedia dell'arte troupes, the family was the preferred model of itinerant theatrical production and distribution. From the perspective of economic sociology, actor-families were classic 'closed-network groups'.[1] Densely self-referential, they have closer relations within than beyond the group and have few bridges to other networks. They are self-contained units of theatrical production and are therefore less likely to innovate, because they have difficulty forming multiple 'weak' alliances. This principle is illustrated by the Bandmann family or families, which was itself a kind of theatrical actor network. Both parents, Daniel E. Bandmann and Millicent Bandmann-Palmer, were prominent actors, and his sister, Lily, pursued a career together with her husband as a respected touring actress in the English provinces.

It is also important to locate the Bandmann family network within the emerging biopolitical regimes of the late nineteenth and early twentieth centuries: the world of censuses, shipping records and, after the outbreak of the First World War, requirements to carry passports. Biopolitical

---

[1] Ronald S. Burt, *Brokerage and Closure: An Introduction to Social Capital* (Oxford: Oxford University Press, 2005), 12.

24

data provide one of the keys to reconstructing Bandmann's personal and theatrical life and that of his family. If family and kinship can be seen as 'the deployment of alliances', then the Bandmann theatrical network was deployed to great effect, as both children, despite being the product of a dysfunctional marriage, immediately embarked on the same career as their estranged parents and no doubt profited from the experience and contacts they provided.[2] Theatrical families in the Victorian period functioned 'as engines of induction, training and inheritance within the profession', as Jacky Bratton has argued, and this was certainly the case for the Bandmanns, a family in which the parents inducted both children, albeit reluctantly.[3]

The theatrical history of the Bandmann family (which endured but two full generations) coincides with what has been termed the largest migration flows in history, with tens of millions of people emigrating to the New World and beyond.[4] Both parents and children were caught up in those flows, which also exerted considerable influence on theatrical culture as it followed the migratory movements and expanded exponentially. Migration and the modern nation state emerge at roughly the same time, which is paradoxical, as Charles Tilly argues, because the latter is predicated on sedentary populations.[5] The nation state's fundamental premises – territory and borders, clearly defined citizenship and sovereignty, statistical accountability and predictability – are challenged by people who move. There are moments when the biopolitical regime pins down the peripatetic actor, when he or she applies for naturalization papers, for example, or is required to fill out a census form. But these are nothing more than brief snapshots and not even necessarily accurate when they give false information, as Daniel Bandmann was wont to do. From a biopolitical perspective, then, the Bandmann families defy prevailing understandings of the family as a localized unit, accessible to governmental surveillance: they appear only sporadically

---

[2] Ştefan-Valentin Voicu, 'Making the Family: Actors, Networks and the State', *Journal of Comparative Research in Anthropology and Sociology* 3 (2012): 117–27, here 119.

[3] Jacky Bratton, *New Readings in Theatre History* (Cambridge: Cambridge University Press, 2003), 178.

[4] Reliable figures are impossible. From Britain alone 22 million people emigrated to the United States and British colonies between 1815 and 1914. See John Darwin, *Unfinished Empire: The Global Expansion of Britain* (London: Penguin, 2012), 95. See also Adam Mckeown, 'Global Migration, 1846–1940', *Journal of World History* 15 (2004): 155–89. It is important to note that migration was multi-directional, involving large numbers of Chinese and Indians as well. See Geoffrey Barraclough, ed., *Times Atlas of World History*. 3rd ed. (London: HarperCollins, 1989), 208–9.

[5] Charles Tilly, 'Migration in Modern European History', in W. H. McNeill and R. S. Adams, eds., *Human Migration: Patterns and Policies* (Bloomington: Indiana University Press, 1978), 48–72.

in the biopolitical regimes of statistical analysis such as censuses, birth certificates, ships passages and passport applications. Of which 'population' are these peripatetic actors in fact a part? Maurice travelled on an American passport, although he never lived in the United States. Such biopolitical data that have survived provide, however limited they may be, the means to follow the Bandmanns' travels and cast particular spotlights on processes of mobility.

As actors, the parents were highly visible, and their careers – especially in the case of Bandmann senior – better covered in the press than that of the son. Maurice was professionally active, however, and he was also present in the press, especially outside Britain, and so it is possible to trace his activities and movements from the moment he becomes a professional actor. His media presence was a prerequisite for his work. All theatre, but itinerant theatre in particular, has a symbiotic relationship with the press, and Maurice Bandmann utilized all the familiar devices to keep himself and his companies in the public eye.[6]

The Bandmann theatrical lives raise ethical questions, too – especially father and son. In his discussion of Thomas Betterton, David Roberts defines actors as social beings in three senses: as professional artists in company with others, as performers who embody and inflect ideas about society, and as people who have lives beyond the theatre. Heeding Levinas, Roberts urges the biographer to find the 'being rather than the concept', but because of the intrinsically mediatized nature of theatrical lives, this is easier said than done.[7] All the Bandmanns lived highly public lives, and their private misdemeanours were frequently an integral part of their professional activities, on occasion blurring the distinction between the two dimensions.

Daniel E. Bandmann

Maurice Bandmann's father, Daniel E. Bandmann (1837–1905), epitomized the actor-manager model of the nineteenth century, which he practised in three countries and three languages. Born in Cassel, Germany, in the Jewish faith, he probably emigrated to the United States in 1852 with his parents and obtained citizenship in 1858, before

---

[6] As the father was mainly active in the United States and that country has by far the best coverage of digitalized historical newspapers, the information on his activities is disproportionately good.

[7] David Roberts, 'Writing the Ethical Life: Theatrical Biography and the Case of Thomas Betterton', in Claire Cochrane and Jo Robinson, eds., *Theatre History and Historiography: Ethics, Evidence and Truth* (Basingstoke: Palgrave Macmillan, 2016), 33–47, here 36.

returning to Germany that same year and making his professional debut at the Court Theatre of New Strelitz, also in 1858.[8] He plied his trade as a young actor at various theatres in German-speaking Europe before returning in 1863 to New York, where in January of that year he made his English-language debut at Niblo's Garden as Shylock in *The Merchant of Venice*. Billed as 'the celebrated German tragedian', Bandmann effectively switched languages within a very short time. According to one account he gave in Australia, he had been performing in German in the New York Bowery district (the German quarter) when he was urged to try his hand at an English rendition of Shylock and learned the part in six weeks with the help of an 'English lady'.[9] By September, he had added the title role in *Narcisse or The Last Days of the Pompadour*, and Hamlet, which, together with Shylock, he performed to great acclaim throughout his career. From New York he toured across the country and acquired not only modest theatrical fame but also his first wife, Anne Herschel of Davenport, Iowa, whom he married in 1865; however, the union seems to have been short-lived.

In February 1868, Bandmann made his first appearance in London at the Lyceum Theatre in *Narcisse* under his preferred stage name of Herr Bandmann, which intentionally foregrounded rather than concealed his German origins. The play was an adaptation of Emil Brachvogel's popular German play dealing with Madame Pompadour and the twilight of the ancien régime. Bandmann's calculation that he could only make an impression in a little-known play paid off.[10] *Narcisse* garnered both critical acclaim and trenchant criticism ('Narcisse is but a melodrama and not a lively specimen of its class') but was a commercial success.[11] One of the supporting actors was a twenty-three-year-old actress by the name of Millicent (Milly) Palmer. A year later, they married. As a sign of his newly won prominence, Bandmann was invited in April 1868 to address the annual dinner of the Royal Theatrical Fund, where

---

[8] This is the information he provided to the 1900 federal census, which is, however, not entirely reliable. He claimed to have been married to his last wife, Mary, for eleven years, although the couple were only legally married in 1893; he also claimed to have been born in 1840, which is not correct, but his given age at 64 is accurate. Ancestry.com: 1900 United States Federal Census. There exist naturalization papers for a Daniel Bandmann for the year 1858.

[9] 'Herr Bandmann', *The Argus* (Melbourne), 17 September 1869, 5.

[10] This argument was made after the successful London premiere: 'A new actor, especially if he happens to be also a foreigner, enjoys more likelihood of success in an unknown work than by attempting to attach interest to his exertions in a hackneyed part. If the new play succeeds the new actor almost invariably succeeds with it.' *Pall Mall Gazette*, 21 February 1868, 10.

[11] Ibid., 11. *Punch* found it excessively wordy and published a satire on its loquacity and Bandmann's accent.

he delivered a controversial speech, claiming Shakespeare as a German author.[12] Despite this act of sacrilege, Bandmann formed a deep connection with his wife's country and language, eventually becoming a naturalized British subject.

In August 1869, Bandmann and Milly embarked for Australia, where they began an extended tour that was punctuated by court cases against Daniel for various misdemeanours ranging from slander to assault. Early in the tour, 'Herr Bandmann', as he was figured in all advertising, was fined for forcibly removing photographs of himself from a photographer's shop because they were caricatures rather than the role portraits he had sanctioned.[13] The tour was exceptionally well documented in the local newspapers. The articles alternated between hyperbolic puff, which Bandmann wrote himself or dictated to willing journalists, and more critical reviews and reports on his on- and offstage (mis)deeds, which included inadvertently stabbing the actress playing Emilia to Bandmann's Iago (Fig. 1.1).

The Sydney season in 1870 was judged highly successful, with Bandmann's company providing a standard mid-nineteenth-century repertoire of Shakespeare (*Hamlet*, *Othello*, *Merchant of Venice*, *Richard III*, *Macbeth*) and melodrama (*The Corsican Brothers*), as well as some other works with more advanced literary pretensions, such as Schiller's *The Robbers*. The Bandmann company continued to play there until June, including a two-week run of Goethe's *Faust* in an opulently staged version by Tom Taylor – a somewhat unusual offering for the English-speaking stage, with Rosa Cooper playing the male lead (Faust) to Milly Palmer's Margaret (Gretchen) and Bandmann's Mephistopheles.

The tour continued to Melbourne and then Adelaide. Here reviewers began to comment on Bandmann's German accent, a topic that would dog him throughout his early stage career.[14] This was, however, more a problem for certain 'discerning' critics than for the public at large, which tended to respond favourably to his forceful acting style. The tour continued in Australia until December 1870, when the couple sailed to Auckland for a short season in a local music hall before shifting to the more commodious Theatre Royal. By this time, Auckland

---

[12] *London Evening Standard*, 9 April 1868, 6.
[13] *The Argus* (Melbourne), 21 September 1869, 5.
[14] *South Australian Register*, 9 August 1870, 8. A reviewer for the *Border Watch*, of 13 August 1870, stated that Bandmann has a 'disadvantage of an accent and also moves in a foreign way', 108–9. Other reviewers praised him for his complete lack of a German accent. Over time, his accent became less pronounced, but it could always be used as a weapon against him.

Figure 1.1 Daniel E. Bandmann. (Billy Rose Theatre Division, The New York Public Library for the Performing Arts, Astor, Lenox and Tilden Foundations.)

and other cities in New Zealand had become of ports of call on the Pacific tours of itinerant troupes, despite quite small populations.[15] The Bandmanns began by giving Shakespearean recitals before acquiring local actors necessary for the larger-cast productions. But even so, performances were often marred by the lack of rehearsals, poor blocking and dropped lines. The season continued until the end of January 1872, when the couple sailed for San Francisco via Honolulu.

The years 1872 to 1878 were spent touring the United Kingdom with a Shakespearean repertoire plus some newer plays such as *Dead or Alive*, a melodrama by Tom Taylor. In August 1873, Bandmann was

---

[15] In 1878, Auckland had a population of 29,000; in 1870, it was probably closer to 20,000. *Brett's New Zealand and South Pacific Pilot* (Auckland: Henry Brett, 1881), 31.

convicted of assaulting the manager of a Manchester theatre, one of his many court cases which invariably involved verbal and sometimes physical violence. In 1878, a short tour to the Continent was included where Bandmann performed in France and Germany in those countries' respective languages. In 1879, the Bandmanns returned to New York for a season at the Standard Theatre, which although a critical success was marred by indifferent houses. A short season in Boston on the way to Canada was more successful, while the Toronto season at the Grand Opera House met with disaster when the theatre burned down and Bandmann lost over $20,000 in lavish costumes.[16] Soon afterwards, the couple separated and Milly returned to England with the two children. A return season in New York in June 1880 at the Standard Theatre was underwhelming, with the critic of the *New York Times* remarking, 'Mr. Bandmann brought his own company with him, and a worse assemblage of bad actors it has seldom been the misery of men to look upon. ... Mr. Bandmann's Hamlet was, to say the least, a very unfortunate performance, pretentiously original, but in fact, false to the core.'[17]

Shortly afterwards, Bandmann embarked for Australia on his second 'world tour', a journey that would last nearly four years and include New Zealand, India, Hong Kong, Shanghai and Hawaii. The company also included a new leading lady, the twenty-one-year-old French-Canadian actress and singer Louise Beaudet (1859–1947). The couple, whose relationship was more than strictly professional, were dubbed mischievously by the San Francisco press as 'the great B and the little B'.[18]

Bandmann was, of course, still remembered in Australia, especially for stabbing his co-performer, Mrs Steele, with a real dagger ('Why is Bandmann the cleverest man in the world? Because he can draw blood out of Steele!').[19] The fourteen-strong troupe, billed occasionally as the Bandmann-Beaudet Company, continued on to New Zealand, where over the course of 1881 they literally played the length and breadth of the country, from Invercargill in the south to Auckland in the north, visiting around a dozen towns (some twice) and providing free readings for school pupils. The company returned to Australia

[16] *The New York Times*, 30 November 1879, 7.
[17] *The New York Times*, 13 June 1880, 10.
[18] 'The Critic', *The Observer*, 25 September 1880, 14. Beaudet stayed with Bandmann for the rest of the decade before moving to London (in 1895), where she performed to great acclaim at George Edwardes' Daly Theatre and became a dominant figure on the English musical comedy and vaudeville stage. She returned to New York shortly before the First World War, alternating between stage and screen before finally retiring in 1934.
[19] 'The Critic', *The Observer*, 11 December 1880, 111.

in December 1881, where Bandmann divested himself of most of his actors before continuing on to India accompanied by a skeleton company, some of whom had to pay their own way.

He recorded the second trip, in considerable self-congratulatory detail, in a book entitled *An Actor's Tour; or, Seventy Thousand Miles with Shakespeare*.[20] Bandmann's three-and-a-half-year, 70,000-mile tour with Shakespeare was remarkable for the sheer length of time he was away and the number of places he played in, some of them extremely remote. Daniel Bandmann travelled the world – or at least many parts of it – not just to spread the word of Shakespeare but also to make money. He employed about a dozen actors and actresses for the roles besides his own, paid them little and kept the bulk of the profits for himself. For the two-month Calcutta season alone he claimed to have made £4,000 'clear profit'.[21]

The *Actor's Tour* book itself is part travelogue, part theatrical diary, and while being somewhat pedestrian in style, it nevertheless provides a fascinating account of what it meant to tour a stock company through Australasia and Asia in the 1880s. By his own account – which is substantiated by contemporary press reports – the Bandmann-Beaudet company was a theatrical sensation, especially because of the heavy Shakespearean repertoire, unusual for the time. The Shakespearean performances drew almost entirely Indian audiences in Calcutta and Bombay, the Bard being too highbrow for the English colonials, who preferred burlesque and light comedy. Bandmann's son, Maurice, perhaps drawing on his father's experiences, only occasionally toured a Shakespearean company and seldom under his own brand.

After completing the 'world tour', the Bandmann-Beaudet company resumed performing in the United States with a mainly Shakespearean repertoire supported by the old standards, *The Corsican Brothers* and *Narcisse*. Bandmann and Beaudet parted company at the end of the decade only to encounter one another again in court in 1892, when Beaudet sued Daniel for withholding monies owed to her. In July 1888, Bandmann purchased two ranches in Hellgate Canyon near Missoula, Montana, which became his home. Although he regularly announced the end of his stage career, he in fact continued to perform until shortly before his death. In the late 1880s, he attempted unsuccessfully to reconquer the London stage with an adaptation of Robert Louis Stevenson's novella *The Strange Case of Dr Jekyll and*

---

[20] Daniel Edward Bandmann, *An Actor's Tour; or, Seventy Thousand Miles with Shakespeare*. Ed. Barnard Gisby (Boston: Upham and Co., 1885).
[21] Ibid., 144.

Mr Hyde. Bandmann had reportedly seen the first adaption by the young actor-manager Richard Mansfield in New York and promptly commissioned his own version. Like *The Corsican Brothers*, the subject matter provided potential for virtuosic acting, with both title roles being played by one actor. Although the American stage, with its lax copyright laws, could quite happily accommodate two or more adaptations of the same work, the situation in London was different. When Bandmann opened his version at the Opera Comique, London, on 6 August 1888, he was immediately issued with a writ by Mansfield, who had begun a season at the Lyceum two days earlier. Bandmann's production closed after three performances, and he returned to the United States.[22]

The years 1892 and 1893 were dominated by two high-profile court cases which put Bandmann back in his preferred state of being in the limelight. In May 1892, he married a young actress, Mary Kelly, after she gave birth to a daughter, Eva, in January of that year. In June, Louise Beaudet brought a lawsuit for monies owed to her from the Australian-Asian tour, and in July, Millicent filed a suit to have the marriage with Mary annulled because she and Daniel were still legally married.

The Beaudet case, heard at the circuit court in Helena, Montana, proved to be a crowd pleaser, because both plaintiff and defendant were present and both played to great effect.[23] Beaudet claimed that Bandmann had invested the proceeds of their tours (estimated at around $50,000) in the ranch, thus depriving her of her rightful share. Unfortunately for Beaudet, all agreements had been verbal. Bandmann treated the courtroom like a stage, and his testimony resounded with dialogue reminiscent of his melodramas: 'I was madly in love with the girl. I want the truth to come out. I have only to fear my folly. There can be nothing against my honour. She had open checks of mine till the November following separation, when I found out her treachery.'[24] He repeatedly pronounced in court how he had loved 'that woman', prompting his own counsel to remark, 'Oh, leave the sentiment out.' Beaudet, in turn, made the dramatic revelation that Bandmann had forged a

---

[22] For an account of the stage history, see Martin A. Danahay and Alex Chisholm, *Jekyll and Hyde Dramatized* (Jefferson: McFarland, 2005). On 10 August 1888, the *New York Times* reported that Bandmann had been threatened with contempt of court for not closing immediately, and several days later that Mansfield had sold the provincial rights of his adaptation for a large sum while reserving rights for the larger provincial centres (*The New York Times*, 10 August 1888, 1, and 19 August 1888, 1).

[23] Beaudet's case is outlined in detail in 'Beaudet the Soubrette', *The Helena Independent* (Helena, MT), 10 June 1892, 5.

[24] *The Anaconda Standard*, 10 December 1892, 1.

letter she had ostensibly written outlining their business arrangement.[25] The dramatic encounter became so intense that the local newspaper was moved to speculate that 'they (might) join hands again in the profession, kiss and make up, and once more put the old, two star combination on the road'.[26] Finally, the case was annulled because of a lack of documentation of the parties' financial affairs.

The divorce case was more clear-cut. Millicent Bandmann-Palmer was able to provide definite evidence from London that the marriage was never legally dissolved, rendering the new marriage bigamous. Bandmann thereupon began divorce proceedings and made the perjurious claim that he had no contact with his wife, not even knowing where she resided. This was quickly proven false with the help of testimony from his son, Maurice, who signed an affidavit stating that his father knew full well where his wife lived and that he had met his father in London in 1888 and subsequently accompanied him to Missoula in that year as well as on a theatrical tour in 1890. Furthermore, the younger Bandmann stated 'that he had seen indications of adultery on the part of his father and that in his early youth he had seen his father drag his mother by the hair and threaten to kill her with a knife'.[27] In her own affidavit, Millicent claimed that 'for 11 years he treated her with cruelty; that he was guilty of adultery, and she therefore left him and returned to her home'.[28] The final divorce settlement left Millicent with the family house in Gloucester Road, Kew, Surrey, and a monthly alimony of $25 (which Daniel later tried to suspend claiming undue financial hardship).

Indeed, the years 1892 and 1893 were burdensome for Daniel. He lost most of his money in a stock market crash (but retained his ranch), had to finance two trials and was soon father of three children (a fourth child, Daniel E., was born in 1905 just before Daniel senior's death). During the rest of the 1890s, he established himself as a rancher and horticulturalist of some note. He continued to perform with local (often amateur) companies the old reliables such as *The Merchant of Venice*, *Narcisse* and *The Corsican Brothers*. In 1901, he returned to New York with a stock company and reprised many of his famous roles at the Murray Hill Theatre. By this time, however, the stock company star system with its changing bills was giving way to the more economical long-run approach, and a heavy Shakespearean repertoire could only be sold at discount prices. He also tried his hand on the vaudeville circuit, with short excerpts from his Shakespearean roles.

---

[25] Ibid.
[26] *The Anaconda Standard*, 25 December 1893, 5.
[27] 'Stage and Green Room', *The Anaconda Standard*, 16 July 1893, 7.
[28] Ibid.

On 23 November 1905, home on his ranch, Bandmann dropped dead of heart failure brought on by acute indigestion. Depending on the sources (Bandmann tended to make himself younger), he was probably aged sixty-eight. His death generated numerous obituaries, which testified to his importance as an old-style tragedian intent on promoting Shakespeare and legitimate drama to an increasingly disinterested audience. His irascible temper, litigious temperament and even propensity for violence were often enumerated. Perhaps the most damning résumé came from Australia, where the magazine *The Bulletin* published a scathing account of his acting ability and character defects:

Daniel Bandmann, alleged tragedian has gone where his dreadful accent doesn't matter. Bandman [*sic*] was an inflated, unbearable and insulting German who drifted to Australia on two occasions many years ago, looking as if the world existed by his permission. ... He made his wife's life a misery; Millie Palmer was a vastly better actress than he was an actor, but he regarded her as something not much better than a door mat and a little worse than a dog. Shakespeare turned in his grave every time Bandmann played one of his characters, and as Bandmann was always playing his characters the Bard of Avon was kept revolving busily.[29]

Most obituaries refrained from such extreme denigration, while recognizing his character faults. The question of his prowess as a Shakespearean actor divided the eulogists between those who accepted that he had indeed brought recognizable 'Germanic' innovations to the English-speaking stage and those who tended to dismiss his performances as loud, heavily accented bellowing. Most commentary focuses on his renditions of Hamlet and Shylock, the latter being the part to which he gave the most original twist. As Nicole Anae argues, 'Bandmann's own Jewish background was central to his conception of the role', in combination with the themes of money, power and usury underpinning the dramatic trajectory of the play.[30] This may also explain why he played it in three languages: he assayed Shylock in French in 1878, playing in Paris in December 1878, then a month later in Berlin in German, and the next month in London in English.[31] His was an interpretation which could transcend niceties of accent

---

[29] *The Cobargo Chronicle* (NSW), 26 January 1906, 5. Reprinted from *The Bulletin*.
[30] Nicole Anae, '"The Majestic Hebrew Racial Ideal": Herr Daniel E. Bandmann's Shylock on the Australian Stage, 1880–1883', *Shakespeare Jahrbuch* (2014), 128–45, here 131.
[31] *Le Gaulois*, 5 December 1878, 3.

to impart the humanity of the character rather than the red-bearded comic figure that dominated into the nineteenth century.

Although a naturalized American and British citizen, Bandmann remained resolutely German, never attempting to assimilate; indeed, the use of the German 'Herr' as his stage name underlined rather than disguised his origin. He crossed the Atlantic and changed languages in order to participate in the economic potential offered by the American and English stages, which were expanding rapidly and, in comparison with the strictly regulated German theatres, offered possibilities for financial gain for the entrepreneurially inclined – almost unheard of in Germany. Bandmann then became an actor-manager, which required that he build his business around his persona and performance capabilities. Each of his long-term partners – Millicent Palmer, Louise Beaudet and Mary Kelly – shared both the stage and his bed and thereby fitted with him the mould of the actor-manager couple. The first two were major performers in their own right, which created tensions and jealousies. His relationship with his estranged family (Milly, Lily and Maurice) was clearly dismal. After the separation, Daniel appears to have had only sporadic contact with his first wife and children. While there is no record of any contact with Lily, Maurice did visit his father on summer vacations and even go on tour with him. The divorce suit revealed what had been alluded to in the press for years: that he mistreated and even physically assaulted Milly.

Millicent Bandmann-Palmer (1845–1926)

Of all the members of the Bandmann theatrical family, Millicent – Maurice's mother and Daniel's wife and stage partner for some ten years – is probably the best known today. This has to do with her brief mention in James Joyce's *Ulysses* when Leopold Bloom pauses before a billboard advertising a performance of *Leah*, which reminds him that she had played *Hamlet* the night before – a 'male impersonator', he thinks.[32] Indeed, Millicent attained considerable prominence as Hamlet, among many other roles, and was a fixture on the metropolitan and provincial theatre circuit for almost three decades.

Born Melicent Farmer on 12 October 1845 in Lancaster, she probably changed her surname to the less agrarian sounding Palmer when she

---

[32] The play, *Leah, the Forsaken* (1863), which deals with a Jewish girl forsaken by her Gentile lover, is an adaptation by Augustin Daly of S. H. Mosenthal's German play *Deborah* (1849). The role was also popularized by Sarah Bernhardt.

went on the stage.[33] She first appeared aged eighteen as Milly Palmer at the Theatre Royal, Liverpool, in February 1863 in an assortment of plays and pantomimes, including a version of *Goldilocks and the Three Bears*.[34] Her early career was without doubt meteoric. Quickly advancing to leading roles by the following year, her performances in Liverpool were exceptional. She debuted as Juliet – the litmus test for any up-and-coming young actress – playing to Alice Marriot's Romeo in July 1864: 'Miss Palmer's rendering was so instinctual with dramatic force and variety, that had it taken place on the metropolitan stage it could not have failed to procure for her a chorus of authoritative laudation.'[35]

Her performances in Liverpool were so strong that she soon attracted the attention of metropolitan managers. Her London debut at the Strand Theatre in the role of Pauline in the light comedy *Delicate Ground* by Charles Dance was purposively designed to introduce her to metropolitan audiences and critics, both of whom she impressed: 'one of the most accomplished actresses whom the London stage has witnessed for many years', remarked the *Standard*.[36] This assessment was echoed by *Bell's Life*: '[She] is young, pretty and intellectual, and possesses capabilities of enacting parts of more weight.'[37]

Milly returned to Liverpool in Dion Boucicault's Irish melodrama *Arrah-na-Pogue*, playing Arrah, for which role she toured for over a year. She reprised Juliet in 1867 in London, playing the role again alongside a female Romeo, this time the German opera singer and tragedian Felicitas Vestvali (who also performed Hamlet). By 1868, she had become a member of the Lyceum Theatre, where she encountered Daniel Bandmann, and garnered significant acclaim for her rendition of the actress Doris Quinault in *Narcisse* alongside her future husband. The couple married in February 1869 after a protracted provincial tour of *Narcisse*. She assumed the role of leading lady to Bandmann's leading man and obtained equal billing as 'Miss Milly Palmer' alongside Daniel's 'Mr. Bandmann' even though they were now married. The couple left for Australia in July 1864. This double billing was discontinued in Australia (presumably because of Milly's pregnancy), where Daniel changed to the German title 'Herr Bandmann'.

---

[33] According to birth records, a Melicent Farmer was born on that date in Lancaster. In her will, she mentions her 'late brother Captain John Farmer', so it is highly likely that Farmer was her actual surname.
[34] *Liverpool Daily Post*, 28 February 1863, 1.
[35] 'Miss Milly Palmer', *Cheshire Observer and Chester, Birkenhead, Crewe and North Wales Times* (Chester, England), 2 July 1864, 2.
[36] Cited in T. Edgar Pemberton, *The Birmingham Theatres: A Local Retrospect* (Birmingham: Cornish Brothers, 1890), 32.
[37] *Bell's Life in London and Sporting Chronicle*, 12 November 1864, 10.

Milly gave birth to a daughter, Lily Clementina Bandmann, on 25 December 1869, and two months later (the tour had now moved to Sydney) Milly announced her first appearance in Australia at the Adelphi Theatre in a performance of *Romeo and Juliet*.[38] The pre-announcement included over twenty citations of glowing reviews from London papers of her ten-week season at the Lyceum. In Sydney, Milly again played to a female Romeo (Rosa Cooper, the manager of the Adelphi), thus continuing the London practice. The tour returned to Melbourne and Adelaide, where Milly changed her billing from Milly Palmer to Mrs Bandmann. This would change again later to the more distinguished Millicent Bandmann-Palmer, the stage name she retained until the end of her life. By the time the couple returned to England via a US tour in early 1872, they were an established actor-manager company. En route to England, Millicent gave birth to Maurice in New York in April 1872.

An actor of remarkable versatility, Millicent was by far Daniel's equal if not superior on the stage. The two were frequently compared in notices – and sometimes not to Daniel's advantage. The relationship deteriorated throughout the 1870s, and their frequent disputes included episodes of violence against Millicent which became common knowledge. Early in 1880, the couple separated after an eight-month North American tour, and Millicent returned to England. A notice in *The Era* in May 1880 puffed the extent of the tour (20,000 miles, 288 'legitimate performances' in both English and German, audiences numbering 200,000 people) but also stated that Mrs Bandmann returned alone while Daniel remained to complete a season in San Francisco. Perhaps to counter rumours, the notice explicitly stated that he would 'join her' in England, which he never did.[39]

Throughout the first half of the 1880s, Millicent disappeared from the public eye, something highly unusual for a high-profile actress. Only later did readers learn that from 1882 to 1886 she had gone to Germany for very grave health reasons.[40] An article published much later in *The Sketch* referred to a 'long and apparently incurable illness [that] caused her to take up her residence in Germany, and here after many months of suffering, she finally recovered her health'.[41] Whatever malady she had, it did not prevent her from learning German and devoting four hours a day for two years in order to master the language to such a level that she

[38] *The Sydney Morning Herald*, 24 February 1870, 8.
[39] *The Era*, 23 May 1880, 13.
[40] The England and Wales census of 1881 records a Maurice E. Bandiman and Lily C. Bandiman (*sic*) residing at 35 Gloucester Road, Richmond, Surrey, which was the family home: www.FamilySearch.org; National Archives reference RG11/Folio 0845/126.
[41] *The Sketch*, 3 June 1896, 231. 'Here' was probably the spa town of Wiesbaden.

could act in it. Although friends tried to dissuade her from attempting such a Sisyphean task, she succeeded: 'The difficulties of the sonorous tongue of Schiller gave way before her energy and perseverance.'[42] In December 1886, she appeared at Dresden's court theatre in *The School for Scandal* playing Lady Teazle in German. According to one German review, the debut was a triumph, declaring in martial metaphors a clear victory: 'Among all the foreign artists who have struggled for success in Germany Mrs Bandmann-Palmer is the only one who can boast that she has fought on German ground with German weapons and has held the field in triumph.'[43] The success led to several more documented performances. There was a dramatic recital by Royal command of the Queen of Saxony in Dresden in February 1887, where she offered a selection of poems and speeches in English and German, including Arrah Meelish in her best Irish brogue.[44] She followed with a series of similar soirées in Berlin in March 1887, including a legendary performance in Berlin before eighty royal personages, which garnered not just personal compliments but also a gold medallion from Crown Prince (later emperor) Frederick.[45] Mention of this imperial gift recurs throughout her later life in numerous press reports about her fame and standing as an actress. The performance remained for her the high-point of her career.[46]

Why Millicent attempted to perform in German – and succeeded – remains a mystery. Apart from the performances in Dresden and Berlin, there is no record her going on tour or trying to establish herself on the German stage. One can only speculate that her relationship with Daniel, who quite literally changed languages, provided a major motivation to rival him in this unusual feat of histrionic code-switching. But whereas he had to change languages to acquire access to the huge theatrical market of the Anglophone world, she did not.

Millicent finally returned to the London stage in 1888 as Lady Macbeth, the press still fondly remembering her as Milly Palmer.[47] She had to slowly rebuild her career by touring the provinces, beginning with a programme of dramatic recitals in Scotland featuring herself

---

[42] 'Success of an English Actress in Germany', *Dundee Evening Telegraph*, 2 December 1886, 3.

[43] Ibid. The original German source is not known.

[44] 'Honour to an English Actress', *Dundee Advertiser*, 1 March 1887, 10.

[45] *Berliner Tageblatt*, 3 March 1887, 2.

[46] *The Sketch*, 3 June 1896, 231.

[47] In May 1888, she published a brief notice in *The Era* that she had returned to England and was 'disengaged', i.e. open for employment: *The Era*, 19 May 1888, 2.

with daughter Lily on the piano. By 1889 she was touring as Millicent Bandmann-Palmer with her own company, offering the new Danish social play *Tares*. Thereafter she embarked on annual tours with a mixed repertoire and a heavy Shakespearean emphasis, including her Hamlet and Juliet, although she was by now in her fifties. After 1892, she included her children, Lily and Maurice, and they obtained their first direct acting experience, with Maurice even playing Romeo to his mother's Juliet. However, the children quickly launched separate careers: Lily married the actor William Maclaren, with whom she set up an independent company, and Maurice began managing multiple companies.

From 1890 to around 1909, Millicent's year was divided into clearly defined phases and places. The company toured through the United Kingdom, playing in larger cities like Liverpool, Manchester and Glasgow, as well as in the provinces (Ilkeston, Jarrow-On-Tyne, Smethwick, etc.). Very seldom did she perform in London, and most stops were part of a regular circuit. An exception to this touring routine was a much-vaunted Shakespearean tour to India – planned for late 1908 and early 1909 to coincide with her son's newly opened Empire Theatre in Calcutta – which was cancelled at the last minute due to her sister's death.[48] It is noteworthy that at age sixty-three she was still willing to undertake a major tour to India. Advertised as the 'Bandmann-Palmer Shakespearian Company', its repertoire was to comprise also *Mary Queen of Scots* and *The School for Scandal*. Touted by the *Times of India* as 'a splendid German scholar' and repeating the story of the imperial audience in Berlin of 1887, her company was termed a 'classical' one. Had the tour eventuated, it would have been Maurice's first attempt to promote a Shakespearean tour in India.

By 1910 she had retired from regular touring, only to re-emerge for a number of benefit performances after 1914 in aid of the war effort. She resided, or rather presided, at 36 Gloucester Road, Kew, until her death, in 1926, from the effects of a paralytic stroke aged eighty years. Her funeral was attended by major figures from the theatre world, including Margaret Kendal, Frank Benson, Edith Craig (Edward Gordon Craig's sister) and Edith's partner, the artist Clare Atwood.

Although Millicent clearly still had many friends in the theatrical and artistic community, she also had many enemies. Like Daniel, she died a representative of the 'old school' of acting and theatre management. An idea of how she (and many others) operated is related by Mrs Patrick Campbell (the original Eliza Doolittle) in her memoirs. After debuting

---

[48] 'Bandmann's Opera Company', *The Times of India*, 9 January 1909, 7.

at the Alexandria Theatre in Liverpool, Campbell was hired by Millicent in 1889 to join her nation-wide tour of the Danish play *Tares*, adapted by (Mrs) Oscar Beringer.[49] The contract provided for a weekly wage of £2 for the part of Rachel Denison, understudying 'all other parts for which you may be cast' and payment of her own rail fare to the opening town plus outfitting herself with the appropriate dresses.[50] The working relationship was not a happy one, perhaps because by this time a young actress such as Campbell contrasted markedly with the older Millicent and her now stout figure. Millicent referred to Campbell as belonging to the 'school of squirmers', which, whatever it meant, was not intended as a compliment, and before long Campbell gave notice.[51] Receiving a wage at all was by no means automatic for a novice actress, as Millicent followed the practice of 'employing' what were termed 'premium' or 'pupil' actors, meaning that the neophytes paid her a negotiable fee (her opening offer was £40) for the privilege of learning the trade on the road. A fictionalized but well-researched account of the practice can be found in Bamber Gascoigne's novel *The Heydays* (1973), which relates the adventures of a young actress on tour with Millicent in the early twentieth century (Fig. 1.2).

Although a formidable presence and a less-than-generous employer, Bandmann-Palmer was highly respected as an actress of considerable intellectual acuity. In interviews, she repeatedly stressed that she had studied *Hamlet*, the main role of which she claimed to have played a thousand times, since her childhood: 'It is the philosophy of Hamlet that has been so attractive to the actress, and she, I believe, made herself familiar with every Shakespearian commentator.'[52] Although her repertoire included many hardy annuals such as *East Lynne* or Rowe's *Jane Shaw*, without which no stock company could succeed, she also pursued a more demanding repertoire of legitimate drama, even including German plays such as *Mary Queen of Scots* (an adaptation of Schiller's *Maria Stuart*) and works by the German naturalist-dramatist Hermann

[49] For a discussion of playwright Aimée Beringer, see Katherine Newey, 'Feminist Historiography and Ethics: A Case Study from Victorian Britain', in Claire Cochrane and Jo Robinson, eds., *Theatre History and Historiography: Ethics, Evidence and Truth* (Basingstoke: Palgrave, 2016), 85–102.
[50] Mrs Patrick Campbell, *My Life and Some Letters* (New York: Dodd, Mead and Co., 1922), 52–3.
[51] Ibid., 53–4.
[52] 'Some Woman-Hamlets', *The Sketch*, 31 May 1899, 244. See also Tony Howard, *Women as Hamlet: Performance and Interpretation in Theatre, Film and Literature* (Cambridge: Cambridge University Press, 2007). Howard stresses that she merged both an older German tradition with 'a fin-de-siècle image linking beauty, opulence and death', here 84.

MRS. BANDMANN PALMER.

Figure 1.2 Millicent Bandmann-Palmer as Hamlet. (*London Illustrated News*, 1 July 1899. Private collection.)

Sudermann.[53] However, it was as a Shakespearean actor that she was best known, a dedication that by the mid-1890s already carried a faint whiff of the old-fashioned. As *The Sketch* noted, Bandmann-Palmer 'contributed to keep Shakespeare's memory green in many a township of Greater Britain where the light of the divine William seemed in danger of being extinguished by the sacred lamp of burlesque'.[54] The trend towards musical comedy, vaudeville and farce that her son Maurice so energetically promulgated on his circuit was not her world.

Millicent died a relatively wealthy woman: her net estate at probate was estimated at around £10,500, which was a considerable sum for the time. She was able to settle an annuity of £100 a year on daughter Lily, who by this time had ceased touring. She settled the same amount

[53] Millicent produced and performed in the controversial *Sodoms Ende* (adapted as *The Man and His Picture*) for which her acting partner and later adopted son, Farmer Skein, had acquired the rights.
[54] *The Sketch*, 3 June 1896, 231.

on her married granddaughter, Millicent Jane Prattent (née Maclaren), Lily's daughter. Interest on the remaining capital was to be divided amongst Maurice's three daughters when they turned thirty, under the condition that they not 'adopt the theatrical or music hall calling' in accordance with Maurice's wish that 'they should not go on the stage'.[55] Her resolve to cut the chain of theatrical enculturation was aimed at the third but not the second generation, because Lily appears to have been groomed for a theatrical career.

Lily C. Bandmann

Lily Clementina Bandmann (1869–1935) was born on Christmas Day 1869 in Ballarat, a gold-mining town in Victoria, during the first Bandmann Australian tour. We know next to nothing about her early life except that it was spent largely on tour until Millicent and Daniel parted ways in 1880. Her schooling was presumably a mixture of private tutoring and, between 1882 and 1886, at a German school in Wiesbaden. We do know that by age eighteen she was an accomplished pianist and able to assist her mother on the latter's 'come-back' tour of Scotland in 1888. In the extensive notices of the 'dramatic recitals' in which her mother delivered a mixture of poetry, dramatic monologues and dialogues (Millicent played both interlocutors), Lily gained favourable mention for her piano playing and her physical similarity to her mother: 'Her daughter, Miss Lily Bandmann, who agreeably diversified the programme by her fine playing, is very like her mother. When they were both on together it was no stretch of fancy to imagine them sisters.'[56] Lily's repertoire was mainly limited to incidental music during the interval, but it also included accompanying her mother during the musical numbers.

Lily soon graduated from pianist to actress, and by 1892 she was touring with her brother and mother in the latter's company. Lily played Ophelia to her mother's Hamlet and several other important supporting roles such as Queen Elizabeth to Millicent's Mary Stuart. One of the tours included a young Scottish actor from Glasgow, William Maclaren, who became her husband. The couple married in London on 8 June 1895.

In the first years on stage, Lily performed under the name of Lily Clements, a reference to her middle name, Clementina. It is unclear why she initially disavowed the Bandmann brand – perhaps at the urging of her mother, who may have wished to avoid confusion in the notices. After

---

[55] Will of Millicent Bandman Palmer, 6 January 1926, 6. HM Courts & Tribunals Service Probate Search Service.
[56] 'Ladies Column', *Dundee Evening Telegraph*, 25 October 1888, 4.

Figure 1.3 Lily C. Bandmann as Almida in *Claudian* by Wilson Barrett, postcard. (Private collection.)

her marriage, she toured with her husband and performed henceforth under the name Lily C. Bandmann. Around 1899, the couple formed their own company. Like her parents, they were a husband-and-wife stock company touring a repertoire of suitable but conservative vehicles.

Their most popular works were the melodrama *Alone in London* (1885), a variation of *Oliver Twist* predicated on great scenic effects (the highlight was the so-called sluice scene in which the stage was flooded) and a breeches part for Lily as the young waif. Equally popular was Wilson Barrett's *Claudian* (1883), a 'Roman' melodrama that involved a 'thrilling story of profligacy published, of a terrible curse, and final catastrophe'.[57] It also provided a vehicle for Lily as Almida, the female lead, which became her most iconic role (Fig. 1.3). They also toured

---

[57] *Nottingham Evening Post*, 25 January 1916, 3.

other Barrett melodramas such as *The Sign of the Cross* (see Chapter 4) until 1924. Although extremely popular, Barrett's plays required a proverbial 'cast of thousands', or at least fifty to sixty performers, which the Maclaren-Bandmann company could still muster (with the help of local extras) until the beginning of the First World War.

Their enterprise was much more modest than that of Lily's brother, despite being very active. In 1905, *The Era* lists their respective companies in its 'Dramatic Cards' section. Lily is featured, both under her maiden and married name: 'Mr. and Mrs. McLaren (Miss Lily C. Bandmann) touring own Co. July 10. County T., Kingston-on-Thames'. Maurice, in contrast, advertises immodestly but accurately his 'Annual Tour of the World'.[58]

In 1922, the Bandmann family network presented, albeit briefly, its third generation. A review notes the appearance of Lily's daughter, Millicent Maclaren, as Nero's empress in *The Sign of the Cross*.[59] Soon afterwards, she took over the part of the 'chaste Christian maid', Mercia – hitherto her mother's preserve. However, her stage career was short-lived, as she seems to have forsaken the theatre once her parents stopped touring around 1924, when they retired to Devon. Lily died there on 20 June 1935, aged sixty-five. This meant that they effectively retired from the stage in their mid-fifties, with very little income. This can be seen by the modest size of Lily Bandmann's estate, which amounted to a mere £416 on her death. As mentioned earlier, she had been provided for in her mother's will with an annuity of £100. Her husband survived her by ten years.

On the final tour in 1924 of *The Sign of the Cross*, William Maclaren claimed that the play had been performed 25,000 times since its premiere in 1895. However, by this time the play and the infrastructural organization required to mount it and its ilk were coming to an end. Melodramatic large-cast plays which could still find an economically viable audience on the provincial touring circuit were a thing of the past, as was the husband-and-wife actor-manager model. It was Lily's brother who worked out a new way to manage theatre on a global scale and make it pay.

Maurice E. Bandmann

According to his passport, Maurice Edward Bandmann was born in New York on 11 April 1872. He was baptized on 30 July of that year in Camden, London.[60] His childhood was spent with his parents on tour and then in Germany with mother Millicent and sister Lily, where he

---

[58] *The Era*, 8 July 1905, 4.
[59] *The Stage*, 7 September 1922, 10.
[60] Ancestry.com: London, England, Births and Baptisms, 1813–1906.

remained until 1890 to complete his schooling. According to an inter-view given many years later in Hong Kong, Maurice was destined for the bar or the medical profession, professional paths he avoided, he claimed, by escaping out West to become a rancher, but in fact to join his father on tour. His cowboy dreams were clearly short-lived, because in 1890 *The Era* announced with some prescience that

Maurice E. Bandmann, a youth of eighteen, and son of Mrs Bandmann-Palmer, who has for some years been studying at the classical gymnasium at Wiesbaden, has decided to adopt the stage as a profession, and will make his appearance in connection with Mrs. Bandmann-Palmer's next tour, playing Careless in *School for Scandal*, Benvolio in *Romeo and Juliet* etc. He is thought to have talent, and he is known to have ambition, and his career will doubtless be watched with considerable interest.[61]

He very soon graduated to Romeo, playing to his mother's Juliet. By 1892, all three members of the family were on tour together in a com-pany which also included Gertrude Evans (Maurice's first wife) and William Maclaren (Lily's future husband).

The 1890s was a turbulent and exciting decade for Maurice. He established himself both as a versatile actor and as the youngest the-atre manager in England; co-authored a play, *The Egyptian Idol*; married and appeared as a co-respondent in a divorce case; and embarked on his first overseas tours around the Mediterranean. During these early years, the family network offered crucial support. His mother provided instruction in acting and in the rudiments of running an itinerant com-pany, while Lily joined his first Manxman tour to play the female lead, Kate Cregreen, with Maurice performing the male role of Pete Quilliam (Fig. 4.1). Although the three eventually parted ways in the mid-1890s, each running their own companies, there can be no doubt that the fam-ily remained close knit and provided a useful deployment of alliances. Despite his evident loyalty to Millicent, Maurice maintained contact with his father, with whom he appears to have gained his first experi-ence of theatrical touring. In summer 1888, he accompanied his father back to the United States and a year later joined him for part of the *Austerlitz* tour, acting as his theatrical agent.[62] Maurice appears also to have dabbled with acting, although not in any prominent part (Fig. 1.4).

---

[61] *The Era*, 20 December 1890, 10.
[62] 'Daniel Bandmann's son M. E. Bandmann is acting as theatrical agent for his father', 'Stage Gossip', *Australian Town and Country Journal* (NSW: 1870–1907), 1 March 1890, 33. *Austerlitz* was a reworking of Tom Taylor's historical melodrama *Dead or Alive*.

MAURICE E. BANDMANN.

CORK

Figure 1.4 Maurice E. Bandmann aged nineteen. (Houghton Library, Harvard University, TCS 1.1058.)

Maurice's first recorded professional appearance is in London on 12 November 1891 with his mother's company, playing Mortimer to Millicent's Mary Stuart in the Schiller tragedy: *The Stage* termed it 'a fine performance'.[63] For the next three years, he worked as an actor of some note, a reputation that crossed the Atlantic, and in 1894 he was engaged by New York manager Gustave Frohman to play the part of Lord Windermere in a touring production of Oscar Wilde's *Lady Windermere's Fan*. A short notice in the *New York Dramatic Mirror* even featured a photograph of the 'talented young actor…a son of Daniel Bandmann, with whom he made quite a reputation in the West a few seasons ago'.[64] The same year, Maurice acquired the rights to Wilson Barrett's hit *The Manxman* and set up two companies – The Manxman

[63] *The Stage Archive*, 12 November 1891, 13.
[64] 'Said to the Mirror', *The New York Dramatic Mirror*, 24 March 1894, 9.

A-North and B-South – to extract maximum profit from the expensive rights. He acted the lead in one and employed a manager in the other (see Chapter 2). Aged twenty-two, this move brought Bandmann the accolade of being the youngest actor-manager in the business.

The Egyptian Idol

Having acquired at considerable expense the provincial rights to Wilson Barrett's *The Manxman* and other London hits such as *Trilby*, Bandmann realized what profit dramatic authorship could bring. It is therefore not surprising that he joined forces with fellow actor Richard Saunders to produce what seemed a sure-fire success: *The Egyptian Idol* is a drama of intrigue set in a melodramatic world of impoverished aristocrats, upstart Americans, women both deceitful and virtuous, a mysterious idol and a spectacular setting by the Niagara Falls – all of which are dramatized with a vigorous use of exclamation marks. The four-act play begins at a garden party in New York hosted by a wealthy banker, Mr Vanderguard.[65] The guests include an assortment of neglected wives, aristocrats, uncouth Americans and a mysterious fortune teller. The central figure is Arthur Chumley, the footloose and impoverished Lord Dunmersey, who has nothing to offer but his title to Vanderguard's daughter, Celia. His real affections are towards Beatrice, sister of his friend Julian Heritage. In the second act, Beatrice has the misfortune to lock herself in a cabinet concealing the eponymous idol and promptly suffocates. For reasons not entirely made clear, Dunmersey throws her body out his window into the Hudson River, pretending that it was suicide. For no particular reason, the third act is set at the Niagara Falls by moonlight and culminates in Julian Heritage losing his footing after a fight with Dunmersey and plunging into the falls. The fourth and final act takes place in New York again and opens with the news of Julian's survival ('What a marvellous escape he had, half stunned by the fall, with one arm broken to cling to a projecting tree into which he fell until assistance arrived.' III, 1). Despite these glad tidings, Dunmersey is determined to end his own miserable life:

Dunmersey: (Looking at Idol). Can it be any truth in your history? – you Idol of the East! Can it be possible that you have been the cause of my misfortunes, and that the curse once put upon you has come to pass – yes – yes. It's true, I see it all now – but for you – you graven image – the cabinet would not have

---

[65] All quotations are from the typescript from the Lord Chamberlain's collection at the British Library, Add MS 53584, number 261.

been opened – she would never have made that terrible mistake which cost her life – and ruined mine – (dashes down Idol into fireplace) (IV, 13) [...]

(Shoots himself... staggers back on stage): Ah, Julian, good-bye! Good-bye! and forgive – forgive – Oh... VERY SLOW CURTAIN (IV, 16)

The Egyptian Idol was licensed by the Lord Chamberlain on 18 October 1895 and had its opening, copyright performance at the Theatre Royal, Sunderland, on 16 December.[66] Notices were largely positive, praising the acting and scenery and sometimes even the writing, in as much as it provided unusual variations of melodramatic themes: 'The villain is not all villainy... He is not a heartless roué nor a coarse bully – he is politeness itself to his man-servant.'[67] The third act showing the Niagara Falls, 'with a panoramic view showing the falls in motion', was invariably singled out for comment.[68] Despite the favourable notices, however, *The Egyptian Idol* was not the next *Trilby* or *Silver King*. It toured for a year and then disappeared from Bandmann's repertoire. A projected London performance at the Opera Comique was cancelled due to 'sudden and unforeseen circumstances', which was shorthand for serious differences of opinion between Bandmann and the producers.[69] No doubt the much-promoted 'four tons of scenery' required to stage it may have contributed to a reluctance on the part of other companies to take it on.[70]

Deployment of Alliances

Continual touring meant that there was practically no distinction between the professional and the personal spheres, as partners were invariably recruited from within the profession, even the same company. While the kinship network of the Bandmann nuclear family remained remarkably stable and resilient over three generations, the same did not hold for Maurice's own relationships. In October 1895, Maurice married Gertrude Evans, an actress in one of the Manxman companies, at St. Matthew's Church, West Kensington. A few months later, he appeared as co-respondent in a petition for divorce brought by fellow actor Percy Evans (known as Percy Mortimer), Gertrude's brother, against Percy's wife, Muriel. The court was told that Bandmann had begun an affair with Evans's wife in March 1895 while on tour in Manchester, where the

[66] 'The Egyptian Idol', *The Era*, 21 December 1895, 9; 'The Egyptian Idol', *The Stage*, 19 December 1895, 14.
[67] 'The Egyptian Idol', *The Worcester Chronicle*, 22 February 1896, 6.
[68] 'Notes from the Theatres', *The Sketch*, 28 August 1895, 278.
[69] *Dundee Advertiser*, 8 January 1897, 5.
[70] Advertisement in the *Hull Daily Mail*, 14 May 1896, 2.

two masqueraded as Mr and Mrs Barton; the petition documents adultery on numerous occasions. A letter from Percy to his wife was cited in excerpts and bore a marked resemblance to a number of dramatic works he was performing in: 'Ah you loathsome, hard-hearted, cruel fiend in woman's shape! How God allows such wretches as you to live and spread your poison, I do not know.' Percy Evans estimated his loss (i.e. his wife's worth to him) at £100, and the judge awarded Percy £125 in damages and granted a decree nisi with costs.[71]

Against this background, it is perhaps little wonder that Bandmann's marriage to Gertrude Evans did not flourish. In fact, it hardly seems to have existed, as both partners immediately embarked on separate tours. It ended eventually in divorce, in 1904, on grounds of his 'desertion and misconduct'. Described in the press as a 'leading lady', Gertrude's appearance in court had a touch of the stage. Maurice, being on tour, was not present. By this time, she was performing alongside Lily Bandmann in the Maclaren-Bandmann company. Soon after their marriage, Maurice had departed on his first Mediterranean tour, where, it was stated in court, 'one of the ladies seemed to have attracted him a great deal'. Gertrude did not accompany him, 'as she was not equal to a long voyage',[72] yet she managed a voyage to South Africa on a separate tour, so the couple spent very little time together. At the end of 1898, he wrote to her 'that months ago, and immediately after we were married, we both had made a fatal error. We have practically not lived together for the last two years, and if we did so again our existence would be a miserable one.' Gertrude consulted a solicitor, who 'caused inquiries to be made' and ascertained 'that in 1896 Mr. Bandmann had misconducted himself with a young woman'. This was probably a Miss Florence Fletcher, who stated at the trial that she had had a child by him.[73] Gertrude obtained a decree nisi with costs.[74]

After such highly publicized appearances, it is perhaps understandable that Bandmann avoided the sanctity of marriage, preferring to lead a bachelor's life on his continuous tours. The 1911 census finds Bandmann residing at 28 Burstock Road, Putney, as a boarder, an address he shared with a Miss Laurie Dean, although there is no record of any connection between them.[75] His marital status changed two years later when he

---

[71] *The Times*, 6 February 1896, 14. The original petition and Bandmann's denial of the charge of adultery is contained in a file at the National Archives J 77/570/17428.

[72] 'Actress's Marriage Story', *The Daily News*, 30 January 1904, 7.

[73] *Sheffield Daily Telegraph*, 30 January 1904, 7. This may be the child Doris Lilian Lapointe, who died in Montreal in 1917 aged nineteen, described as 'the daughter of Maurice E. Bandman'; *The Stage Archive*, 7 June 1917, 14.

[74] '"A Fatal Error": Leading lady in a divorce court role', *Daily Mail*, 30 January 1904, 3.

[75] 1911 census of England and Wales – household transcription. www.findmypast.co.uk. RG14, piece 2433. He gave his occupation as 'Gentleman'.

Figure 1.5 Maurice and Moyna Bandmann shortly after their marriage, Calcutta, 1913. (Vanessa Lopez Family Archive.)

married a soubrette from the Bandmann Opera Company, Moyna Hill, on 12 September 1913, at London. Moyna, born Hélène Moyna Hill on 25 June 1892 in London, began acting professionally at age eighteen. She joined the Bandmann Opera Company in 1912. Moyna advanced quickly to major roles, and a relationship was formed with Maurice. News of the wedding reverberated around the Bandmann Circuit. The *Japan Gazette* reported that the announcement 'will not excite much surprise among those who saw how the two were attracted during the latest tour'.[76] This marriage seems to have been a happy one, at least initially, and three children were born in quick succession: Millicent in 1914 and the twins, Moyna Patricia and Sally, in 1916 (Fig. 1.5).

[76] Cited in *The Japan Weekly Chronicle*, 30 October 1913, 796.

Judging from the series of passport applications to US consulates for himself, wife and daughters, the Bandmann family appears to have spent time together on the circuit. The last application was in 1920, and after that the relationship deteriorated. In October 1921, Moyna petitioned the divorce court for 'restitution of conjugal rights'. In the petition she claimed that Maurice had deserted her in November 1920, not having lived with her since then, although he had resided in England in the meantime. The petition contained a copy of a letter she wrote to him from a hotel in Bournemouth:

Dear Maurice,

It is now nearly twelve months since you left me to go to India and though you have been back in England you have made no attempt to see me or return to me. I am anxious to make an effort to persuade you to live with me again. Will you think this over and let me hear that you will try again. I would join you wherever and whenever you like and I ask you to make a home for me and the children once more. Your wife, Moyna.[77]

Maurice's reply to this carefully worded entreaty is not recorded, but it was clearly not positive. On 3 March 1922, Moyna was granted her petition and Maurice was formally requested by the divorce court to 'render her conjugal rights'. Failure to comply would have given Moyna the right to an immediate legal separation, the basis for a divorce if adultery could be proven. The formal nature of her letter (compared to the impassioned epistles of the earlier cases) suggests that Moyna was performing the necessary legal steps to procure a divorce on terms beneficial to her.[78] Six days later Bandmann was dead.

Bandmann's Will and Testament

When Bandmann arrived in Gibraltar on 2 February 1922 to supervise the opening of the New Empire Theatre, which he had renovated at considerable expense (see Chapter 7), he was already seriously ill with 'enteric fever' (i.e. typhus), which he had contracted in Egypt. He was hospitalized at the Colonial Hospital, where he died on 9 March 1922. There is evidence that his illness was quickly recognized as serious,

---

[77] National Archives (Kew), J 77/1832/7170.

[78] 'The Matrimonial Causes Act 1884 reformed the law so that a refusal to restore conjugal rights no longer led to imprisonment but was deemed to be desertion, which was then grounds for divorce. From then, wives are found applying to court for "the restitution of conjugal rights", not because they wanted their husbands to move back in, but as the first step towards getting a divorce.' www.historyofwomen.org/marriage.html (last accessed 1 April 2019).

because close friends and family members were present at his funeral a day later when he was buried at the North Front cemetery. Mourners included Annie Lewinstein (known as Nancy Lewis), Bandmann's secretary, to whom he bequeathed a quarter of his estate. Also present at the funeral was his niece, named as Miss Bandman McLaren, the daughter of his sister, Lily. Either she had been accompanying him or had travelled to Gibraltar on learning that he fallen seriously ill. Others present were William Freear, the manager of the New Empire, and Annie's brother, Charles Lewis (Charles Lewinstein, who was named in Maurice's will as a trustee). The latter had hurried to Gibraltar on 17 February 1922 and arrived before Bandmann died. Also present was the US vice-consul; Bandmann's solicitor in Gibraltar, Adolphus Montegruffo; and J. R. Crook, the government engineer with whom he had negotiated the renovation of the theatre.

Bandmann's death was reported throughout the East, from Gibraltar to Japan. With the exception of *The Stage*, however, no English paper printed an obituary. This indifference shows that by this time his reputation was primarily offshore, as an entrepreneur of empire but not of home. The English press accorded more interest to his will, which was dated Gibraltar, 13 February 1922, and executed on 31 March 1922. The will was written or updated there and witnessed by his solicitor Montegruffo and by William Freear, his local manager. Clearly Bandmann knew that he was dying and wished to put his affairs in order. Press interest was directed at the first provision, that one quarter of his estate was to go to secretary Annie Lewinstein, who was the daughter of a Jewish tailor from Hackney who had emigrated from Riga. 'In recognition of her loyal and faithful services', she also received all his silver, his jewellery, his household effects and his Renault motor car. One-half of the estate went to his three daughters, to be invested in trust securities and the interest to be divided equally throughout the course of their lives. This investment was also to be used to pay their nurse, Lilian Hill, £2 per week throughout her life. The will thus suggests that the children were in the care of the nurse and not their mother, Moyna. The other main beneficiaries were his mother, Millicent, and his niece, Millicent, both of whom received £1,000.

He listed his assets in Table 1.1. He described himself in the will as half-owner of the Empire Theatre in Calcutta and adjoining grounds: 'my interest in these can either be sold for the benefit of the Estate or if my trustees consider it more beneficial to continue to let the Theatre they can do so'. The estate was officially calculated to be worth £33,057 (roughly the total of the cash and bonds), which means that Bandmann

Table 1.1 *List of assets contained in Maurice E. Bandmann's will, 1922*

Deposit with Chartered Bank of India, London	£14,000
Deposit with Westminster & Parrs Bank, London	£12,000
Current account	£1,000
	£3,000 in Chinese bonds 5%
	£3,500 in Brazilian bonds 5%
Deposit with Hong Kong & Shanghai Bank, Calcutta	Rs 18,500 (= £1,200)
Deposit with Hong Kong & Shanghai Bank, Calcutta	5,400 Bandman Variety Ltd shares
Deposit with Hong Kong & Shanghai Bank, Calcutta	30,000 Russian Roubles War loan at 5½%
Bandman Eastern Circuit, Ltd	50,000 shares = £5,000
Total	£33,057

lived and died a relatively wealthy man.[79] Administration was granted to Annie Lewinstein and trustees, including his mother and Charles Lewinstein.[80] The will contained no mention of Moyna, who promptly contested it in court, claiming undue hardship after being sued for unpaid bills. She asserted that he allowed her £1,000 per year, of which she spent about £200 on clothing. His own annual income was estimated at around £3,000 per annum.[81]

Although the Bandmann companies continued to operate after his death under the directorship of various associates (see Chapter 2), his death clearly marked a caesura in the Bandmann family network. The family ties remained strong to the end: Millicent and Maurice provided for each other in their respective wills, although the latter made no mention of Lily, providing instead for her daughter, Millicent Jane, who by this time had already embarked on a career on the stage with her parents. As we saw with Millicent Bandmann-Palmer, Maurice was strongly against his own children entering the theatrical profession. The disavowal of the stage as a career by both son and mother documents a break in the theatrical genealogy studied in this chapter. It was motivated no doubt by upheaval in the theatre industry itself. Whereas both Millicent and Maurice could make a very good living, this was no longer the case by the 1920s.

[79] It is difficult to calculate currency conversion across time, but one estimation suggests that £33,000 corresponds to a fortune worth around £1,354,943 in 2017. See the currency convertor of the National Archives: www.nationalarchives.gov.uk/currency/default0.asp#mid (last accessed 2 April 2019).
[80] Will of Maurice Edward Bandman, HM Courts & Tribunals Service, 31 March 1922, F399.
[81] 'H. M. Bandman's Will', *The Straits Times*, 2 March 1923, 9.

Although it is possible to reconstruct the lineaments of Bandmann's private life through biopolitical regimes and his encounters with the legal system (which tends to have longue durée archival systems), the political person is less clearly delineated. There is no doubt that he was an imperialist, an advocate of empire, on which his business so clearly depended. A member of the Eccentric Club in London, which harboured other actors and theatre people, Bandmann certainly evinced Tory leanings, but he steered clear of direct involvement in politics. Of the many interviews he gave throughout his career, only one contains an explicit political reference. In Hong Kong in 1910 he was asked about the impending election in Britain, and he expressed support for a Conservative government: 'All knew full well that the Conservatives were the only Government which looked properly after the colonies and one could tell a vast amount of difference when the Liberals were returned. He hoped sincerely that the Conservatives would be the next Government.'[82] Bandmann's fears were realized: the election produced a hung parliament, which resulted in a Liberal government under Asquith. In his support for a colonialist Conservative government, the private and the political converged.

In its obituary, the *South China Morning Post* in Hong Kong described Bandmann as 'cheery and breezy'. He possessed considerable powers of persuasion, even charismatic appeal, in his many dealings with performers, administrators and business partners.[83] He was also ruthless and ready to litigate to protect his business interests, which while profitable were always tenuous, dependent as they were on fickle tastes and various exigencies ranging from the weather to shipping costs. As will be shown in Chapter 2, the economic model of itinerant theatre based on the actor-manager lay in the past. Whereas Maurice earned his fortune through expanding the radius of touring and many other business activities globally, the old system of the touring stock company had passed its heyday. It could only survive by expanding into the colonies under beneficial economic and political conditions.

From a biopolitical perspective, births, deaths, marriages and divorces provide an accurate pathway into the business model of the theatrical family. Although not all Bandmann marriages were characterized by dysfunction, adultery and violence, discord was certainly widespread. It led directly to the dissolution of the Bandmann-Palmer two-star enterprise

---

[82] 'New Theatre for Hong Kong: Mr. Maurice Bandmann's Views', *South China Morning Post*, 17 January 1910, 4.
[83] 'Bandmann's Exit', *South China Morning Post*, 17 March 1922, 6.

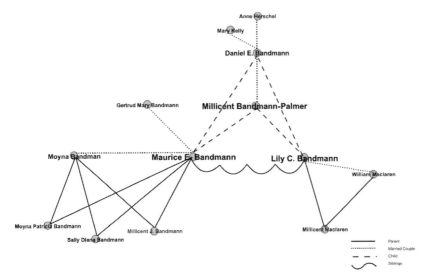

Figure 1.6 The Bandmann family networks, illustrating a high degree of homophilic interconnection between spouses and children. Except for Maurice's own children (Millicent, Sally and Moyna), all were involved in theatre. Maurice, Daniel and Millicent Bandmann-Palmer have the highest betweenness centrality.

and also to the failure of the similarly organized Bandmann-Beaudet company. Maurice Bandmann's first marriage, although to a fellow actor, never functioned on the actor-manager model. Marriages and families are prototypical cases of strong networks marked by homophilic connections (see Fig. 1.6). They are also strongly hierarchical, albeit on the smallest scale, with the paterfamilias usually controlling all activities, although in nineteenth-century theatre there are notable examples of the wife controlling the family network.[84] Because they are strongly homophilic, actor-manager families are also relatively self-contained and do not necessarily forge links with other entities. According to network theory, this means that they are not particularly innovative and above all cannot grow because of their lack of connections with other networks. Although there are examples of actor-manager families being active well into the twentieth century (such as the Kendall family in India immortalized in

---

[84] See Tracy C. Davis, 'Female Managers, Lessees and Proprietors of the British Stage (to 1914), a Database Collected and Introduced by Tracy C Davis', *Nineteenth Century Theatre* 28(2) (2000: Winter): 115–44.

the film *Shakespeare Wallah*), by this time they were an anomaly.[85] The actor-family enterprises had next to no legal basis; the actors were often employed on the basis of verbal agreements, sometimes even without pay, as in Millicent's 'pupil' system. They were designed to extract the maximum profit for the pater- or materfamilias. Maurice, in contrast, set up limited companies and eventually companies listed on the Indian stock market. These had more robust legal foundations, and all employees had contracts which could be, and frequently were, tested in courts of law. If the parental companies were held together by affective affinities, Maurice's companies were cemented by ironclad contracts that even prevented actresses from marrying while on tour.

Maurice inherited a model of theatrical production based around the touring family involving mainly a husband-and-wife double act and sometimes including the children. The actor-manager family enterprise did not 'network' well; it tended to remain a mobile, self-contained unit with weak connectivity. Bandmann's innovation was to recognize that this model, so dependent on kinship and affective affinities, was not able to provide the necessary stability for the large-scale multi-company touring that he envisaged. Homophilic networks marked by strong ties such as family and kinship are relatively stable internally but often lack the openness to form alliances with other networks. The latter situation can be better effected by networks with weak ties, which for all their instability do lend themselves better to strategic alliances, however short-lived. Multiple ties were a precondition for the Bandmann Circuit to function. These were lateral, not hierarchical, but their very laterality or low homophilic connectivity meant that they could be quickly formed and detached as the situation required.

---

[85] See also the memoirs by Geoffrey Kendal, *The Shakespeare Wallah: The Autobiography of Geoffrey Kendal with Clare Colvin* (London: Sidgwick and Jackson, 1986), and Felicity Kendal, *White Cargo* (London: Michael Joseph, 1998).

2 Mobile Enterprises

> Yet his means are in supposition. He hath an argosy bound to Tripolis, another to the Indies. I understand moreover, upon the Rialto, he hath a third at Mexico, a fourth for England, and other ventures he hath squandered abroad.
>
> *The Merchant of Venice*, 1.3.17–21[1]

Bandmann's career spans a fundamental shift in the way theatrical entertainment was organized, financed and delivered in the transition from the nineteenth to the early twentieth centuries. The period of his active professional life – roughly 1892 to 1922 – coincided with significant changes that saw small-scale theatrical family 'firms' being challenged if not largely replaced by joint-stock limited companies run by managers who often had no direct artistic input; they were neither actors, directors nor writers but rather entrepreneurs who excelled (and sometimes failed) in one of the more 'speculative forms of industrial art'.[2] In his own career, Bandmann moved from being a small-scale actor-manager (the quintessential family firm) to an entrepreneur running limited companies that were traded on the Indian stock market. He organized mergers and formed partnerships like any other industrial capitalist. A major difference was that he owned very little material stock. Like Antonio in *The Merchant of Venice*, his means were very much 'in supposition', a combination of mobile human capital and copyrighted works moving around the world on his circuit. The special qualities of Bandmann's enterprises were both symptomatic of wider developments in British and European theatre and also highly specific because of the global extent of his operations.

---

[1] *The Complete Oxford Shakespeare*, ed. Stanley Wells and Gary Taylor, Vol. 2 (Oxford: Oxford University Press, 1987), 606.
[2] 'Theatre and Music Hall Companies', in Lionel Carson, ed., *The Stage Yearbook* (London: The Stage, 1917), 65.

If we view the Bandmann Circuit, as it came to be known, as a net-work and not just a succession of ports of call, then it will become clear how it was distinguished by heterophilic ties. It intersected not just with the performers in the troupe but also with venues, copyright holders, the stock market, colonial and municipal officials, and business partners. The Bandmann network was also able to incorporate other smaller, family-based troupes, such as Allan Wilkie's and Matheson Lang's Shakespeare companies, both of which toured successfully under Bandmann's management (and both of which depended on husband-and-wife couples).[3] The long-distance touring practised by Bandmann created an intermediary form merging some of the qualities of the actor-manager family model (Bandmann was a kind of paterfamilias) and the more complex hierarchical managerial structures typical of entrepreneurs such as J. C. Williamson and his ilk.

The Managerial Turn

We can observe in the late nineteenth and early twentieth century a 'managerial turn' in the theatre and entertainment industry in the sense that they were the main drivers of innovation and diffusion. Yet the role of managers in these processes during the first phase of globalization has been largely overlooked by scholars. Even defining theatrical management is not easy because the terms are unstable. Tracy C. Davis has referred to a 'muddle of theatrical nomenclature' and confusion between a set of often-interchangeable terms: propri-etor and patentee, lessee and manager, impresario and entrepreneur.[4] Whatever the differences between these positions, they all entail a managerial function in some way. More importantly, they are, to use Ronald Burt's term, 'brokers' who enable connections and can bridge the 'structural holes' between networks where weak ties are lacking.[5] In actor-network-theory terminology, we could speak of 'intermediaries' or 'mediators'. Bandmann's special ability consisted in his ability to recognize and act on opportunities to fashion connections between

---

[3] For a discussion of this model in the West End during the Victorian period, see Jackie Bratton, *The Making of the West End Stage: Marriage, Management and the Mapping of Gender in London, 1830–1870* (Cambridge: Cambridge University Press, 2011).

[4] Tracy C. Davis, *The Economics of the British Stage, 1800–1914* (Cambridge: Cambridge University Press, 2000), 167.

[5] On the concept of 'structural holes', see Ronald S. Burt, *Brokerage and Closure: An Introduction to Social Capital* (Oxford: Oxford University Press, 2005).

the various networks of his companies, venues and the local political and economic networks that he needed to harness.

In order to study the reorganization of theatrical entertainment in this period, particularly outside of the main metropolitan centres, we need a concept of managerialism that encompasses the dynamics of both theatrical production and reception. Such a notion requires, however, that we distinguish heuristically managing from managers, the complex set of tasks and activities from the persons carrying them out. The distinction can only be a heuristic one, because in practice, management in the new sense was created by biographical persons whose actions contributed to the creation of the new concept.

The *locus classicus* of this development is Frederick Winslow Taylor's *Principles of Scientific Management* (1911), an analysis of 'task' management to improve efficiency in the workplace on the basis of 'scientific' principles, the goal being to free management from the serendipity of relying on 'some unusual or extraordinary man'.[6] Although in theatre studies we tend to associate Taylorism, as it came to be called, somewhat eccentrically with Meyerhold's biomechanics, Taylor's own less-than-modest aims suggest very much an all-encompassing shift or turn in modern life: 'the same principles can be applied with equal force to all social activities: to the management of our homes; the management of our farms; the management of the business of our tradesmen, large and small; of our churches, our philanthropic institutions, our universities, and our governmental departments'.[7] While theatre management is far from Taylor's mind, it is nevertheless imbricated in these defining elements of modernity. Drawing on economic historian Alfred Chandler's work, Tracy C. Davis points to the late nineteenth-century roots of modern management in the theatre and theatre's leading role in this development: 'entertainment may be among the first sectors of the British economy to evince the organizational characteristics of centralized management and integrated production and distribution'.[8] These organizational characteristics refer to multi-unit, modern corporations with simultaneous investment in manufacturing, marketing and management.[9]

---

[6] Frederick Winslow Taylor, *Principles of Scientific Management* (New York: Harper & Brothers, [1911] 1919), 7–8.

[7] Ibid.

[8] Davis, *Economics of the British Stage*, 181. See also Alfred D. Chandler, *The Visible Hand: The Managerial Revolution in American Business* (Cambridge, MA: Harvard University Press, 1977).

[9] According to Davis, the 'theatrical corollary to manufacturing is the centralized brokering of talent, such as a London agency putting together whole packages of music hall or theatre programmes for distribution on tour to distant provincial or foreign locations'. See Davis, *Economics of the British Stage*, 182.

In addition to the adoption or even pioneering of such techniques, in theatre the managerial turn was mostly linked to a high-profile personality, whose function was no longer primarily performance-related in the sense of acting, singing, dancing or writing but where the personal or company name came to assume its own artistic dimension in the sense of standing for quality and often genre. Managerial theatre is an early form of theatrical branding.[10] Theatre managers of the new type seldom ever bestrode the stages they managed, yet they became as closely identified with them as any virtuosic actor: Max Reinhardt, George Edwardes, Diaghilev, J. C. Williamson, Isidore Schlesinger and, here, Maurice E. Bandmann, all had brand recognition. In Bandmann's case, this was even utilized for advertising purposes, as an endorsement for Dunlop tyres illustrates (Fig. 2.1).

As the name suggests, the actor-manager model – associated with nineteenth-century theatre but in fact with its roots in the early modern period – highlights the double function of artistic and business activities in one and the same person, whereby the brand recognition was directed at the artistic, not the business, activity. The actor-manager configuration in this sense could range from the highly capitalized operations of a Henry Irving and a Herbert Beerbohm Tree to those of the myriad lesser- to better-known actors and spouses who plied their trade with the help of a small number of usually underpaid actors, some of whom were recruited on site. An itinerant actor-manager of the lesser (rather than the virtuosic) variety would typically acquire the rights to a certain repertoire if it was in copyright, hire a group of supporting performers and journey from venue to venue. They would either rent the venue from a lessee or proprietor and then pocket the box office or divide it up according to an agreed-upon percentage. This was a high-risk undertaking dependent on the play or the leading actor(s) to attract an audience. Although such performers were labelled 'managers', the term itself was used fairly loosely and often applied to 'anyone connected with the business affairs of a traveling troupe'.[11] Although some actor-managers such as Henry Irving and Sarah Bernhardt did become exceptionally wealthy, and some new managers were rendered impecunious, the important distinction was not so much wealth as the separation of managerial activity from the artistic sphere.

[10] See here David Savran, 'Trafficking in Transnational Brands: The New "Broadway-Style" Musical', *Theatre Survey* 55(3) (2014): 318–42.
[11] Levi Damon Phillips, 'Uses of the Term "Manager" in 19th Century U.S. Theatre', *Theatre Survey* 20(2) (1979): 62–3, here 63.

Figure 2.1 Bandmann endorsing Dunlop tires. (*The Singapore Free Press and Mercantile Advertiser*, 14 March 1912, p. 10. Singapore National Library.)

Victorian, and particularly Edwardian, theatre is replete with managerial theatre, which replaced the small-scale, family-style operation, although the latter continued to exist. Management in this newer sense is linked more closely to entrepreneurialism than the task management described by Taylor. Looking beyond Britain and the United States, we find spectacular examples of managerial theatre which combined entrepreneurial elements of risk-taking, creative investment, planning and producing, as well as the use of managers and management in the administrative sense to run highly dispersed organizations. The Australian manager J. C. Williamson, who was originally an American actor, created a theatrical empire in Australia that continued until 1976. The name J. C. Williamson meant control of venues (whether by lease or ownership), organization of 'product' (touring artists and productions), innovative and aggressive publicity, and the employment of mid-level site managers to administer local arrangements. Although Williamson died in 1913, his company, known simply as 'The Firm', actually grew significantly under his successor, George Tallis (1869–1948), until it became the largest theatrical company in the world. The characterization of Tallis in the *Australian Dictionary of Biography* provides a succinct summary of the new breed: 'He was a born manager whose talents blended creative perception, visual imagination, good taste, intuition and courage.'[12]

The structural characteristics of theatrical managerialism in the early twentieth century follow a set of shared principles. These attributes emphasized generic *pluralism*: theatre was understood as spectacle and entertainment in the broadest sense. For this reason, theatre, variety and the new medium of cinema were not regarded as competing entertainment forms but rather as components of a varied assortment of products. In this period, cinema was just one element of a broad selection of theatrical entertainments ranging from puppet shows to magicians, from musical comedy to drama – anything in fact that would fill a theatre. Especially outside the main centres, theatre was in the truest sense of the word a *theatron* – a place where one came to see something.

---

[12] Mimi Colligan, 'Tallis, Sir George (1869–1948)', *Australian Dictionary of Biography*, National Centre of Biography, Australian National University, http://adb.anu.edu.au/biography/tallis-sir- george-8744/text15313 (last accessed 1 March 2019). The only serious rival to 'The Firm' in Australia came from the brothers J. & N. Tait. In 1920, the J. & N. Tait and J. C. Williamson interests combined, with J. & N. Tait continuing as a separate company to promote celebrity artists. Such mergers were typical of the managerial dynamism of the period; in this respect, theatre was no different from other spheres of business.

Managerial theatre was *monopolistic*. It tended towards vertical and horizontal control of as many levels of the production and distribution of a theatrical product as possible, as well as the actual theatres themselves whether by purchase, lease or construction of new venues. This trend reached its apogee in the infamous turn-of-the century US syndicates like the Shubert Brothers and the eponymous Theatrical Syndicate, which between them controlled the touring business throughout most of the United States.

Like enterprises in other sectors, managerial theatre was predicated on *diversification and capitalization*. A common feature of large-scale theatrical management, the creation of multiple, public companies traded on the stock market meant that they not only did business with each other but also engaged in non-theatrical business activities such as real estate. The organization as public companies ensured a much higher degree of capitalization than even the most celebrated traditional actor-managers could achieve.

The managerial turn is characteristic of early theatrical globalization, understood as a rapid expansion of theatrical infrastructure driven mainly by touring companies. The key innovation that Bandmann introduced concerned the unusual combination of touring, management of venues, and stable partnerships across an extraordinary geographical range and involving numerous cities, languages and political regimes.

The Business of Theatrical Mobility

In 1895, the British theatrical trade paper *The Stage* conducted a survey amongst readers to ascertain the burden of rail costs for itinerant theatre companies. The article noted that 'Mr Maurice E. Bandmann headed the list who reported paying as much as £1,300 in fares and goods rates'.[13] By this time, Bandmann had left his mother's company and set up his own, touring Wilson Barrett's smash hit *The Manxman* and featuring his sister, Lily, in the role of Kate Cregreen (the play is discussed in Chapter 4). While it was standard practice for a small touring company to ply its trade with a successful play and some less successful ones to complement the repertoire, Bandmann set up two companies in 1894 devoted to the same play – *The Manxman* A-North and B-South companies – to extract more profit from the expensive (although by no

---

[13] 'Railway Reform', *The Stage*, 31 October 1895, 11.

means exclusive) rights he had acquired.[14] He performed in and managed the A-North company and installed a manager, E. H. Nelson, for company B. The use of these two troupes – and a year later he would add two more – explains Bandmann's record-breaking transport costs.

Managing multiple touring companies was not his invention, of course. The colourful actor and impresario Ben Greet (1857–1936) had begun touring West End successes in the 1880s and at his peak could boast '25 fit-up companies travelling under his banner'.[15] By the turn of the century, around 200 companies small and large were on the road criss-crossing the country. The infrastructural background to this boom in theatrical touring was the rapid expansion of provincial theatre-building since the 1880s. Between 1895 and 1900, the number of theatre buildings in Britain, excluding music halls, increased from 319 to 343.[16] These new venues, which were all run on a commercial basis, produced a huge demand for theatrical product.

From the many reviews the touring companies generated, one can see that the Bandmann *Manxman* companies clearly had a reputation for excellence, which was by no means the norm for such troupes. A three-night stint at the Theatre Royal in Edmonton near London prompted *The Era*'s correspondent to claim that it was 'one of the best, probably the best, company that has ever visited Edmonton'.[17] Regardless of a good reception, however, the economic problem of the touring companies remained the short sojourn: the provincial centres were unable to sustain the long runs that made possible the successful productions in London which generated the huge returns. An analysis of the *Manxman* companies between 1895 and 1896 demonstrates remarkable mobility as well as extremely short performance runs. In 1895, *The Manxman* A-North company (which included Bandmann as lead actor) performed in forty-six different theatres (some theatres were visited twice), whereas the B-South company managed forty-seven. Often, the companies operated in close geographical proximity to one another, so

[14] In November 1894, *The Sketch* announced that Barrett had sold 'the No.1 and No.2 rights' to H. Cecil Beryl and that 'a clever young actor, Mr Maurice Bandmann' had obtained 'certain other rights to the play', *The Sketch*, November 7 1894, 82. In *The Era*, Bandmann announces that he has acquired exclusive rights to the play for the provinces, except for those held by Barrett himself. Performances are booked out until 3 February 1896 and 'all scenery carried with both companies'. *The Era*, 13 July 1895, 2.

[15] Claire Cochrane, *Twentieth-Century British Theatre: Industry, Art and Empire* (Cambridge: Cambridge University Press, 2011), 50.

[16] Ibid., 19.

[17] *The Era*, 23 May 1896, 18.

that the designations North and South were not indexed to particular regions. For instance, on 7 January 1895, company A performed in Llanelly, South Wales, while company B-South appeared in Abercarn, roughly sixteen miles away. The frequency meant that both companies averaged at least one different theatre per week; the mean duration was little more than one or two nights per town.

Managerial and proprietorial arrangements were highly volatile in the itinerant theatrical world, and companies were continually being reorganized, renamed and repackaged. By 1897, the Bandmann Répertoire Company was on the road; a year later, it appeared as Thomas Verner's Bandmann Répertoire Company, advertising a Mediterranean tour, although the repertoire (*The Manxman*, *Trilby*, *David Garrick*, etc.) was largely the same and a number of the actors remained relatively loyal amongst the normal fluctuation.

Also in 1897, Bandmann's touring operations took on a new quality and range when he joined forces with Malcolm Wallace to form the English Comedy Company to tour the Mediterranean. The first port of call was Gibraltar, which the company reached in late September. After a ten-day season at the Theatre Royal, they continued on to the British colony and naval port of Malta. As will be explained in more detail in Chapter 3, Malta would assume a special significance for Bandmann. On this first visit, the company played a remarkable two-and-a-half-month season, finally leaving at the end of December to continue on to Alexandria and Cairo. The evident artistic and financial success of the tour motivated Bandmann not only to return annually but also to embark on a new business model. Later he claimed that the first tour had been a disaster; the second, however, made him a profit of £1,000 in six months, with excellent business in Egypt.[18]

Bandmann Ltd

Encouraged by this financial success, on 27 July 1900, Bandmann registered the Mediterranean and the East Entertainment Syndicate Ltd as a 'Company Limited by Shares and the Companies Acts, 1862 to 1893'. The memorandum of association contains both general

[18] 'The Bandmann Company: A Chat with the Man at the Head', *South China Morning Post*, 9 March 1906, 2.

stipulations regulating any limited-liability company as well as more specific rules pertaining to theatrical management. These included:

(b) To carry on at any place or places both in the United Kingdom or else-where the business of Theatrical Agents, Proprietors, and Managers, and in particular to provide for the production, representation, and performance of opera, stage plays, operettas, burlesques, vaudevilles, ballets, pantomimes, spectacular pieces, promenade and other concerts, and other musical and dramatic performances and entertainments.

(d) To enter into agreements with authors or other persons for the dramatic or other rights of operas, plays, operettas, burlesques, vaudevilles, ballets, panto-mimes, spectacular pieces, musical competitions and other dramatic and musical purposes and entertainments, or for the representation thereof in the United Kingdom and elsewhere, as well as of foreign, colonial and American rights, and to enter into engagements of all kinds with artists and other persons.[19]

Article (b) groups together the different activities of agents, proprietors and managers into one legal category encompassing broadly all forms of performance and extends jurisdiction to the 'United Kingdom or Elsewhere', thereby taking cognizance of the fact that theatrical tour-ing is not bounded by national borders. Similarly, article (d) recognizes that a theatrical limited company will be operating in multiple copy-right jurisdictions ('foreign, colonial and American rights').

The Articles of Association, a separate document, outlines the appointment of Bandmann as governing director at an annual salary of £225. The summary of capital and shares, dated 6 October 1900, stated the nominal capital as £500, divided into 500 shares of £1 and owned by seven shareholders (Table 2.1).

The majority shareholder was Blanche Forsythe (1873–1953), the company's leading lady and a member of Bandmann's companies since the mid-1890s.[20] The division of shares indicates that Forsythe was the major investor in the company, while Bandmann as 'Governing Director' was its major financial beneficiary, claiming roughly 50 per cent of the share capital as a salary.

By setting up a limited-liability company, Bandmann was keeping abreast of new developments in the entertainment world. It reflected

---

[19] Mediterranean and the East Entertainment Syndicate Ltd: Memorandum and Articles of Association, National Archives, London: BT 31/8984/66396.

[20] Advertised as 'England's greatest emotional actress' at a screening of the film *East Lynne*, she toured in the 1890s with Bandmann's *Manxman* company, playing Kate Cregeen and Trilby. She was also a member of the Bandmann Opera Company on the Bandmann Circuit. *Burnley News*, 3 December 1913, 3.

Table 2.1 *Shareholders of the Mediterranean and the East Entertainment Syndicate Ltd*

Name	Occupation	Number of Shares (in £)
Forsythe, Blanche	Spinster	150
Forsythe, Blanche	Spinster	220
Herbert, Arthur	Actor	1
Durie, Charles	Gentleman	1
Austin-Leigh, Anthony	Theatrical manager	125
Godwin, Richard C.	Stockbroker	1
Chester, J. F.	Clerk	1
Ellis, W. J.	Clerk	1
		500

the significant shift from the family firm model of theatrical management to a corporate enterprise, albeit a small and undercapitalized one. Economic historians have emphasized the revolutionary nature of this form of corporate organization, which entailed a relatively high degree of potential return on investment at low personal financial risk. While the older form of joint-stock company that emerged in the early modern period meant equal investment and risk for shareholders, the new form that developed in the nineteenth century enabled greater leverage for less personal financial investment, and above all liability. The successive development of the Companies Acts meant a progressive reduction of personal liability and was a significant factor in helping the burgeoning manufacturing industry attract investment. For the theatre industry, this meant the ability to gather capital for expensive building projects and also to manage other assets such as copyrighted works. The shift to the joint-stock, limited-liability company in the theatre begins mid-century and is characterized by a small number of investors – over half had less than ten. The minimum number of shareholders was seven, which was lowered to three by the end of the century.[21] Because of the small numbers of shareholders, such companies were seldom traded on the stock market and functioned more as a means to limit risk for a small group of investors while offering them the potential for considerable financial gain.

[21] See Davis, *Economics of the British Stage*, 173, and Cochrane, *Twentieth-Century British Theatre*, 48.

Unfortunately, the Mediterranean and the East Entertainment Syndicate Ltd generated neither profit nor a risk-free investment. It advertised for performers for a projected Mediterranean tour in September 1900, which did in fact take place, with Malta again being the main port of call.[22] In July 1901, a large advertisement by the company appeared in *The Era*, announcing 'Artistes Wanted' for the syndicate. It listed Maurice E. Bandmann as governing director under the 'immediate patronage of His Highness the Khedive, the Viceroy of Egypt H.E. Viscount Cromer', and other notables. It claimed to be on a 'Fifth year of tour' (which pertained to Bandmann's touring activities since 1895 and not the business operations of Mediterranean and the East Entertainment Syndicate per se). Tour A was devoted to England and the West Indies, lasting from September through December, while Tour B focused on the Mediterranean, leaving England in December and returning in May. The tours were evidently planned to run successively, as the syndicate was not able to field two full companies simultaneously.[23]

Both tours took place, yet not under the aegis of the Mediterranean and the East Entertainment Syndicate Ltd. In the West Indies, the Bandmann Opera Company undertook visits to Jamaica, Barbados, Trinidad and even Guyana, which lasted from mid-October 1901 until January 1902. The repertoire ranged from light opera (*The Mikado*), to melodrama (*Trilby*, *The Sign of the Cross*) and featured both Bandmann and Blanche Forsythe in leading roles. The tour was instigated by the shipping company Elder, Dempster and Co. to publicize their new direct steamship service between the UK and the West Indies. Prior to that time, the company, the largest in the UK, mainly serviced West African ports, where it played a significant role in the British colonization of the region.[24] In September 1901, a number of newspapers carried the same report that 'Messrs. Elder, Dempster, and Co. have made arrangements by which an opera company of 35 to 40 artistes will sail for Jamaica by the Port Royal [the shipping company's new ship for the West Indian run] on the 28th September'.[25] The article explicitly

---

[22] Newspapers in Malta record in detail performances by the Bandmann Comedy Company and the Bandmann Repertoire Company under the 'direction of Mr. A. Austin Leigh'. There are almost daily reviews in the *Daily Malta Chronicle* between 2 January and 11 March 1901, which attests to the capability of the island to host exceptionally long seasons.

[23] *The Era*, 6 July 1901, 31.

[24] Paul Wood, 'The History of Elder Dempster', www.rakaia.co.uk/assets/elder-dempster-history-summary.pdf (last accessed 2 April 2019).

[25] Cited here in the *Manchester Courier and Lancashire General Advertizer*, 13 September 1901, 8.

mentions Bandmann as director and lists part of the repertoire: *La Cigale*, *Little Christopher Columbus*, *The Geisha* and *The Casino Girl*. This was the main repertoire of the Bandmann Opera Company, which also included comedy and melodrama. The Bandmann Opera Company became the core company for the later Bandmann Circuit but at this time does not appear to be part of another limited-liability company, being run instead on the old method of a 'family firm'.

The collaboration with a shipping company such as Elder, Dempster, and Co. is significant because it demonstrates how the network principle could be utilized to the mutual benefit of interested parties. For the shipping company, the transportation of a high-profile theatre company guaranteed attention; for the Bandmann Opera Company it meant cheap transportation to a distant market where there was practically no competition; for the audiences and local theatre managers in the West Indies it meant access to professional theatre. The shipping company, in turn, was reacting to a political initiative by Joseph Chamberlain to reinvigorate the West Indian economy after the collapse of the sugarcane industry caused by the introduction of beet sugar. The plan was to cultivate the West Indies as a source for tropical fruit. The deal was, in a nutshell, opera for bananas.[26]

By September 1901, just as the Bandmann Opera Company was about to embark on its first tour to the West Indies, the Mediterranean and the East Entertainment Syndicate Ltd was already in liquidation. The 'gentleman', actor-manager and shareholder Charles Durie (one share) was appointed as liquidator. Since Durie was continually on the move with the Carpenter & Crichton Company in the 'new musical comedy' *The Lady's Maid*, the process dragged on for another year. On 27 November 1902, Durie finally submitted a signed affidavit confirming that the company had neither assets nor liabilities, the 'total amount of capital paid up in cash was £275' and £225 had been 'issued otherwise than cash'.[27] It is unclear why the company went into liquidation so quickly, presumably because of personal differences rather than financial burdens. *The Times* records a court case between Bandmann and the company of which he was the governing director, so there had evidently been friction among the shareholders.[28] By this time, Bandmann had begun to shift his operations westwards as well as eastwards. In 1903 he undertook further tours to the West Indies and visited several countries in South America.

---

[26] For the link between the fruit industry and the new shipping line, see *Ocean Highways: Illustrated Souvenir of Elder, Dempster & Co.* (Liverpool: Shipping Gazette and Lloyd's List, 1902), 40.
[27] National Archives, London: BT 31/8984/66396.
[28] 'Law Notices', *The Times*, 1 February 1902, 5.

Bandmann and Partners

To reach audiences, Bandmann required, in ANT terminology, inter-mediaries and mediators of different kinds. Of these intermediaries, business *partnerships* were perhaps the most important, often connecting the peripatetic entrepreneur with the culture of the locale, which became a distinguishing characteristic of the Bandmann network. In comparison with normal touring, where an artist or company would pass through a city with little long-term impact, Bandmann attempted to forge lasting ties with the important centres on his circuit. This involved leasing theatres, not just for his companies but for other troupes and artists as well. Most significantly, he planned to, and indeed did, build new theatres. The fact that Bandmann built or attempted to build modern theatres in many of the cities on the circuit suggests that his investment was long term and predicated on a growing public for theatrical entertainment. It also shows that his network was designed for permanence rather than quick profit.

Bandmann's first major partnership outside Britain, however, was not local but of a peripatetic kind. In 1904 he formed an alliance with the actor Henry Dallas. The latter's Dallas Musical Comedy Company and the Bandmann Opera Company appeared as a double act until the two impresarios fell out and undertook litigation against one another. Contractual partnership rather than joint stock was the dominant theatrical business arrangement in this period. Henry Dallas, the stage name of James Ryder (?–1917), was already well established in the East. After a short period working as a sailor, Ryder soon switched to acting. As his obituary noted, he was determined 'to carve out a career for himself in lands overseas, where Britons congregate'.[29] He first embarked on this mission in the mid-1890s on a tour to South Africa and then further afield to India in 1900 with the George Edwardes musical comedies *The Geisha* and *The Runaway Girl*. His circuit and repertoire closely paralleled Bandmann's, although he appears to have started somewhat earlier. It was therefore perhaps logical that the two manager-performers soon formed a partnership.

The partnership was presumably necessitated by disputes over the musical comedies for which Bandmann had obtained exclusive rights in the British colonies in 1903. Rights to the hugely popular George Edwardes' musical comedies were clearly a key to the partnership and had to be safeguarded at all costs against competitors. In July 1904, Dallas published a strongly worded notice in the Singapore *Straits Times*

[29] 'Death of Mr. Henry Dallas', *The North-China Herald*, 30 June 1917, 763.

warning 'proprietors or lessees of theatres or Halls, resident or touring managers and companies' that the 'Dallas & Bandmann Opera Company' possessed 'sole rights of the following plays, viz: "The Cingalee", "The Country Girl", "The Duchess of Dantzic", "The Orchid", "Madam Sherry", "The Girl from Kays"'.[30] In any case, the two companies were supposed to act in tandem rather than as a merger, with Dallas working the eastern portion of the circuit, roughly India to Yokohama, while Bandmann concentrated on the Mediterranean, the West Indies and South America and the eastern side of Canada.[31] According to an article published in *The New York Clipper* in February 1905, the Bandmann Dallas Opera Company played for nine successful nights at the opera house in St Johns, Newfoundland. The article describes the company as 'globe trotters':

as their engagements extend to nearly every part of the world. They have already toured South America, West Indies, and they go from here to Boston where they embark for Gibraltar, going from there to Malta, thence to Egypt and India, where they join another of the Messrs Bandmann-Dallas companies. They will then *proceed to Java*… Maurice E. Bandmann, the senior member of the firm, is English, as is his company, and is a son of Daniel Bandmann, the well-known tragedian.[32]

In the same month, the Dallas-Bandmann Opera Company (note the changed order of names) was performing in Singapore.[33] During the same season, the Dallas Opera Company also appeared there under its own name, so clearly the affiliations were loose and primarily motivated by copyright exigencies.

The partnership with Henry Dallas was to prove a fractured one, with the two managers communicating more frequently via litigation in court than through gentlemanly agreements. Trouble began as early as 1905, only a year after the partnership had been made public. In June 1905, Bandmann announced in the Singapore *Straits Times* that he was severing all ties with Dallas:

I beg to inform you that the combine that existed between Mr. Henry Dallas and myself is at an end, I having cancelled same. From now on this gentleman has no right to connect my name with his in any shape or form, nor has he any right to play any of Mr. George Edwardes' or the Gaiety pieces. My company in the future will be known as before by the name of the Bandmann Opera Co.[34]

[30] 'The Dallas & Bandmann Opera Co.', *The Straits Times*, 11 July 1904, 4.
[31] See the article 'Theatrical Partnership', *Singapore Free Press*, 4 June 1904, 2.
[32] 'St John', *The New York Clipper*, 25 February 1905, 25.
[33] See the article 'The Dallas Bandmann Opera Company', which highlights 'this strong combination', *The Singapore Free Press and Mercantile Advertiser*, 7 February 1905, 5.
[34] 'The Dallas-Bandmann Co.', *The Straits Times*, 7 June 1905, 5.

According to a case heard in the Supreme Court in Penang in June 1906, brought about by two former members of the Dallas-Bandmann Opera Company who were stranded there, Bandmann disowned any direct liability for the financial operations of his partner:

Mr. Bandmann whose evidence was taken on commission denied that he was connected with the 'Dallas-Bandmann Company', which engaged the plaintiffs. He was touring with his own company, in which no one but himself had any interest. His name was associated with Mr. Dallas merely to enable Mr. George Edwards [*sic*] Gaiety pieces, of which Mr Bandmann had the sole right of performance to be played in certain places, including the Straits Settlement. Mr Dallas was the only sub-licensee under him.[35]

The company had encountered financial difficulties in Shanghai, where Dallas and his wife left the performers, taking with them the 'reserve fund' (the company's cash flow). This forced the actors to borrow money to get as far as Hong Kong, then Singapore and finally Penang, where the company dissolved. All the while, Bandmann had sent messages disowning any financial responsibility for the Dallas Company, although his name adorned stationery and all publicity material. A year later, in April 1907, Bandmann petitioned the High Court in Calcutta to wind up the partnership with Dallas, to which the latter replied with a defamation suit in May 1907. In a private letter to Dallas, Bandmann had made accusations that the former regarded as libellous and defamatory. We can only speculate what these accusations were, but from the suit brought in Penang it is clear that Dallas was – in Bandmann's eyes – financially irresponsible and that his business planning did not extend much past the next port of call. Although it was not unusual among itinerant touring circles for companies to be stranded without funds – a few bad houses were enough to exhaust the reserve fund – there is no record of Bandmann ever doing this.[36]

Despite this acrimony, business exigencies seem to have won over, because by the end of 1907, Bandmann and Dallas had reconciled their differences and reformed the partnership, with Dallas running the opera company again and performing the lead comic roles. In an interview given in Calcutta, Bandmann stressed that the new agreement pertained only to the opera troupe and not to his other companies. The disputed partnership agreement had, he claimed, curtailed his theatre-building activities in particular: 'Before I was afraid to do anything lest the law step in and say that Mr. Dallas was entitled to a half share in

[35] 'Theatrical Law-Suit', *The Straits Times*, 16 June 1906, 5.
[36] 'Eastern Tours', *The Stage Archive*, 20 October 1921, 6.

all I did.'[37] Inevitably, this partnership also was of brief duration, and Bandmann resumed his touring activities under his own name.

Of key interest is the legal and commercial status of a partnership as a way of running theatrical operations. Partnerships are, as Tracy C. Davis notes, 'frequently short-lived business structures, readily disbanded or reconstituted'.[38] They also constitute the secondary stage of business organizational forms evolving from family firms, through partnerships and on to larger corporate structures, which also holds true for theatre in the nineteenth and early twentieth centuries. Partnerships tend to demonstrate specialization of function and arise when more profit can be gained for both parties and when there is little or no direct competition between partners. Although a formal contract was not necessary, as opposed to setting up a limited-liability company, some kind of agreement in the form of an exchange of letters was usually enacted. This seems to be have been the case with Bandmann and Dallas, although the reconstitution of the partnership in London only took 'half an hour', according to Bandmann. Partnerships have, on the one hand, the advantage of being relatively informal arrangements requiring neither complex legal agreements nor large investments of capital. On the other hand, they also mean that partners are liable for each other's debts, which was a key problem of the Bandmann-Dallas partnership, where the latter was evidently financially irresponsible.

Partnerships lend themselves more readily to a greater degree of institutionalization than do family firms, because they require a more precise calculation of tasks, divisions of responsibility and judgements regarding operational decisions.[39] The Dallas-Bandmann partnership can be seen, therefore, as an intermediary step between the family firm and the corporatization that would eventually characterize Bandmann's operations. It was perhaps also the logical step towards more complexity after the short-lived attempt to form a joint-stock, limited-liability company in the form of the Mediterranean and the East Entertainment Syndicate Ltd. However fractious the relationship was, there evidently existed a greater degree of mutuality than competition. Dallas, who had been building audiences since the mid-1890s, was the trailblazer of the Eastern circuit and had been providing audiences with theatrical fare that was identical to that offered by Bandmann. He appears also to have begun somewhat earlier than Bandmann with the performance of Edwardian musical comedy, which did not feature at all in Bandmann's English and first

---

[37] 'The Bandmann-Dallas Combination', *The China Mail*, 27 November 1907, 2.
[38] Davis, *Economics of the British Stage*, 245.
[39] Ibid., 246.

Mediterranean tours of the 1890s. Touring musical comedy was a more complex matter than doing so with comedy or drama because it required musicians, musical directors and specialist performers, as evidenced by the advertisements for the Mediterranean and the East Entertainment Syndicate Ltd, which specified in great detail vocal and physical requirements. By securing the rights for the George Edwardes musical comedies for the British Empire, Bandmann had effectively made Dallas dependent on him, because the enforcement of performance rights was becoming more effective and more of an issue as touring activities intensified. Bandmann, in turn, needed Dallas's performance expertise for this new repertoire and, initially at least, his knowledge of the routes around South East Asia and the Far East.

Building Partnerships

Bandmann's partnership with Henry Dallas was based mainly on short-term mutual benefits, and Bandmann maintained it as long as it served his purposes. After 1908, it was dissolved again, but without public recriminations or legal action.[40] By this time, Bandmann had established himself in India, where he had been active on a regular basis since 1905, although his first tour to that country dates to early 1901. Calcutta, still the British colonial capital of India, became his headquarters. By 1907 he was sole lessee of the Theatre Royal there and proprietor and manager of the Grand Opera House 'in the course of erection'. An advertisement in *The Stage* in October of that year (Fig. 2.2) speaks explicitly of 'Maurice E. Bandmann's Circuit' and lists the touring companies. Apart from his core companies, the Bandmann Opera and the Bandmann Comedy companies, he mentions another opera company and, more importantly, 'The London Bioscope and Variety Company', which documents his early involvement in cinema, in combination here with variety (see Chapter 7). A year later, he advertised in the English-language Indian paper *The Amrita Bazar Patrika* a 'Grand Re-Opening under entirely new Management' as being the 'sub-lessee of the Lily Theatre', which was considered one of the Indian theatres (the notice includes mention of 'special accommodation for Zenana Ladies').[41] Here he presented Tom Lilliard's New Bijou Troubadours, an Australian children's troupe and a selection of films from the Alhambra Theatre, London. As sub-lessee,

---

[40] In 1913, Bandmann was hosting the Dallas Comedy Company at the Theatre Royal in Calcutta and was helping Dallas promote his latest tour; see 'Mr. Maurice Bandmann and the New Dallas Comedy Co.', *Ceylon Observer*, 12 January 1913, 65.
[41] 'Amusements', *The Amrita Bazar Patrika*, 27 February 1908, 3.

INDIA   and   THE   FAR   EAST
_____

MAURICE E. BANDMANN'S CIRCUIT.
The Premier Theatres of the East.

_____

Maurice E. Bandmann controls now the
only circuit of theatres in the East.
Proprietor and Manager.
GRAND OPERA HOUSE, CALCUTTA
(now in the course of erection).
Holds, at ordinary prices, £850.
Sole Lessee and Manager.
THEATRE ROYAL, CALCUTTA
Holds, at ordinary prices, £250
Two Resident Scenic Artists, Band and Full Staff
Companies Touring:-
THE BANDMANN OPERA COMPANY.
THE BANDMANN COMEDY COMPANY,
THE O'CONNOR OPERA COMPANY
and
THE LONDON BIOSCOPE AND VARIETY
COMPANY.
Required, First-class Attractions of Every
Description. Rent, Share, or Certainty.
Address all communications.
MAURICE E. BANDMANN, Theatre Royal,
Calcutta.
Telegraphic address, "Svengali. Calcutta"
ALFRED DOVE, 28. Gerrard Street, London, W.
London Representative.
Telegrams, "Turridu. London."

Figure 2.2 Advertisement for the Bandmann Circuit and the Theatre
Royal, Calcutta. (*The Stage*, 17 October 1907, 28.)

Bandmann placed himself in a somewhat precarious position at the lower
end of the theatre managerial food chain, and the project does not seem to
have lasted long. Cinema was, however, to become a significant, although
never central component of his business operations. The goal of advertisement was to attract touring companies and acted to fill the theatres. The
advertisements show that his financial investment had grown. By leasing
the Theatre Royal (an older theatre building in Chowringhee Street), he
had financial commitments, which had to be met.

The mention of the 'Grand Opera House in the course of erection' refers to the Empire Theatre which would open just over a year later. Here Bandmann proclaims himself 'proprietor', which was only half-true. He had, however, formed a partnership with a local Armenian-born businessman, Arratoon Stephen (1861–1927), and together they planned and executed the building of the Empire. The partnership with Arratoon Stephen was to prove the most successful and long lasting. Stephen, whose full name was Arratoon Stephen Hyrapiet Gregors Bashkoom was born in Julfa, Ispahan (in present-day Iran), into an Armenian family of jewellers. At the age of seventeen, he travelled to Calcutta, where family members were already resident. Here he established a successful jewellery business and gradually moved into property. He bought and sold properties, including in the mid-1890s No. 16 Chowringhee, containing the dilapidated Theatre Royal. He successively purchased or leased the adjoining buildings and turned them into attractive shop fronts and hotels, including the Grand Hotel.[42] In this partnership, Stephen provided most of the capital and Bandmann the know-how, just as he would two years later with the Parsi coal merchant J. F. Karaka in Bombay in order to build the Royal Opera House there. Once the Empire opened, Bandmann always advertised himself as 'half-owner', which he remained until his death.

The partnership deal was signed on 17 December 1907, 'for the purpose of managing, maintaining and otherwise utilising for profit the theatre and building … known as the Empire Theatre and also the Theatre Royal'. The partners jointly appointed Warwick Major as manager.[43] The move into theatre ownership was motivated by the rapidly growing costs of leasing theatres in Calcutta and Bombay. On a number of occasions, Bandmann complained to the press of the prohibitively high costs of leasing, which, he claimed, rivalled those in London. In 1907, the Calcutta press published a rumour that Bandmann was bidding for the lease to the Grand Opera House in Lindsay Street against his 'partner' Dallas at a 'probable price of Rs 3,000 a month'.[44] Bandmann subsequently denied the rumour, but the process gives an accurate indication of the liabilities such a lease incurred. Rs 3,000 corresponded to approximately £200 per month.[45] This was cheap in comparison to London, but in the light of the unreliable bookings, it was still a considerable risk. Calculated the

[42] Ranabir Ray Choudhury, ed., *Early Calcutta Advertisements, 1875–1925: A Selection from* The Statesman (Calcutta: Nachiketa Publications, 1992), 580–1.
[43] 'Theatrical Defamation Suit', *The Amrita Bazar Patrika*, 4 January 1910, 7.
[44] 'Theatre Deal – Mr. Bandmann Bids for the Opera House', *The Empire*, 19 October 1907, 3.
[45] The conversion rate of rupees to pounds sterling at this time was 15 to 1. See 'Notes on Currency' in the front matter.

other way, the £250 per house would generate income in the realm of Rs 3,750, enough to pay the lease in one evening. Of course, only a small portion of this would go back to the lessee, but when Bandmann was touring his own companies, he could keep the gross income. Theatrical management could generate large profits as well as large losses.

Bandmann's desire to own theatre houses marked a new stage of theatrical entrepreneurship, which was motivated by a need to increase vertical control of his theatrical enterprises. From a network perspective, Bandmann, by forming a local partnership with a real estate developer, was establishing an alliance or filling a 'structural hole' between two networks – that of theatrical enterprise and the property business of Arratoon Stephen. Bandmann joined this expanding commercial development by offering Stephen his theatrical expertise. He also had a financial interest in two hotels in the same block (including the Albany, where he accommodated his performers), so that theatrical management and accommodation formed an interconnected node.

Partnerships can thus be seen as nodes in a structure of business and artistic relationships (Fig. 2.3). They represent a means by which theatrical networks enabled the relay of people, intellectual property, entertainment, technical know-how and affective relationships around the world. Repeatedly, Bandmann tried and sometimes succeeded in forming such local partnerships either to jointly manage or even own theatre buildings. Apart from the Empire in Calcutta, his most successful venture was in Bombay. In order to build the Royal Opera House there in 1911, at a cost of approximately £33,000, he formed a partnership with a Parsi coal merchant and entrepreneur, Jehangir Framji Karaka (see Chapters 3 and 7). The construction of a theatre – a highly complex operation involving considerable capital investment, local knowledge, bureaucratic negotiations and political savvy – represents in itself the formation of a new network. To build such theatres, the itinerant entrepreneur needed the collaboration of local partners as mediators within the city in question.

The First World War was a watershed for Bandmann, as he expanded his variety business, relocated to Cairo but also increased his involvement in cinema. During these years, he alternately competed and joined forces with the Calcutta-based Parsi businessman Jamshedji Framji Madan (1857–1923), who was expanding his operations in theatre and was shortly to establish the foundations of a local film industry.[46]

---

[46] On Bandmann and early Indian film, see Kaushik Bhaumik, 'Cinematograph to Cinema: Bombay 1896–1928', *BioScope: South Asian Screen Studies* 2(1) (January 2011): 41–67; Sharmistha Gooptu, *Bengali Cinema: 'An Other Nation'* (London: Routledge, 2011), 16.

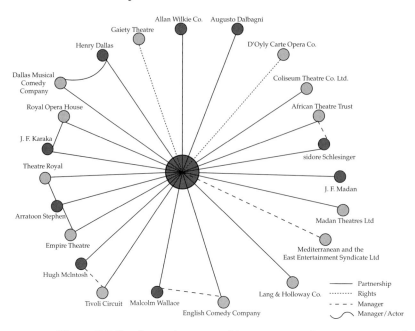

Figure 2.3 Bandmann's partnerships represented as an ego network.

Originally from Bombay, Madan had begun as an actor in Parsi theatre in his home city but later established himself as a merchant supplying the British army with wine and other provisions. This formed the basis of his fortune, with which he began to acquire theatres. In 1902 he relocated to Calcutta at the same time as Bandmann and founded J. F. Madan and Sons there. He bought the Corinthian Theatre, founded the Elphinstone Bioscope Company and began showing films in tents on the Maidan before opening the first dedicated movie house in Calcutta, the Elphinstone Picture Palace. From there, he acquired theatres all over India, became an agent for Pathé and also began producing films. In 1917 his company Madan's Far Eastern Films joined forces with Bandmann to form the Excelsior Cinematograph Syndicate, dedicated to distributing films as well as owning and managing a chain of cinemas. In 1919, Madan, like Bandmann, floated a public company, Madan Theatres Ltd, which incorporated the other companies. It was this company that formed the basis of the remarkable growth of the Madan empire. By issuing shares and generating a much broader capital base, Madan was able to embark on a large-scale program of buying up theatre houses as well as distributing and producing films, both foreign and Indian. Using an initial capital of 100 lakhs (10 million) of rupees, Madan acquired cinemas not just in India but also in Ceylon and Burma.

Bandmann and Madan were both competitors and partners, although after the First World War cooperation dominated. The two companies specialized: Bandmann provided a high-quality theatrical product, which was shown in theatres owned by Madan. The theatrical side of this collaboration broke down gradually after Bandmann's death, when the supply began to decrease, as the Bandmann Eastern Circuit began itself to focus increasingly on cinema and thus became a competitor for the Madan companies. At its height, Madan's business reputedly controlled over one hundred cinema houses and theatres throughout the Indian subcontinent as well as all levels of production and distribution, even including editing and later sound-recording equipment. This virtual monopoly generated, not surprisingly, severe criticism, and in the famous *Report of the Indian Cinematographic Committee* of 1926–27, Madan's operations, then controlled by his son, J. J. Madan, came in for particular scrutiny.

Raising Capital

By 1913, Bandmann's touring activities had reached a peak, with his core companies on the move in a continual rotation system. To expand further, he returned to the model of the joint-stock company. Early in 1914, he registered the Bandmann Variety and Asiatic Cinema Company in Calcutta with a capital of 6 lakhs of rupees (roughly £40,000).[47] This was a far cry from the £500 capital invested and lost in the Mediterranean and the East Entertainment Syndicate. With this new company, Bandmann invested in the burgeoning variety theatre business, which had become a booming branch of theatrical activity. Bandmann acquired all the properties belonging to Asiatic Cinema Ltd to form the joint-stock company. The new enterprise became proprietor of Bandmann's interests in the Empire Theatre in Calcutta, which was renamed as a variety theatre. The business plan included the production of films and the acquisition of cinema studios, which, however, came to little. The soubriquet 'Asiatic Cinema Company' was soon dropped, and the company continued to operate into the 1930s as Bandmann Varieties Ltd.

The new company was designed to capitalize on variety theatre, which with its cognates 'music hall' and 'vaudeville' had become the

---

[47] 'Joint Stock Companies', *The Times of India*, 24 April 1914, 7.

most profitable branch of theatrical enterprise. Bandmann's idea, which he expounded in an extensive interview given to the *Times of Ceylon* in February 1914, was to link together existing nationally based theatre concerns, notably the Tivoli Circuit in Australia and the African Theatre Trust in South Africa, to form a global variety theatre scheme called the 'All-Red Circuit'.[48] Preliminary discussions with Tivoli's founder, Harry Rickards (1843–1911), in Australia were curtailed by the latter's death in 1911.[49] Bandmann renegotiated with Rickards' successor, Hugh McIntosh, who was appointed managing director of the Tivoli Circuit, which was floated as a public company with a capital of £250,000. Bandmann and McIntosh agreed that 'the East would get a weekly supply of the best English artists, tapping at Colombo the supply of artists to and from Australia, contracted for by the Harry Rickards Tivoli Theatre, Ltd'. Arrangements were also made with a 'big company in South Africa', so that a circuit for artists was arranged to extend over forty weeks: 'Eighteen weeks would be spent in South Africa, sixteen weeks in Australia and six weeks in India.'[50] The forty-week engagement meant that the new consortium was in the position to offer 'star' artists long-term contracts by ensuring that there was a minimum of downtime and loss of earnings engendered by travel. This also meant that they were in a position to control the artists who wished to go abroad: 'they could only appear at theatres controlled by the three concerns which had affiliated'.[51] Colombo was intended to be the relay point connecting India, Australia and South Africa, where artists switched between the three circuits.

The 'big company' in South Africa was the African Theatre Trust Ltd., owned and managed by Isidore Schlesinger (1871–1949). Schlesinger was born in New York to a Hungarian-Jewish family. He emigrated to South Africa aged twenty-three and there sold insurance on the goldfields. In 1913 he began acquiring theatres and cinemas until he controlled most forms of performed and screened entertainment throughout South Africa, including Rhodesia and Nyasaland. Amongst theatre managers, Schlesinger was unusual in that he did not have a theatrical background. He is reputed to have said, 'What do I know about theatres? I won't buy any theatres unless

[48] See the article 'Variety Theatres – Big Scheme for "All-Red Circuit" – Mr. Maurice Bandmann's Proposals', *The Straits Times*, 10 March 1914, 2.
[49] See G. M. Anderson, *Tivoli King: Life of Harry Rickards, Vaudeville Showman* (Kensington: Allambie, 2009).
[50] 'Variety Theatres', *The Straits Times*.
[51] Ibid.

I can control the whole theatrical business in South Africa, and put it on a decent business basis.'[52] In effect, that is what he did, as well as establishing a local film industry.

Although live artists, preferably star ones, were the main draw card of the variety business, the new cinematic medium was also an integral part. Bandmann planned to acquire so-called 'first-run films', which meant the first rights to a film after its initial release. The consortium also arranged for the purchase of exclusive rights to films. The cinematic arm of the variety business initially involved showing short films as part of an evening, but as films became longer, they increasingly became an autonomous part of the theatrical business and were shown in the theatres when no live acts were available.

In the period immediately before the outbreak of war, Bandmann was anxious to form business partnerships for investments in all the important ports of call. In Ceylon, for example, he amalgamated his local theatrical interests with the newly formed Coliseum Theatre Co. Ltd., on whose board he had a seat. This company had been formed by local 'gentlemen', with a view to building a new theatre in the city for which Bandmann had been lobbying for some time. The town hall was the only performance space available and inadequate for the demands of high-quality variety. As with many of Bandmann's schemes, the Coliseum did not come to fruition, but the town hall was refurbished to make it more accommodating for itinerant troupes.

The Coliseum Theatre Co. Ltd. is symptomatic of Bandmann's grand scheme to anchor the large 'All-Red Circuit' through smaller local companies. The global circuit or network could only function if local mediating nodes were in place to facilitate the movement and exchange of the troupes. In an interview given to *The Era* in June 1914, he reiterated the main points of the Colombo interview while specifying the importance of local enterprises: 'Local companies are to be formed in the different centres, and eventually one big company will be formed to absorb all these small ones.'[53] Apart from the Tivoli Circuit, he mentions the Honolulu Theatre Circuit and the Western American Vaudeville Association. There is no evidence that he formed any association with US vaudeville circuits, but the mention of them testifies

---

[52] *Stage and Cinema* (Johannesburg), 8 July 1916, 2. Quoted in tlweb.latrobe.edu.au/humanities/screeningthepast/25/rose-of-rhodesia/parsons-1.html (last accessed 2 April 2019).
[53] 'Enterprise in the Far East: New Music Hall for Bombay', *The Era*, 24 June 1914, 17.

to the increasing global interconnectedness of the variety business. Bandmann envisaged a world-spanning circuit:

Artistes going to or returning from Australia on the Rickards tour will break the journey at Colombo for six weeks, and will play a week in Colombo, a fortnight in Calcutta, a week or ten days in Bombay, and one week in Rangoon. These artistes are not only the pick of the variety stage in England, but also those booked for Australia from the United States, who will go via the Far East to Australia and return to their own country by way of India, Egypt, and England. Thus, when the scheme is matured and is in full working order, there will be a constant chain of music-hall artistes girdling the greater part of the world.[54]

A month later, war broke out, which frustrated Bandmann's Arielesque scheme of a constant rotation of music-hall artistes 'girdling' the world.

The First World War both curtailed and stimulated his theatrical activities. Travel became more difficult, male performers enlisted for military service and merchant shipping was redirected to aid wartime activities. War could, however, also provide opportunities for a theatrical entrepreneur. War meant large movements of troops and thus men (and some women) concentrated in tents and barracks, desperate for distraction. War also meant propaganda, a new word for an old activity, which all sides of the conflict engaged in by utilizing the new medium of cinema. Bandmann became involved in both troop entertainment and war propaganda by cinematic means (see Chapter 7).

The largest concentration of Allied troops outside Europe was in Egypt, near Cairo, where preparations were under way for war with the Ottoman Empire. This lead to the disastrous Gallipoli campaign and later to the slow reconquest of Palestine, Syria and Iraq. Although Bandmann had been a frequent visitor to Egypt since the 1890s (see Chapter 3), it had only been one stop on the circuit. During the First World War, Bandmann temporarily relocated the centre of his operations there, where he entered into a partnership with the Italian 'Chevalier' Augusto Dalbagni (1874–1951), who had been an Egyptian resident since the 1890s and had established himself as an impresario. Together they owned and managed three theatres in Cairo – the Empire, the Kursaal and the Piccadilly – as well as the Alhambra in Alexandria. They also forged plans to control further theatres in Haifa, Beirut, Damascus, Aleppo, Jaffa and Jerusalem.[55] The partnership in Cairo functioned mainly on the level of repertoire, while advertising material for the Kursaal theatre presented both men as equal partners of the enterprise (see Fig. 2.4).

---

[54] Ibid.
[55] 'Mr. Bandman's Plans – the Theatre in the East', *The Times of India*, 30 September 1919, 11.

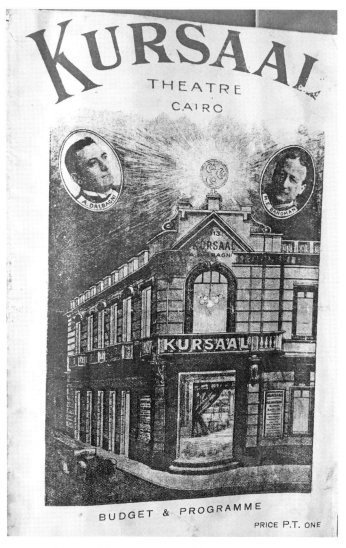

Figure 2.4 Programme of the Kursaal Theatre, Cairo, featuring
Bandmann and A. Dalbagni as partners, ca. 1915. (Vanessa Lopez
Family Archive.)

Postwar Activities

Bandman Varieties Ltd continued to operate after the war ended, although conditions for theatrical touring had deteriorated. In its six-monthly report for the year ended 31 March 1920 (Table 2.2), the company showed a profit on revenue of Rs. 51,383 (approximately £3,425). After deductions for fees, legal charges, depreciation and 'managing director's remuneration' (i.e. Bandmann's emolument), the report showed a net profit of Rs. 41,599 (£2,773). After paying a share dividend of Rs. 19,701, the remaining balance of Rs. 21,898 (£1,460) was to be allocated to a capital redemption fund and an extensions account. Clearly the company was not flourishing, and the report strongly recommended remedial action 'owing to the recent activity in India in theatrical matters'.[56] Although not exactly specified, the 'recent activity' referred to a decline in attendance due to competition from cinema, increased transportation costs and static ticket prices. The report strongly suggested that the company 'provide a continual supply of high-class attractions' to meet a demand which clearly existed. It should also improve its negotiating position in regard to theatres by providing good-quality productions.

The Indian press reported that touring companies were having severe difficulties competing with cinema because of the latter's cheap prices.[57] This pressure on costs, combined with a drop-off in audiences, led to a dearth of high-quality theatre. The solution for Bandmann was to join forces with J. F. Madan and thus gain access to his chain of theatres at reasonable prices; for Madan, Bandmann's theatre companies offered additional revenue and perhaps a cachet of cultural respectability that his cinematic offerings certainly did not have.[58]

Shortly before his death, Bandmann floated the Bandman Eastern Circuit Ltd. as a limited liability company, with his long-term associate Warwick Major as director and producer.[59] The Eastern Circuit had been in existence for some years as a business name, but only now did he actually incorporate the company by issuing shares. In his will, Bandmann noted that he owned 50,000 shares of the concern, which owed him in turn 'roughly about £ 5000'. This company, as well as

[56] 'Bandman Varieties Ltd. Theatrical Activity in India', *The Times of India*, 26 May 1920, 10.
[57] 'Bombay Theatre Prices – the Touring Company', *The Times of India*, 7 October 1920, 11.
[58] 'Trade and Finance', *The Times of India*, 14 May 1921, 6.
[59] See 'Death of Mr Bandman: An Eastern Impresario', *The Times of India*, 11 March 1922, 12.

Table 2.2 *Bandmann Varieties Ltd: Six-monthly report to 31 March 1920*

Liabilities	Rs.
Capital	1,50,840
Reserves	27,931
Debts	54,303
Profit and loss	41,599
Total	2,74,673
Assets	
Goodwill	50,000
Furniture and fittings	34,659
Bar stock	7,573
Outstandings	16,139
Cash and invests	1,66,302
Total	2,74,673

Bandmann Varieties Ltd., continued to operate for some years after Bandmann's death, under the directorship of Warwick Major. It organized, together with Madan, the hugely successful tour of Anna Pavlova in 1923, in which she performed at the Empire Theatre in Calcutta, among other cities (see Chapter 8). A theatre programme of the Calcutta performances (see Figure 8.1) states that 'Bandman's Eastern Circuit, Ltd. have the honour to present ANNA PAVLOVA at the Empire Theatre: Lessees Bandmann Varieties Ltd.'[60] The latter was primarily responsible for managing the theatres, whereas the Eastern Circuit Ltd. organized the acquisition of artists and companies. In 1935, Bandman Varieties Ltd. was still operating, although exclusively as a film distribution company specializing in British films, under the proprietorship of Humayan Properties Ltd., a Calcutta-based real estate company that purchased both Bandmann's Empire Theatre and his company.[61]

The Economics of Touring

In 1924, roughly two years after Bandmann's premature death, James McGrath, a former performer in the Bandmann Opera Company turned Bombay-based businessman, announced in *The Times of India*

[60] Theatre programme, Laurence Senelick Collection. For a discussion of Pavlova in Calcutta, see Keith Money, *Anna Pavlova, Her Life and Art* (London: Collins, 1982), 313.
[61] 'British International Pictures', *The Times of India*, 30 November 1935, 11.

Table 2.3 *Estimate of costs for touring companies in India, 1925*

Genre	Costs per Week	Average Receipts per Week
English musical comedy	£700	£1,000 a week
Dramatic star with own company	£700	£1,000 a week
Revue company	£500	£800 to £1,000
Comedy company (newest London plays)	£400	£600 a week
Concert party	£300	£400 to £600

Source: 'Theatrical Fare: A New Bombay Syndicate', *The Times of India*, 29 January 1924, 10.

that a new syndicate would attempt to reinvigorate Bandmann's touring activities. No company had really emerged to follow in his footsteps. He explained that one reason why the gap left by the Bandman Co. still remained unfilled was that 'in those days' expenses were considerably less. Increases in hotel accommodation, salaries and fares all made touring a less attractive business proposition. The only concessions that could be obtained were 'from the railway companies'. According to McGrath, capital of £5,000 or £6,000 would be required 'to build up a repertoire of modern plays as extensive as that of the Bandman Company, whereas Bandman was able to do it on a capital of £2,000'.[62] The costs could be roughly divided into the previously mentioned categories of salaries, accommodation and transport. Royalties were usually calculated on a percentage of box office, so they varied greatly. McGrath estimated the following broad costs for the different companies, which followed the Bandmann mould (Table 2.3).[63]

McGrath's estimates are rough and probably somewhat optimistic, especially regarding the receipts. To calculate the incomings and outgoings of an itinerant troupe precisely and over the period of time Bandmann was active would require a lot more data than have survived.

If we compare, however, the passenger fares between 1913, at the height of his touring activities, and 1922, the year of his death, then we can see that costs had quite literally doubled. Bandmann usually paid his actors for second-class fares. A second-class passage from Liverpool

[62] 'Theatrical Fare: A New Bombay Syndicate', *The Times of India*, 29 January 1924, 10.
[63] Ibid.

to the East Coast of the United States, for example, cost £13 in 1913 on the *RMS Carmania* of the Cunard line. The same passage on the same ship in 1922 cost just over £31.[64] This meant that the large-scale companies like the Bandmann Opera Company became increasing uneconomical. After the First World War, there is a noticeable decline in the activities of this company and a shift towards the Bandman Comedy Company, small revues and single acts such as the Russian dancers Thamara Swirskaya and the already mentioned Anna Pavlova. The Bandmann Opera Company completed its final tour in 1921 and did not survive the death of its namesake.

In the heyday of long-distance theatrical touring, roughly the period between 1900 and 1918, it was certainly possible to generate considerable profits, although not on the scale that a North American tour of a successful play or musical could provide. The assets consisted of copyright-protected works, in particular those of George Edwardes' Gaiety Theatre, which were next to Gilbert and Sullivan, whom Bandmann also represented – by far the most valuable theatrical commodities in the English-speaking world. He also secured the rights to successful comedies and melodramas, some of which were hardy annuals, others novelties. These assets also had their costs in the form of royalties, which had to be remitted regularly to the rights holders.

A major expense was that of the venues. These also varied widely. In 1907, the Gaiety Theatre in Bombay, a 'native theatre', cost £100 a week for Europeans to rent, at which price it could not be made to pay a profit, according to Bandmann. He also turned down the offer to lease the Empire Theatre in Bombay at a cost of Rs. 2,250 (£150) per month.[65] The Grand Opera House in Lindsay Street, Calcutta, cost Rs. 3,000 (£200) a month to lease.[66] In this period, he planned to build new theatres or lease existing ones so that he could discount this expense. The downside of this arrangement was the need to make the theatre pay throughout the year when his own troupes were not present.

Theatre management on a lessee basis was calculated according to how much revenue it could generate on average, an equation based on the number of seats plus their average price. These figures were used to

[64] D42/PR3/7/38 Minimum Fares (November 1913), and D42/PR3/9/46/1, Sailing List (February 1922), University of Liverpool, Library.
[65] 'Bombay Amusements: Mr Bandmann's New Theatre', *The Times of India*, 5 June 1907, 8.
[66] 'Theatre Deal – Mr. Bandmann Bids for the Opera House', *The Empire* (Calcutta), 19 October 1907, 3. The Alhambra in Alexandra cost £40.00 per week in 1920, which was definitely on the low side.

attract potential companies and artists to hire the premises, the prerequisite for any successful lessee arrangement. In 1907 while the Empire in Calcutta was under construction, Bandmann puffed its earning potential at around '£850 at ordinary prices', whereas the smaller Theatre Royal, which he also leased, was advertised at £250. The latter included two resident scenic artists, a band and a full staff.[67] This meant that a touring company did not need to transport and pay for support staff. These figures referred to the maximum gross revenue per performance. More accurate estimates are those that he gave in 1911 in an interview to *The Referee*, when he stated that the Theatre Royal and the Empire generated income of £350 and £400, respectively.[68] The capacity – £350 or £400 – reflects the potential revenue for a company, which would operate on a profit-share basis.

Of equal importance was the human capital contained in the companies – i.e. the performers, conductors and stagehands who had to be paid. The overall salary bill was the largest cost factor for the touring impresario. Records of his companies in Alexandria at the Alhambra Theatre in 1920 show an average salary bill of around £160 per week for a variety company numbering around ten to twelve members. This was a vast reduction when compared to the fifty-odd members of the Bandmann Opera Company that was the norm before the war.[69]

Bandmann was also an impresario in the more technical sense of someone who organized and promoted a company or artist for a limited time or tour.[70] These enterprises usually involved high-profile artists who were paid a fixed sum for a tour. In 1910, he reportedly negotiated a tour to South Africa, India, the Far East and Australasia with the violinist Miss Marie Hall, at very generous terms. For two hundred concerts, she was to receive the guaranteed sum of £10,000 plus a share in the profits of each concert over £50.[71] Such figures were part of pre-tour promotion and need to be treated with care. More accurate figures were those provided by two Shakespeare tours that Bandmann organized and ran almost parallel to one another.

---

[67] 'India and the Far East', advertisement in *The Stage Archive*, 17 October 1907, 28.

[68] 'Mr Maurice Bandmann: His Theatrical Enterprises in the East', *The Straits Times*, 5 August 1911, 3.

[69] Source: Vanessa Lopez Family Archive. The actual sum is 21.929,80 Egyptian piastres, which converts at an exchange rate of approximately 137 piastres to £1. See 'Notes on Currency' in the front matter.

[70] For this definition, see Davis, *Economics of the British Stage*, 166.

[71] 'Miss Marie Hall's Tour – Unique Trip of the Famous Lady Violinist', *The Straits Times*, 8 September 1910, 8.

In 1911, Bandmann signed a contract with Canadian-born Matheson Lang, who was by this time a moderately famous Shakespearean actor who had learned his craft in the companies of Frank Benson, Ellen Terry and Lillie Langtry. He formed his own company in 1910 and went into partnership with another actor, John Holloway, in order to embark on a tour of South Africa, which, after Bandmann's intervention, was extended to include India and the Far East. The initial capital of the company was £2,000, a modest sum on which to launch such an undertaking. Bandmann offered the new enterprise an additional £300 a week and 60 per cent of box office plus half the second-class fares from South Africa and back to England.[72] The ten-week season in South Africa ended with a profit of £4,800 on the books.[73]

Almost at the same time, the Shakespearean actor Allan Wilkie toured India and the Far East under Bandmann's banner after first touring for Bandmann's Calcutta competitor Elias Moses Cohen. According to figures tabled during a court case, Cohen paid Wilkie a total of Rs. 55,951 (£3,730), out of total gross receipts of Rs. 76,100 (£5,073). Wilkie received £300 per week while performing in Calcutta and £200 in other towns, out of which he had to pay his company.[74] These were the same amounts that Bandmann was paying Matheson Lang. Once expenses were deducted, such tours could be extremely lucrative. On their second visit to Bombay, a local paper claimed that Matheson-Lang had 'netted twelve thousand pounds in less than five months'.[75] Ultimately, the ten-month Lang-Holloway tour of the Far East, despite good-to-excellent houses, little more than broke even, as much-touted excellent houses were followed by dismal ones. Nevertheless, well into the 1920s, a full house in India was still called a 'Lang House'.[76]

Such tours were an integral part of Bandmann's enterprises, but they represented more the pecuniary icing on the cake than the bread-and-butter revenue of his own companies. One source we have for actual income generated from performances of the Bandmann Opera Company is the Royalties Book, no. 2, of the George Edwardes Gaiety Theatre Company.[77] This ledger contains remittances for royalties for

[72] For the details, see David Holloway, *Playing the Empire: The Acts of the Holloway Touring Theatre Company* (London: Harrap, 1979), 133.
[73] Ibid., 138.
[74] 'Theatrical Dispute – Mr Allan Wilkie in the Box', *The Englishman*, 1912. This dispute is discussed in detail in Chapter 6.
[75] 'Bombay Amusements – the Opera House', *Bombay Gazette*, 9 May 1912, 3.
[76] Holloway, *Playing the Empire*, 153.
[77] V&A Theatre & Performance Collections, Gaiety Theatre Co. Ltd, Royalties Book no. 2.

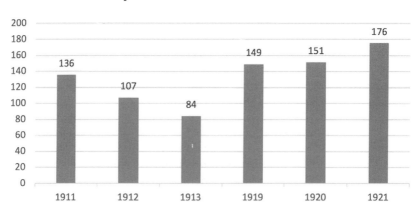

Figure 2.5 Average receipts per performance in sterling, 1911–1920. (Gaiety Royalties Book, Theatre Museum, London.)

the years 1911–1913 and 1919–1921. Although the accounts do not seem to be in any way complete, we have at our disposal data for seventy-six performances in seventeen different cities, which give some indication of the economics of touring on the Bandmann Circuit. Tracy C. Davis has already noted in her analysis of the Royalties Book that profits were 'not huge: in 1912, eighteen performances of *Peggy* and *Our Miss Gibbs* in Asia yielded £103 for the London office, or about £5.15.0 per performance'. She contrasts these minor sums with royalties from settler colonies such as South Africa, Australia and New Zealand, which were substantially higher.[78]

Davis's analysis is based on the perspective of the Gaiety Theatre in London and how much (or little) income it gained through royalties. From Bandmann's perspective, the calculation was a different one. The remittances were divided into three different kinds: a lump sum of £3 for *The Shop Girl* and *A Runaway Girl*, 5 per cent of box office or a lump sum of £5 for the other works. The lower sum for the two 'Girls' was presumably due to their age (1894 and 1898, respectively); they were older commodities whose use-by date was well past. For approximately half of the performances, the minimum sum was remitted.

If we look at gross income (Figure 2.5), then we can gain a better idea of what kind of revenue Bandmann's performances actually generated.

[78] Davis, *Economics of the British Stage*, 351–2.

The most detailed data exist for 1912, with exact receipts for twenty-three performances in sixteen cities. Although the overall value of £107 is lower than that from 1921, the latter is only represented by six cities.

Income from performances had to be calculated against salary costs. Average weekly salary payments for the Bandmann Varieties Co. after the First World War in Alexandria amounted to £160. Salaries plus rental costs for the Alhambra Theatre resulted in an overall profit of merely £43 for the week. Although this translates to approximately £1,250 in today's currency, and only represents one week's returns in a city that was possibly not the most profitable, it still demonstrates the increasingly precarious nature of itinerant theatre.[79]

After the end of the First World War, the equilibrium of theatrical and cinematic entertainment shifted significantly as the business of touring live theatre became less profitable. This was due to several factors. The rise of cinema meant competition on the entertainment market that forced troupes to charge ticket prices that were little more than those for the cinema. Advertisements on the amusements pages of the local English-language Bombay or Calcutta newspapers show an overwhelming preponderance of films, while a Bandmann troupe often provided the only professional theatrical shows on offer. In 1920, *The Times of India* analysed the situation in terms of ticket prices, which had remained unchanged for a decade while the travelling expenses of a theatrical company had doubled compared to before the war. This pressure on costs, combined with a decline in audiences, led to a dearth of high-quality theatre.[80]

In an era predating state subsidies, theatre and cinema needed to be traded for a profit, and they could be highly profitable. Bandmann certainly made a modest fortune, Madan an even greater one, while J. C. Williamson died a multi-millionaire. In the context of imperial politics, theatrical management needs to be understood not as a mere administrative task but perhaps as the most important activity in a complex network linking entrepreneurial vision, existing distribution networks, marketing strategies and fundamental unease about 'theatrical business' in a time of war. If we review the three categories defining theatrical managerialism in the early twentieth century – pluralism, monopolism and diversification – then we can find both confirmation

[79] Source: Vanessa Lopez Family Archive. This calculation is based on the year 2017 and uses the currency convertor of the National Archives: www.nationalarchives.gov.uk/ currency/default0.asp#mid (last accessed 2 April 2019).

[80] 'Bombay Theatre Prices – the Touring Company', *The Times of India*, 7 October 1920, 11.

and modification of the three concepts. Pluralism was inherent in the theatre business: outside the metropolitan centres, managers such as Bandmann traded in spectacles ranging from magicians to cinema. But all the large-scale theatre managers operating 'abroad' attempted to establish monopolies, and they were largely successful. Diversification meant creating groups of companies under one controlling figure; in this respect, Bandmann and Madan were similar, with their respective companies trading with each other.

Perhaps the most important dimension of the Bandmann Circuit was its complex networked structure that formed relations with a multitude of partners and other networks. In the capitalist-driven, entrepreneurial world of itinerant theatre in the first phase of globalization, to network meant not only to survive but was the precondition for expansion. It meant the difference between remaining an ad hoc itinerant troupe (such as that of Henry Dallas) and becoming a publicly traded company or set of companies. Bandmann exploited opportunities that arose and responded to exigencies that posed themselves; in both cases, they required the formation of relations with local partners, whether political, economic or affective. The exigencies of locality determined the exact nature of these relations: to these we turn in Chapter 3.

3 The Micropolitics of Locality

The Bandmann Circuit comprised roughly two dozen towns and cities that the companies visited on a regular basis (Fig. 3.1). If the commercial operations were on one level largely de-spatialized (the companies performed a standardized repertoire wherever they went), each locality still required specific knowledge regarding venues, press and municipal authorities. The infrastructure was highly disparate, and local cultural politics varied in the extreme. This chapter will explore how the Bandmann Circuit was imbricated in these diverse locales. The argument can be made that what distinguished Bandmann's itinerant theatre practice from that of the many other troupes that passed through the same cities and venues was not only the recurrence but also the commitment to and investment in locality. Acquiring property, leasing buildings, even constructing theatres mitigated against what has been termed a purely 'extractive' institutional relationship with the host culture.[1] These factors all contributed to the formation of networks on a local level which were tied in turn to the macro-network of the circuit.

Bandmann's engagement with the many towns and cities along his circuit needs to be understood both in economic and political terms. His interests always concerned his companies and business endeavours, which, as we will see, primarily meant securing high-quality performance venues. To achieve this, he needed to engage with the many localities on the circuit in more profound ways than were normally expected of an itinerant impresario. This engagement required a certain degree of political activity at a level which will be termed here *micropolitical*. This term combines genealogically both economic

---

[1] On the difference between 'extractive' and 'inclusive' economic institutions, see Daron Acemoglu and James Robinson, *Why Nations Fail: The Origins of Power, Prosperity, and Poverty* (New York: Crown, 2012). This is not to say that Bandmann's enterprises were altruistically inclusive, but they were not exclusively extractive, either.

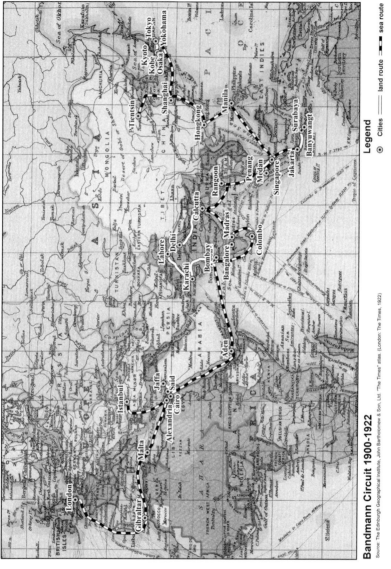

Bandmann Circuit 1900-1922

Source: The Edinburgh Geographical Institute, John Bartholomew & Son, Ltd. 'The Times' atlas, (London: The Times, 1922)

Legend

◉ Cities ═══ land route ▰▰▰ sea route

Figure 3.1 Map of the main localities of the Bandmann Circuit.

and political perspectives, or rather it highlights the latter in the former. The concept was first proposed in the early 1960s by the organizational sociologist Tom Burns to describe political manoeuvrings and competition within organizations, mainly companies, as a struggle for resources and how this can lead to innovation.[2] The term was redefined in the 1990s in the context of historical anthropology to describe patterns of patronage in the early modern era. In the German historiographical context, it is mainly linked to the work of Wolfgang Reinhard, who, inspired by Ruth Benedict's *Patterns of Culture* (1931), began to investigate the interconnection between patronage and power within the Roman papal state.[3] Micropolitics, as Reinhard understands the concept, is not just a synonym for patronage or, in its modern variation, cronyism, but rather an anthropological constant that underpins all forms of political activity. He glosses the term to refer to all forms of personal connections and networks and how they function in a political context.[4] In keeping with the ethnological perspective of historical anthropology, the view is very much one from below. In this sense, micropolitics is not a 'pre-modern' stage that was overcome with the introduction of Weberian rationalized bureaucracy in the modern era but in fact underpins all forms of politics. Although seen from below, the telos of this approach is politics in its accepted sense: the actions of politicians, officeholders and the institutions they seek to control as they interact with individuals and enterprises requiring this influence.[5]

The concept of micropolitics proposed here is a marriage of the original term proposed by organizational sociology and management studies and its more complex elaboration in the work of historical anthropology. Its micro-perspective also coheres with most forms

---

[2] Tom Burns, 'Micropolitics: Mechanisms of Institutional Change', *Administrative Science Quarterly* 6 (1961): 257–81.

[3] Wolfgang Reinhard, 'Die Nase der Kleopatra', in Peter Burschel, ed., *Geschichte als Anthropologie* (Köln: Böhlau, 2017), 273–308.

[4] For a recent survey of the term *micropolitical* and its applications, see Volker Köhler, *Genossen – Freunde – Junker: Die Mikropolitik personaler Beziehungen im politischen Handeln während der Weimarer Republik* (Göttingen: Wallstein, 2018). Köhler restricts his use of the term to competition for state resources.

[5] Another use of the term *micropolitical* can be found in Deleuze and Guattari's *Thousand Plateaus*, where they postulate that 'every politics is simultaneously a macropolitics and a micropolitics', which refers not to a question of scale – society versus individuals – but to the interpenetration of flows of desires between the 'molar' realm of representations and the 'molecular' realm of beliefs and desires; Gilles Deleuze and Félix Guattari, *A Thousand Plateaus* (Minneapolis: University of Minnesota Press, 1987), 213 and 219.

of network analysis, including actor-network theory, which, as outlined in the Introduction, also follows an ethnographic methodology
of following people, objects and processes. The origins of the term
in management studies are also relevant. Bandmann was a manager
who ran companies and who needed to negotiate different forms of
support, patronage and business partnerships in highly diverse cultural environments. The overriding political framework was colonial
rule, but his partnerships were often with local businessmen as well
as municipal authorities and the colonial public sphere. The activities
examined in this chapter are therefore studies in micropolitical networking: the forging of alliances, the garnering of symbolic patronage
and the concluding of partnerships. While much of this activity was
invisible, a certain amount was communicated through the local press
and occasionally as highly theatricalized communication via gala performances and ceremonies. In such cases, the micropolitical networks
are made manifest.

Locality needs to be understood economically, politically and culturally as a connecting point or node linking other localities. The
Bandmann Circuit capitalized on the fact that many of the locales it
visited on a regular basis were interconnected entrepôts. *Entrepôt* is used
here in both a literal and metaphorical sense. Some of the cities along
the Bandmann Circuit – such as Singapore, Hong Kong, Shanghai,
Manila and Yokohama – were quite literally entrepôts because of their
special legal status. If we extend the concept to include the broader
notion of hub, then Bombay and Calcutta as well as Alexandria and
Cairo could be understood in these terms as well. Both Indian cities
were important as centres with relatively large theatre-going populations, but they were equally significant as stopping-off points for
extended tours throughout the Indian subcontinent. Coming from the
West, Bombay or Colombo were usually the first ports of call where
the repertoire was tested. The response was invariably reported in the
press both inland and further long the circuit. In Japan, Yokohama had
the same function.

Etymologically, *entrepôt* derives from the Latin *interpositum*, meaning
literally 'between places' or to 'place between'. The state of in-betweenness
and the temporary emplacement of goods for later redistribution is an
accurate description of particular nodes on the Bandmann network.
It does not refer to every and any place of performance but only to
those with a magnifying, redistributory function. A major challenge for
itinerant theatre in the Far East was the generation of audiences receptive to Edwardian musical comedy or any of the other genres on offer.
The larger centres provided not only a crucial amplificatory function,

generating advance publicity for smaller ports of call along the route, but they provided economically the potential for longer sojourns and hence the possibility to generate revenue. Theatrical entrepôts also gradually gained a more localized function as, in Bandmann's case, he established partnerships and theatre-building schemes. This represents on the surface a counter movement to entrepostian trade by deepening locality through the investment of capital in a building rather than just leasing the theatre as a warehouse for performances. But on closer inspection, as we shall see, the localization engendered by theatre-building or leasing can also be seen in terms of a mediating function for the circuit as a whole.

If we conceptualize theatrical entrepôts in terms of actor-network theory, we can view them as intermediaries and mediators. Both have a relay function and are, in Latour's terminology, 'building blocks of the social world'.[6] They differ considerably, however, in the transformative force of moving or relaying from one entity to another. Intermediaries transport without transformation, where inputs and outputs are practically identical. Mediators, on the other hand, 'translate, distort, and modify the meaning they are supposed to carry'.[7] In the narrower sense of warehousing for rapid redistribution, entrepôts are intermediaries, but in the broader sense they can be mediators because their trading function very often results in the emergence of cultural 'contact zones' – in Mary Louise Pratt's famous formulation, those 'social spaces where cultures meet, clash, and grapple with each other, often in contexts of highly asymmetrical relations of power, such as colonialism, slavery, or their aftermaths as they are lived out in many parts of the world today'.[8] Most big cities function as mediating contact zones. And port cities in particular are predestined to fulfil this role. They often become cultural hubs by drawing merchants, artists, writers and engineers into one place where they can find manifold opportunities to work and interact with each other. Such hubs are the prerequisite for theatrical cultures to emerge. We can observe the paradoxical development through which entrepôts, despite their ostensible requirement to store and redirect wares with as little transformation as possible, become economically and culturally highly attractive locales with pronounced 'pull factors'.

Localizing the global in terms of actor-network theory requires a perspective that sees locality not just in splendid isolation but as a set

---

[6] Latour, *Reassembling the Social*, 41.
[7] Ibid., 39.
[8] Mary Louise Pratt, 'Arts of the Contact Zone', in *Profession 91* (New York: MLA, 1991), 33–40, here 33.

of interconnected nodes where locality always has a translocal dimension. Latour's distinction between intermediaries and mediators poses the question as to what extent itinerant theatre is more the one or the other – intermediary or mediator? The travelling company which spends a few nights in a town entertaining the local (most often colonial) populace appears on the surface to be largely intermediary, with little transformative power. In this case, it could be argued, such companies are insignificant as objects of research; their cultural ephemerality is an index of their historiographical inconsequentiality. If, however, we can discern evidence of distortion, transformation or modification, then we are, historiographically speaking, back in business. One should not, however, just look specifically at Bandmann or the Ballets Russes or any other itinerant theatrical visitor. Evidence of mediation should be directed, rather, on an institutional level: at the cumulative effects of visiting troupes and the exposure to theatrical culture they brought with them. Of crucial importance is their interaction with local audiences and publics, but also with indigenous performers and entrepreneurs. In the following discussion, we will look at a number of ports of call on the Bandmann Circuit from a twin perspective: in terms of Bandmann's micropolitics and for evidence of how the localities functioned as mediators and how the companies themselves contributed to mediation, which is a reflexive relationship between theatre and the city itself. Because Bandmann visited so many places during his 25-year touring career, including Latin America and the West Indies, the focus will be on those places where he had a long-term recurrent presence (he only visited Latin America twice). The Bandmann Circuit centred mainly around the ports and cities between Gibraltar and Japan.

Malta

The fortress island of Malta had long been an entrepôt in the Mediterranean. Its maritime activities shaded into piracy directed against the Ottoman Empire and its counterparts on the Barbary Coast of North Africa. Today, the island state of Malta is an entrepôt in a double sense: it possesses an entrepôt in the form of a container harbour, Malta Freeport, where goods are transhipped and redistributed around the Mediterranean, and it sees itself as an entrepôt in a cultural, political and economic sense, as a place of mediation between Europe and North Africa. If present-day Malta is both literally and metaphorically an entrepôt, in the 1890s, when Maurice Bandmann first arrived, it was also very much still a fortress. While no longer ruled by the eponymous knights but instead by the British, through whom the island was by then a major naval base for the Royal Navy, it was defined by its actual fortifications and by a population distinguished by different cultural influences. The local language is of Semitic origin, and subsequent major cultural influences were Italian and French, but by the late nineteenth century Malta was already transitioning to English language and culture.

Malta was the main port of call on Bandmann's first major tour outside the British Isles, under the auspices of the English Comedy Company, which he ran jointly with Malcolm Wallace. The company arrived via a short season in Gibraltar in mid-October 1897. Although Gibraltar occupies a special place in the Bandmann Circuit – it was often the first port of call on a tour and was quite literally his last port of call when he died there in March 1922 – it has less significance theatrically than Malta on account of its size. Gibraltar and Malta were both colonies and naval bases and hence interconnected. Malta, however, became the more important centre for Bandmann. The first season there ran for a staggering two-and-a-half months, by far the longest single sojourn at any theatre previously visited (see Chapter 2). The company performed in the centre of Valletta at the Theatre Manoel, a beautiful mid-eighteenth-century baroque theatre and the only other main theatrical venue next to the Opera House, where the resident Italian Opera Company provided a predictable diet of Rossini, Verdi and some Puccini.

On the company's arrival on 17 October 1897, *the Daily Malta Chronicle* extended 'a cordial welcome' and specified which parts of the population were the potential audience: 'We feel sure they will receive a hearty support from the Fleet, the Garrison, and the English-speaking part of the population.'[9] By 1900, Malta's total population was little more than 185,000, of whom only the educated elite used English. Malta hosted one regiment as a permanent garrison, plus the British fleet, whose size fluctuated depending on how many ships were at sea. During the late 1890s, the troop numbers increased dramatically due to the Boer and Sudanese wars, and Bandmann found a large and ready audience, able to support a ten-week season. The company returned prematurely from its subsequent Egyptian tour in February 1898 (the British troops in Cairo departed *en masse* to the Sudan to exact belated revenge on the Mahdi for the death of General Gordon in 1885) to perform for another twelve nights.

If we look at Bandmann's micropolitical endeavours, then one event is of particular interest. The final performance of the 1897 tour was

[9] 'The English Comedy Company', *The Daily Malta Chronicle*, 18 October 1897, 1.

devoted to a locally written play, *A Society Sphinx*, whose author was given as 'Mrs. Alfred Hart'. Nevertheless, or perhaps because of the palpable tie to locality, the performance was patronized by the governor, two admirals of the fleet, a general and numerous officers. *The Daily Malta Chronicle* provides a detailed synopsis which suggests that *A Society Sphinx* belongs to that vast repertoire of rightfully forgotten plays. Its significance lay therefore less in its literary merits than in the fact that the company rehearsed a totally new work featuring its main actors, including Bandmann himself:

> Hearty applause greeted the fall of the curtain and in response to loud and continued cries for 'Author' Mrs Hart came forward, escorted by Mr Bandmann; and amidst continuous applause bowed her acknowledgements, being at the same time presented with a very handsome basket of flowers.[10]

The reviewer generously conceded that 'at a later date with more rehearsing, and one or two alterations such as so frequently are found necessary in every piece, we shall hope to see a reproduction of Mrs Hart's play'. He goes on to list twenty or so 'noteworthy spectators and a large number of other representatives too numerous to mention, from the civil, naval and military communities both Maltese and British'.[11] The press coverage of the whole season repeatedly emphasized the presence of Maltese spectators, so that it is clear that the performance did not just attract military personnel. This performance established a pattern that Bandmann was to repeat many times in the course of his career and demonstrates micropolitics in action. A particular performance is singled out, and important personages are invited to ensure maximum symbolic patronage. This in turn strengthened Bandmann's status and that of his companies.

Two years later, by which time the troupe had become the Bandmann Repertoire Company, the same paper importuned its readers to support the company:

> [S]urely with our large Garrison and Fleet, with our hotels full of visitors and our large number of Maltese and English residents, there is enough to fill the Manoel nightly... what is to prevent your buying tickets and presenting them to those of your less well-off friends and acquaintances who will only be too happy to go and applaud, in your name the BANDMANN REPERTOIRE COMPANY?[12]

---

[10] 'Theatre Manoel', *The Daily Malta Chronicle*, 27 December 1897, 2–3.
[11] Ibid.
[12] 'What About the Bandman Repertoire Company?' *The Daily Malta Chronicle*, 18 November 1899, 2.

Bandmann returned annually, sometimes more frequently, and even became the proprietor of the Empire Theatre, one of many venues on his circuit. This meant that he had a longer-term investment in the locality that went beyond just extracting income for the seasons his own companies were performing. Proprietorship meant running a venue at a profit throughout the year.

Alexandria and Cairo

After Malta, the Bandmann Circuit invariably included Egypt, especially Alexandria and Cairo, and later Port Said and Kantara. Egypt was a de facto British colony (although it was never formally annexed) after the country went bankrupt in 1882, and it became a military and naval base with control of the Suez Canal. Both Alexandria and Cairo had relatively large European populations and theatrical infrastructure of the kind the Bandmann Opera Company required. By 1897, the number of foreigners in Cairo alone was estimated at around 30,000 against a total of 590,000 – a sizable population for cultural activities. This was a colonial class, with Europeans monopolizing most important government posts and enjoying privileges and a style of life that made them the envy of Egyptians as well as their peers at home. As Janet Abu-Lughod notes in her history of Cairo, 'by 1897 the destinies of Egypt and Europe had become inextricably intertwined'.[13]

By the end of the nineteenth century, travel guides for Egypt featured not only the usual sights of Egyptian antiquity and the newly established Egyptian museum but also theatres, both Arab and European. Baedeker's guide to Egypt of 1898 notes for Alexandria three different theatres offering French and Italian operas and operettas.[14] In Cairo, visitors could choose between the Khedival Opera House, the Summer Theatre in the Ezbekiah Garden and also 'Arab Theatres', for information on which the reader should 'see the newspapers'.[15] Port Said also offered entertainment in the form of two café-theatres, one offering musical performances, the other featuring a 'theatre of marionettes', presumably *Aragoz*, the Egyptian version of *Karagöz*.[16] In Cairo, an important addition were theatres such as the Printania, a major venue for touring European troupes, and the Kursaal specializing in music

---

[13] Janet L. Abu-Lughod, *Cairo: 1001 Years of the City Victorious* (Princeton: Princeton University Press, 1971), 99.
[14] *Egypt: Karl Baedeker* (Leipzig: Rpt. Elibron Classics, 1898), 6.
[15] Ibid., 29.
[16] Ibid., 170.

Figure 3.2 Front of the Kursaal Theatre of Cairo, at Emad El-Din Street. (Photo by Max H. Rudmann, Cairo, Egypt, 1916. Bibliothèque nationale de France. Public domain.)

hall (see Fig. 3.2). The latter became Bandmann's headquarters during and immediately after the First World War. A historian of Arabic drama in Egypt, Muhammed Badawi, notes that the turn of the century saw the emergence of a large number of theatre companies that included local actors and playwrights: 'As early as 1900 the Egyptian theatre had become not only a permanent feature of Egyptian urban life, but a political force of some significance.'[17] There is little evidence to suggest that Bandmann or his companies had much interaction with Egyptian theatre, although support by the Khedive for the Bandmann Opera Company generated considerable symbolic and presumably financial capital.

On his first visits to Egypt in 1897 and 1899, Bandmann came with a purely dramatic repertoire. In an interview given in 1899, he looked forward to his second visit to the two cities: 'I like Egypt immensely … and

[17] Muhammed Badawi, *Modern Arabic Drama in Egypt* (Cambridge: Cambridge University Press, 1987), 5.

have great faith in it as a field for English theatrical enterprise. My last tour did remarkably well, and I am in the hopes of one day taking a company of players into the Soudan itself. What do you think of a stock season at the Theatre Royal, Khartoum?'[18] This was a particularly brazen remark, considering that only a year before the British had reconquered the Sudan after the Battle of Omdurman in 1898. Although there is no record of Bandmann ever following through on this plan, Egypt was a crucial link in the network. His predilection for a country or city was determined always by two factors: good theatrical infrastructure and large audiences for English-language theatre.

In terms of infrastructure, Cairo offered the imposing Khedival Opera House built by Khedive (Viceroy) Isma'il Pasha (1830–1895) in 1869 to coincide with the opening of the Suez Canal. Up until the First World War, Bandmann performed at the Khedival Opera House and he evidently enjoyed Khedival patronage. As noted in Chapter 2, Bandmann formed a partnership with Augusto Dalbagni during the First World War. They jointly owned and managed three theatres in Cairo as well as the Alhambra in Alexandria. Before 1914, Augusto Dalbagni had established a reputation for building and managing the Kursaal theatre located on Emad El-Din Street (Fig. 3.2). Next to the Khedival Opera House, it became an important venue for touring troupes, providing a varied programme ranging from opera to tragedy for Cairo's cosmopolitan citizens. With the outbreak of war, Cairo was flooded with foreign (mainly British and empire) troops whose tastes tended towards vaudeville rather than Greek tragedy. Here Bandmann provided the necessary theatrical fare, as he had just completed plans for establishing a circuit devoted entirely to variety theatre (see Chapter 2). By 1920, life in Cairo had returned to normal and Dalbagni terminated the collaboration. He reinstated his pre-war repertoire, which included Italian, French, English, Spanish and Greek companies performing a broad selection of genres ranging from opera, ballet and Greek tragedy to classical concerts and even Futurist soirées.[19]

A Gala Performance, Cairo 1919

In the third week of July 1919, official peace celebrations were organized by Britain and its allies to commemorate the end of the First World War. Although the signing of the armistice in November 1918 had given

---

[18] 'Stage Whispers', *The Westminster Budget*, 24 February 1899, 16.
[19] For information on Augusto Dalbagni, see the website xoomer.virgilio.it/ nuovopapiro/in_egitto_file/dalbagni_famiglia.htm (last accessed 2 April 2019).

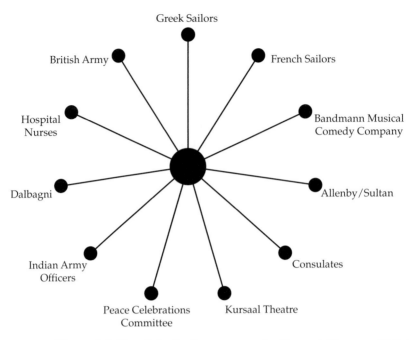

Figure 3.3 The Gala Performance at the Kursaal Theatre, 13 July 1919, represented as an ego network.

occasion for spontaneous celebrations across the world, these were neither organized nor orchestrated. In comparison, the official celebrations were carefully staged and followed a similar playbook. In Egypt, a British protectorate, the celebrations took place at the Kursaal theatre. On 13 July 1919, a 'Grand Gala Performance' was staged, with admission by invitation only. Bandmann and Dalbagni placed the theatre at the disposal of the Peace Celebrations Committee, and the Bandman Musical Comedy Company provided the lion's share of the entertainment. A closer examination of the attendees can serve to illuminate how such a performance served to strengthen network ties on a micropolitical level. Such performances are by nature transitory and function to make visible by means of spectacle the normally invisible ties within a network (see Fig. 3.3).

The event was under the patronage of and attended by the His Highness the Sultan (a title invented by the British) and the special high commissioner for Egypt, General Allenby, who had commanded the Allied troops in the campaign against the Ottoman Empire (including the legendary T. E. Lawrence).[20] The invited guests included members of the Allied consulates and diplomatic corps and a broad selection of Allied service men and women comprising not only British army officers but also NCOs, a company of wounded soldiers in hospital blue (transported by motor ambulances), Indian army officers and men, British and Greek sailors, and a 'very merry party of French sailors and *Poilus*' (i.e. French infantry).[21] The latter created a diversion by arriving 'in state' carrying a large French emblem suitably adorned with lilies and headed by one stalwart mounted on a donkey. The Kursaal itself had been lavishly decorated for the occasion with the flags of the Allies, and a souvenir programme was presented to the audience. A large number of hospital nurses was also present, 'their red and white dress lending most appropriate support to the colour scheme'. Before the rise of the curtain, the orchestra played the anthems of the Allies, and during the interval the audiences were treated to a display, seen from the terraces, 'by illuminated aeroplanes – certainly the first ever seen in Cairo or rather over it. The intrepid airmen performed "stunts" and firing off coloured lights – a really remarkable exhibition'. The main attraction, however, was a farewell variety performance by the Bandman Musical Comedy Company, which provided 'a series of refined and high-class acts'. It was concluded with a finale, when the whole company appeared in 'a patriotic setting, "Peace", a gorgeous tableau personifying the Allied powers'.

A gala performance of this kind mixing the genres of variety show and pageant represents a special kind of network inasmuch as it is ephemeral but the ties it illustrates are durable and can be read in terms of at least two different agendas. For the colonial authorities, represented principally by Allenby and the Sultan as his proxy, the performance served to demonstrate Allied power at a time when the whole region was in flux. The Ottoman Empire was in dissolution, and the British and French were actively supporting Greek military action in Asia Minor (which would ultimately lead to the mass expulsion of Greeks from the region). The invitation of all ranks, including the wounded, underscores – with the exception of the invited diplomats – the exclusively military nature of the performance. The local politics were anything but peaceful.

[20] In 1914, the British had deposed the Khedive and instituted a 'sultanate' headed by a member of the former Khedive's family. It lasted until 1925, when it was replaced by a constitutional monarchy under British control.

[21] All quotations are from a newspaper report 'Kursaal Gala Performance', *Egyptian Gazette*, 18 July 1919, n.p. It is located in the Vanessa Lopez Family Archive. The use of allegorical tableaux vivants was a standard device in imperial pageants.

British authorities had violently suppressed vociferous demonstrations against colonial rule which had begun in March 1919 and were still continuing in July. Against this background, the climatic tableau of 'Peace' illustrated more wishful thinking than any kind of actual cessation of unrest. The demonstrations were no doubt the reason why the performance was an exclusively military affair, as large sections of the Egyptian elite, including upper-class women, were actively engaged in resistance.[22]

For Bandmann and Dalbagni, the performance was no doubt seen in terms of reciprocity. By 'donating' their theatre, they were demonstrating not only allegiance to the colonial power but were also engaging in audience development. Most important on a micropolitical level was the aspect of patronage symbolized by the Sultan and General Allenby, the high commissioner. The large number of military personnel present at the performance reflected the general audience's composition and why Bandmann had shifted his headquarters to Cairo during the war. Despite much demobilization, there were still thousands of servicemen in the country, most of them in or near Cairo. Nevertheless, Cairo was transitioning to a peacetime economy and a gradual reduction in demand for variety entertainment so beloved by the troops.

East of Suez: Theatrical Hubs

Bandmann's operations east of Suez were centred in India, more precisely Calcutta. As the capital of the British Raj until 1911 and the centre of the British opium trade to China, it was a key trading city with a large cosmopolitan population. Around 1900, Calcutta accounted for one-third of total Indian exports. Apart from opium, Calcutta exported sugar, saltpetre, rice, indigo, tobacco, jute and cotton. Bengalis, Parsis, Jews, Muslims and Armenians, as well as the British colonial administration, troops and businesspeople, rubbed shoulders in this bustling, crowded city. Still the largest city in India around 1900, with a population of over one million, of whom 20,000 were Europeans and another 20,000 were counted as Eurasians or Anglo-Indians, Calcutta was not just politically and economically important but a cultural and educational centre as well, with major schools, universities and museums. When Bandmann first arrived there in January 1901 with his musical comedy company, he

---

[22] This uprising is known as the Egyptian Revolution and resulted in over 800 deaths and 1,600 injuries amongst the Egyptian population as well as widespread destruction of property. See the article in the *New York Times*, '800 Natives Dead in Egypt's rising 1,600 wounded', 25 July 1919, 1.

found a city that already had a thriving theatre and performance culture. By the mid-nineteenth century, a Bengali-language theatre had emerged, modelled partly on the European one and engaged in constant exchange with it. Theatres like the Star, the Minerva, the Cornwallis, the Classic and the Alfred offered performances in Bengali and hosted on occasion European troupes. These theatres also advertised in English in papers such as *The Bengalee* and the *Amirita Bazar Patrika*, which were primarily read by the Bengali elite.

Administratively, the theatres were divided into European and 'native', with the latter, which tended to be grouped around Beadon Street in the area of Hatibagan north of the centre, subjected to much stricter supervision and political censorship than the former. They were regularly fined for performing after 2 a.m. Although performances were mainly in Bengali or other Indian languages, there were attempts to appeal to European audiences by providing English synopses of plays.[23] Three main theatres hosted Western performances and targeted a colonial public: the Corinthian, the Royal and the Grand Opera House, all of which were located in the central precinct around Chowringhee Road and opposite the Maidan. Although the Corinthian, where Bandmann first performed, was Parsi owned (after 1900 by J. F. Madan), its management was often European. Lessees changed regularly as they struggled to make a profit in a city where the European theatre-going public was extremely fickle and not inclined to support serious drama. In 1896, shortly before Madan acquired the Corinthian, its lessee, T. V. Twinning, complained to the London magazine *The Sketch* about the difficulties of managing a theatre for a Calcutta public. He bemoaned the fact that the long run was unknown and that he had to change his bill at least twice a week, which meant a larger repertoire and more rehearsals. He could provide, however, a resident orchestra consisting of musicians from Goa.[24] The background to his complaint was a failed tour he had organized the year before, when he was sued by his actors for arrears of salary.[25]

Bandmann's first visit from January to April 1901 coincided not only with the death of Queen Victoria and a temporary lack of interest in musical comedy but also with a rival English company playing at the

[23] See, for example, the advertisement for the Minerva Theatre: 'English Synopsis of Principal Plays Supplied Free to Gentlemen and Ladies Not Familiar with the Bengalee Language', *The Amrita Bazar Patrika*, 28 December 1911, 8.
[24] 'The Indian Stage: A Chat with Mr. Twinning', *The Sketch*, 8 April 1896, 476–7.
[25] See 'Theatricals in India', *The Era*, 9 May 1896, 14.

Theatre Royal. Although the Brough company, as it was called, offered mainly light comedy, it stood in direct competition for almost the whole sojourn. When Bandmann returned to India in 1904, he resolved to form deeper contacts in the city, which became the centre of his theatrical empire. The most important step was the partnership with the Armenian-born businessman Arratoon Stephen, who was already owner of the Theatre Royal and other properties. Bandmann became lessee and manager of the Theatre Royal before embarking on plans to build the Empire in Chowringhee Place.

After Calcutta, Bombay was the most important city in India for Bandmann's companies. Because of its size (it had a population of around one million), it was a popular destination for touring actors and companies, but its real importance lay with the Parsi community, who after 1850 quickly recognized the potential of theatre for educational, reformist and commercial purposes. The Parsis, of Persian origin, were successful merchants and cultural brokers who mediated between the English colonial administration and India's multi-religious and multilingual population. Between 1850 and 1900, Parsis adapted the European proscenium stage and the genres of melodrama, tragedy and comedy and mixed them with Indian and Persian mythological stories to produce a remarkable and commercially successful theatre that travelled all over the Indian subcontinent.

The existing theatres were all controlled by the Parsis, expensive for European companies and of a poor standard; therefore, Bandmann soon began to lobby for a new theatre. This became a pattern of micropolitical activity at all of the main cities on his circuit (see also Chapter 7). In June 1906, returning from one of his Far Eastern tours, Bandmann let it be known to the *Times of India* that he would regrettably be unable to include Bombay on his return journey because the city lacked a suitable venue. The Novelty was being demolished, the Gaiety was not yet completed and construction for the new Empire had only just begun. In 1906, he briefly leased the Gaiety Theatre and installed his friend Warwick Major as manager, but it proved too expensive. Bandmann's complaints about poor or entirely absent performance venues on his circuit were a predictable part of his advance publicity and public discourse. However, the situation in Bombay was worse than usual, if only because it was one of the largest cities on his newly established route and therefore a cornerstone of his business. As a last resort, he applied – unsuccessfully – to the city authorities to use the town hall. He continued to lobby until finally the Bombay City Improvement Trust, which had been established in the 1890s to coordinate and regulate the development of Bombay, agreed to lease him a plot of land for the erection of a temporary theatre.[26] The trust consisted of prominent citizens from the city's main communities and was by no means a simple extension of British colonial rule. In May 1907, the decision became public, and a short but bitter political controversy erupted in English and Indian newspapers because the plot of land was located directly adjacent to Parsi burial grounds.

The controversy was conducted initially in English-language and Parsi newspapers in Gujarati, the Parsis being some of the most vocal critics but also supporters of theatre, as most theatre houses were owned by Parsis. The Improvement Trust appears to have reacted to their objections, and by the end of the month proposed a new location further along the same street. Unfortunately, the newly allocated plot of land was now literally within smelling distance of the Hindu burial grounds. The controversy quickly spread and was discussed in all the main Bombay newspapers, but in particular in the *Times of India*, where vociferous letters to the editor were exchanged under the heading 'the errant theatre'. The *Times of India* was a British-controlled paper but fiercely independent and resistant to government influence and was thus used by different citizens and groups as a mouthpiece. Within days, leading spokespeople of the Hindu community pointed out the impossibility of constructing a theatre so close to *their* burial grounds. The debate also led to a general discussion of the work of the controversial Improvement Trust.

An Indian interlocutor, Narayan T. Vaidya, included in his letter a sketch of the street, thus providing clear visual proof of the nuisance the theatre would engender (Fig. 3.4):

The real danger is this. If the theatre is built on the proposed site its visitors will be subjected to a serious nuisance from at times a noisome stench and discordant and high-pitched music of the backward classes of Hindu mourners, especially as the theatre will be leeward of the burning ground, and any endeavour to abate or put a stop to the nuisance will rouse bad blood between the ruling and the ruled races.[27]

---

[26] Miriam Dossal terms the Improvement Trust 'a supra-municipal body' and its creation 'an admission that the municipal authorities could not cope with the needs of the city'; see her *Theatre of Conflict, City of Hope* (New Delhi: Oxford University Press, 2010), 163. According to Bombay city historians Sharada Dwivedi and Mehrotra Rahul, it was given significant powers to develop land and roads and to ensure quick procedures and a mandatory time limit for buildings to be commenced. It 'transformed the geography of Bombay from a town to a city'. Sharada Dwivedi and Mehrotra Rahul, *Bombay: The Cities Within* (Bombay: India Book House, 1995), 166.

[27] 'The Errant Theatre: Position Examined', *The Times of India*, 4 June 1907, 5.

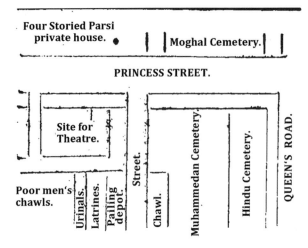

Figure 3.4 Sketch by Narayan Vaidya of proposed theatre on Princess Street, Bombay, next to cemeteries. (*Times of India*, 4 June 1907, 5.)

On the same day, the *Times of India* carried another article on the issue ironically entitled 'Bombay Amusements: Mr Bandmann's New Theatre'. The article opens with a question:

'What will he do with it?' This, the well-known title of a popular novel may be suitably applied to the plot of ground released to Mr Bandmann, on Princes [*sic*] Street, where he contemplates erecting a temporary theatre [...] He arrived in Bombay from Calcutta yesterday morning with 47 members of his new opera company and when visited by a representative of the Times of India produced a copy of the day's paper and looked demurely at the plan of the theatre site given with the letter of complaint by Mr Narayan Vaidya in which the adjacent cemeteries, chawls and latrines are depicted. 'Really,' said Mr Bandmann, 'I had no idea it was half as bad as this ... However, I cater for the public, and cannot of course afford to fall out with the public and if I find on further investigations that the objections to the proposed theatre are well founded then, perhaps, the improvement trust will find me another site ... Bombay must have its European theatre and where is there another site?'[28]

In the end, Bandmann bowed to public pressure, as he had to – 'I cater for the public, and cannot of course afford to fall out with the public' – the public here being not the Europeans but the Indian communities, who

---

[28] 'Bombay Amusements: Mr Bandmann's New Theatre', *The Times of India*, 5 June 1907, 8.

constituted a significant portion of his audience. European spectators were of course important but by no means numerous enough to sustain his operation. The Improvement Trust also bowed to pressure and permitted Bandmann to erect a temporary theatre made of corrugated iron on the Maidan, located in the centre of the city, where he shared the space with tent cinemas until he had finished building the Royal Opera House, to be discussed next.

The errant theatre controversy demonstrates not only how a multi-religious public sphere reacted to proposals to build the theatre contiguous with its holy places, but highlights the cultural complexities at stake when a foreign institution is inserted into an existing cultural matrix. Theatre building was part of the restructuring of Bombay into a cosmopolitan metropolis and an early portal of globalization. The failed theatre highlighted the problem of providing infrastructure as a basic prerequisite for the creation of a theatre-going public. But theatre was arguably still a foreign body, which, although theatres had been built throughout the previous century, was still finding its place in the array of new cultural practices that colonialism engendered. The controversy also highlighted the theatre's function as a medium of the senses. It seemed to concentrate all the existing olfactory, acoustic and visual irritation associated with a quarter of the city reserved for the 'Untouchables'. The latrines, urinals and ramshackle accommodations were evidently a multi-sensorial but necessary eyesore. The plan, however, to erect a European theatre practically in the midst of what Foucault would term a heterotopic space represented a significant disturbance to this cultural matrix.

Singapore

Always an important port of call for Bandmann companies, Singapore became over the period of his visits a theatrical hub on account of its location and cosmopolitan population comprising Europeans, Chinese, Indians and Malays, which by 1900 amounted to approximately 250,000 inhabitants, 165,000 of whom were of Chinese descent. The European and Eurasian population comprised little more than 8,000.[29] Culturally, Singapore was a characteristic port city with a highly diverse mixture of peoples. In his *Handbook to Singapore*, first published in 1892 and

---

[29] Swee-Hock Saw, *The Population of Singapore*, Singapore: Institute of Southeast Asian Studies, 1999, 11–12.

revised in 1907, G. M. Reid evoked the cosmopolitan make-up with a characteristic orientalist gesture:

The streets of the town are crowded and busy at all hours of the day, and in the native quarters at nearly all hours of the night as well. . . . In half-an-hour's walk, a stranger may hear the accents of almost every language and see the features and costume of nearly every race in the world. Amongst the crowds that pass him, he may see, besides Europeans of every nation, Chinese, Malays, Hindus, Madrassees, Sikhs, Japanese, Burmese, Siamese, Javanese, Boyanese, Singhalese, Tamils, Arabs, Jews, Parsees, Negroes, &c., &c.[30]

Within this mix, European society forged its characteristic social institutions comprising clubs, theatres, dances, 'smoking concerts', reading rooms, a public library, a museum and botanical gardens. Because (almost) every European nation was represented on the island, European society was more diversified than in most cities in the Old World. Historians Mark Ravinder Frost and Yu-Mei Balasingamchow argue that by 1900 this lifestyle was increasingly being shared by a new generation of Asian professionals, many of whom had been educated in English-language schools and some even at universities: 'More than their middlemen predecessors in the earlier part of the century, this rising Asian bourgeoisie came to appropriate the lifestyle of their colonial masters. In an age of global communication, European trends had arrived in Singapore and young Asian professionals now had the income (and the wherewithal) to afford and obtain them.'[31]

Singapore was an important port of call not just for European theatre troupes but also for Chinese, Parsi and Malay companies. The latter had created their own version of Parsi theatre known as *bangsawan*. The Opera House Yap Chow Thong, a Chinese theatre, had even performed their version of *Hamlet* before the governor of Singapore. The most important *bangsawan* troupe was Wayang Kassim, which played in Malay for indigenous and European audiences at the Indira Zanibar Theatre a repertoire that included Malay, Javanese and European material.

By 1914, a small entertainment industry had developed in Singapore, with travelling and local groups competing with each other and the new cinematic medium. For example, in the week beginning 6 March 1912,

[30] G. M. Reith, *Handbook to Singapore*, 2nd ed. [1907] (Reprint: Singapore: Oxford University Press, 1985), 35–6.
[31] Mark Ravinder Frost and Yu-Mei Balasingamchow, *Singapore: A Biography* (Singapore: Editions Didier Millet, 2009), 144.

the Bandmann Opera Company at the Victoria Theatre competed with the following performances:

ALHAMBRA:	Thuness Kovarick and His Violin in conjunction with the pick of the production of: Pathé, American Kinema etc.
HARIMA HALL:	Cinematograph offering 'Gaumont's Greatest Graphic'
VICTORIA THEATRE:	Chinese New Year entertainment: Part I 'After the battle'; A sketch by Low Kway Soo; Part II 'Mustapha': A comedy by Lee Choo Neo.
THEATRE ROYAL:	The Star Opera Co. The Dutch and Malay variety entertainers.
PRINCE KOBAT SHARIL:	Come and see: charming actresses, clever actors, competent orchestra, comfortable theatre.
TEUTONIA CLUB:	Kilkare Koncert Kompany.[32]

Significant here is the mixture of cultural offerings, both professional and amateur, catering to Singapore's cosmopolitan population. The advertisements do not include the Chinese theatres, which targeted mainly the local Chinese population. The performance of the Chinese New Year play in two parts in aid of the Chinese Red Cross Society, written by two local authors and presented in the high temple of colonial representation, the Victoria Theatre, documents a growing interpenetration of performance cultures. While the local Chinese opera continued to flourish in its own venues, the special performance was clearly designed as the demonstration of cultural occupation and perhaps even of a certain degree of social mobility in an otherwise highly stratified colonial settlement.

An unusual feature on the colonial theatre circuit was the status of the Victoria Theatre as a municipal building and the use of public funds totalling S$60,000 for its conversion in 1911 into a fully functional theatre, partly as a result of Bandmann's lobbying (Fig. 3.5). In keeping with his usual practice, he had complained about the cramped conditions on several occasions in the local papers.[33]

Despite the newly opened theatre, Bandmann still pursued plans for his own theatre. In 1912, the *London and China Telegraph* reported

---

[32] *Singapore Free Press*, 6 March 1912, 1.
[33] *Singapore Municipal Report* (Singapore: Govt Printer, 1908), 10. National Archives of Singapore.

Figure 3.5 Victoria Theatre and Memorial Hall, Singapore, ca. 1910. (*Scenes in Singapore*, published by Kelly & Walsh Ltd., Singapore. University of Leiden Digital Collection, Creative Commons CC-BY License.)

that 'it is rumoured that Mr. Maurice Bandmann intends erecting his own theatre in Singapore, and that he has purchased Abrams' stables and yard in Orchard-road for the purpose'.[34] Like many of his theatre-building schemes, this one came to nothing and was perhaps always only designed to put pressure on the municipal authorities to expedite renovations of the Victoria Theatre.

The Victoria Theatre reopened in February 1912 and most performances given there were by Bandmann-sponsored artistes or companies. Still, it was not intensively used. Figures for 1916 show that the Victoria Theatre was booked on a total of seventy-two nights for performances of touring companies and local amateurs.[35] In some months, the figures were as low as three or even none. This was still a remarkable improvement over 1914, when only forty performances for the whole year were counted. Wartime disruptions were partially to blame, but overall the figures demonstrate the precarious situation

---

[34] *London and China Telegraph*, 29 April 1912, 447.
[35] *Singapore Municipal Report* (Singapore: Govt Printer, 1916), 74. National Archives of Singapore.

for the lessee of the theatre. A year later, the municipal reports stated that the arrangements for licensing the Singapore theatres were 'still not satisfactory, there is dual control and no control' and proposed that the municipal commissioner should be the licensing officer under 'a new Theatres' Ordinance'.[36] The reference here is not, however, to the Victoria but to the 'native theatres' which operated largely free of regulation. 'Dual control' refers to a division of responsibility between the chief of police and the fire department, with the former being responsible for the licensing and the latter for the regulations. While the municipal fire department was on duty at all performances at the Victoria free of charge (as a municipal institution), they also attended 'a large number of native theatres and cinematograph halls, and for these services earned $2,187.35 ... Licensing arrangements for these theatres were not satisfactory.'[37] However regulatory authority was distributed, the recurrent complaints over division of responsibility show that the-atres were the object of administrative control and were increasing in numbers (Table 3.1).

By the First World War, a theatrical culture had emerged in Singapore that was largely commercial in orientation, culturally diverse and clearly conducive to syncretic recombination of forms and idioms. The multiple strands of theatrical activity – itinerant touring European companies, Parsi theatre but also indigenous South Asian forms such as *bangsawan* – all combined to make Singapore theatrically speak-ing an entrepôt, albeit on a small scale and nowhere near rivalling its importance as the official British entrepôt for opium. The latter still constituted the port's main source of revenue, the colonial government franchising the opium trade to wealthy Chinese businessmen.[38]

Although a frequent and revered visitor, Bandmann did not estab-lish the kinds of ties that he forged in other cities. This would have

---

[36] *Singapore Municipal Report* (Singapore: Govt Printer, 1917), 5. National Archives of Singapore.

[37] Ibid., 10.

[38] The percentage of revenue derived from opium from the colony of the Straits Settlement in the years 1898 to 1906 was between 43.3 and 59.1 per cent. *Proceedings of the Commission Appointed to Enquire Into Matters Relating to the Use of Opium in the Straits Settlement and the Federated Malay States* (p. 42, Microfilm no. NL 14242, London: Darling & Son Ltd., 1909), cited in Naidu Ratnala Thulaja, 'Opium and Its History in Singapore', eresources.nlb.gov.sg/infopedia/articles/SIP_622_2004-12-16.html (last accessed 2 April 2019). See also C. A. Trocki, *Opium and Empire: Chinese Society in Colonial Singapore, 1800–1910* (New York: Cornell University Press, 1990), 1–6, 96–7, who calculates between 30 and 55 per cent for the period between 1825 and 1910.

Table 3.1 *Performances at the Victoria Theatre, Singapore, 1914–1917*

Victoria Theatre Singapore:
Performances by Travelling Companies and Others

	1914	1915	1916	1917
January	6		3	
February	6	6	2	13
March	9*		17	14
April	2*	3*	8	10
May	3	2*	1*	
June	4	3		12
July	7		2*	7
August		1	11*	1*
September		15	12	2*
October	1*	7	3*	4*
November	1	7	7	6
December	1*	4	7*	5*
Total	40	48	76	74

Source: Singapore Municipal Reports, National Archives of Singapore.
* Includes amateur performances.

been different had he realized his building scheme in Orchard Road. Singapore was a fixture, hosting companies at least twice a year, but also a stopping-off point for destinations further east: China and Japan, but also the Dutch East Indies.

Shanghai

Like Singapore, the Chinese port city of Shanghai can be considered a quintessential entrepôt centred on the opium trade and cotton goods. With the establishment of the Shanghai International Settlement in the second half of the nineteenth century, there emerged a Western expatriate zone with British, Russian, American, German, Japanese and French concessions. It was the most northerly of the ports opened to foreign trade under the British Treaty of Nanking (1842), which ended the Opium Wars. The 'Settlement' (concession) had institutional autonomy, with its own police force, fire brigade, schools and soon its own theatre. It had a fast-growing foreign population. A 1905 census counted 12,328 foreigners, which rose to over 14,000 by 1908, exclusive of the French settlement. Of these, the largest group were British, followed closely by the Japanese. Like Singapore, Shanghai had an extremely heterogeneous foreign population representing most European nations plus Indians and Malays. The city boasted five daily and four weekly papers in European languages and about a dozen Chinese dailies.[39]

In 1874, the first Lyceum Theatre was built for the Amateur Dramatic Club of Shanghai (ADC), which was established in 1866. Although primarily a venue for Europeans, the Lyceum assumed an important role as a broker and mediator. It was at the Lyceum that Chinese spectators had their first encounter with European theatre.[40] Bandmann's companies and other Western troupes performed there on a regular basis. The Bandmann productions, which included variety shows, musical comedy, operetta and occasionally spoken drama, were renowned for their high professional quality. Most of these performances were, however, predominantly musical, with spoken drama playing only a subordinate role.

Institutionally speaking, the Lyceum was different from Chinese theatre in terms of its social and cultural function. The theatre was occasionally frequented by Chinese elites, who found it totally different from Beijing-style *jungju* and *kunqu* theatre performed in traditional teahouses. The Chinese theatre here was characterized by noise, cigarette sellers, melon seeds and peanuts, the candy peddlers shuttling back and forth between the spectators. A visit to the Lyceum theatre was a more formal occasion: people dressed smartly, and the usher bowed spectators into the theatre.[41]

For Bandmann, Shanghai provided a large potential market and was a key port of call for his tours. Not only was the potential European audience very large, his theatre-building plans in Shanghai suggest that he also targeted Chinese elites. Although the Lyceum was his preferred place of performance, the company also performed in hotels such as the

[39] *The Directory & Chronicle for China, Japan, Corea, Indo-China, Straits Settlements, Malay States, Sian, Netherlands India, Borneo, the Philippines, &C: With Which Are Incorporated 'the China Directory' and 'the Hong Kong List for the Far East'* (Hong Kong: Hong Kong Daily Press Office, 1910), 835 and 842.

[40] I am following here Siyuan Liu, *Performing Hybridity in Colonial-Modern China*, Palgrave Studies in Theatre and Performance History (New York: Palgrave Macmillan, 2013).

[41] The Lyceum Theatre was a key feature of Western leisure activities: 'They go to balls at the town hall; they ride horses and play cricket at the public recreation ground; they go to the Lyceum Theatre for shows; they visit the public garden…As for Chinese entertainment, the guide's recommendation of a walk around the wall city and a visit to the Settlements' Chinese Theatre is accompanied by a warning not to entertain too high hopes.' Catherine Vance Yeh, *Shanghai Love: Courtesans, Intellectuals, and Entertainment Culture, 1850–1910* (Seattle: University of Washington Press, 2006), 324.

luxurious Astor House Hotel on the North Bund (reputedly the best hotel in the East, to which was attached the Astor Hall, seating 300) or at the hastily refurbished town hall when the Lyceum was not available.[42] A visit by the Bandmann Comedy Company in 1907 tested the renovated town hall and found the stage machinery severely wanting:

> Last night, as far as the auditorium was concerned, the inconvenience caused by the closing of the Lyceum Theatre was reduced to a minimum by the transformation which the Town Hall had undergone with the addition of a sloping floor. It was unfortunate, however, that similar advantages had to be dispensed with on the stage; for the make-shift nature of the stage appliances were apparently responsible for an unconscionable delay at the beginning and long intervals between the acts which prolonged the play until well after midnight.[43]

Because the Lyceum was controlled by the local amateur dramatic society and was not of the technical standard of the Empire in Calcutta, Bandmann included Shanghai in his theatre-building plans to erect bespoke venues for travelling companies. He began lobbying around 1908 and found an interested partner in the owners and shareholders of the Astor House Hotel, who contemplated adding a 1,200-seat theatre to the hotel proper. The plan, one of several for the hotel, made good business sense in terms of multiplier effects. Dinner parties could be expected to dine there before and/or after performances, and the Astor accommodated the majority of theatre companies visiting the city.[44] In the end, to Bandmann's great frustration, the theatre plans came to nothing; instead, small shops for rent were added, plus more bedrooms and apartments.[45]

Hong Kong

The Crown Colony of Hong Kong, which China ceded to Britain in 1841 during the infamous Opium Wars, was established as a naval base and bridgehead for British commercial interests (mainly trading opium) in the Far East. Hong Kong was formally declared a free port in 1842. Kowloon Peninsula across the harbour was added in 1860 and became a military base. Like Singapore, to which it had close commercial ties, the colony's economy was inextricably linked to opium; in fact, loans

---

[42]   See, for example, 'The Bandmann Company at the Astor Gardens', *The North-China Herald*, 15 June 1906, 625.

[43]   'The Bandman Comedy Company', *The North-China Herald*, 12 April 1907, 87.

[44]   'New Theatre in Shanghai', *The North-China Herald*, 11 October 1913, 34.

[45]   'Astor House Hotel Co., Ltd.', *The North-China Herald*, 3 October 1914, 38–9.

contracted for public works were secured through opium revenue.[46] Gradually, all the institutional accoutrements of British colonial rule were added: a clocktower, waterworks, a lunatic asylum, a college, a hospital, botanical gardens, a city hall, various clubs, including the famous Hong Kong Jockey Club, and a Theatre Royal, as part of the city hall. In 1910, the city also had two large Chinese theatres which performed almost all year round. Four daily newspapers and three weekly English papers as well as eight Chinese newspapers were published. By 1900, the economy had diversified to include sugar refining, cotton spinning and various other types of manufacturing. The total population in 1906 amounted to 319,000, of whom 12,415 were non-Chinese. To this number should be added a military population of near 10,000.[47]

Bandmann performed at the Theatre Royal, which opened in 1869 and had already accommodated his father in the 1880s. It seated 500 and was a typical multi-purpose colonial venue showing a mixture of stage performances, both professional and amateur, concerts and boxing matches. By 1900, it also exhibited films. Like the Victoria in Singapore, it was integrated into the city hall and was therefore subject to municipal administration. After undergoing extensive renovation in 1903 – just before Bandmann began touring there in 1905 – it obtained better sightlines, acoustics and lighting. Although he visited Hong Kong annually, often twice a year, the city's theatrical infrastructure was still deficient, at least for his needs. The 500-seat capacity of the Theatre Royal was insufficient to meet the economics of touring the Bandmann Opera Company. On a number of occasions, but most actively in 1909 and 1910, he expressed the desire publicly to build a theatre in the colony along the lines of his theatres in Calcutta and Bombay. He frequently used the local press to create a public discussion and thereby acquire local, financially potent partners. In November 1909, Bandmann let it be known to the *South China Morning Post* that he was contemplating building a 'modern theatre on the Gaiety principle in Hongkong provided he can obtain a good site'. He was already negotiating with authorities in Shanghai for the erection of a Bandmann theatre there (which ultimately came to nothing): 'He has in view, we believe, the erection of theatres after the London Gaiety pattern in all the chief ports his companies have been in the habit of annually visiting.' The paper fully supported Bandmann's entrepreneurial endeavours by pointing out that there was constant growth in the foreign population

[46] *The Directory & Chronicle for China, Japan*, 1086.
[47] Ibid., 1095.

in each of the centres he visited which was bound to continue in the foreseeable future: 'The man who is first in the field should therefore be the one to reap the golden harvest.'[48]

The paper pointed out that sites for a new theatre on the 'Gaiety principle' were not over-abundant, which meant a building like the Empire in Calcutta. Bandmann continued his campaign when he returned in January 1910, giving interviews to the local papers: 'As Mr. Bandmann pointed out, if he were to bring a big and expensive company here, he could not recoup himself as there was not enough room in the Theatre Royal. At the present rate of exchange, a full house did not leave a very big profit.'[49] If a site could not be found, then he suggested that the Theatre Royal be reconstructed and expanded to provide more capacity: 'What was needed was to bring the seats on the ground floor, so that people could walk straight in from the road-way. A dress circle and a gallery could then be built, and the whole of the building would be changed and made more convenient... If the theatre were made to hold, say, about 660 more persons, that would be all that would be required in Hongkong.'[50] What was meant by 660 'more' persons was in addition to the existing 500, and therefore a capacity of almost 1,200, which would have brought it into line with the Empire or the Royal Opera House in Bombay.

The years 1910 to 1912 mark the highpoint of Bandmann's theatre-building schemes, when he planned to erect no less than twelve new theatres in the Far East. In the case of Hong Kong, he offered to practically rebuild the Theatre Royal in return for a twenty-year lease. This was not intended, he claimed, to secure a monopoly but simply to ensure that Bandmann companies would be given priority of occupancy. He argued repeatedly that poor venues would not induce companies to include the Far East in their itineraries.[51]

Like many of his other theatre-building plans, this one also came to nothing – whether for lack of a good site or because of governmental obstruction, it is not clear. One effect was, however, the improvement of the Theatre Royal, as one of many obituaries in 1922 made clear:

When Mr. Bandmann first came to Hongkong, he was quick to note the inadequacy and inefficiency of the City Hall for such entertainments as he had to offer. Suggestions for its improvement were made by him through the Press

[48] 'Proposed New Theatre: Mr. Bandmann Fancies Hongkong', *South China Morning Post*, 8 November 1909, 6.
[49] 'New Theatre for Hongkong: Mr. Maurice Bandmann's Views', *South China Morning Post*, 17 January 1910, 4.
[50] Ibid.
[51] 'New Theatres in the Far East', *The Straits Times*, 27 January 1910, 7.

and other channels – he even went so far as to study out the matter of build-ing his own theatre here – with the result that the Theatre Royal, although it still leaves much to be desired, is a better house of entertainment to-day than it was.[52]

The Dutch East Indies

Until 1949, the many islands large and small that comprise present-day Indonesia belonged to the Dutch colony known as the Dutch East Indies. Its most important ports were Batavia (Jakarta) and Surabaya on the island of Java, as well as Medan on the north Sumatran coast. Batavia boasted a municipal theatre since 1821 (the Schouwburg), and by 1900 a thriving hybrid performance culture had emerged, including a local adaptation of Parsi theatre. Drawing on newspaper advertise-ments of the time, Matthew Cohen and Laura Noszlopy describe urban Javanese entertainment as an eclectic mixture of

circuses, magic shows, European social dancing, organ grinders, string orchestras, phonographic demonstrations, magic lantern shows, variety shows, marionette companies, English operetta companies, French and Italian opera, ring toss games and tombola stands, Japanese and Chinese acrobats, firework displays, panoramas, waxworks, cinematic projections, dog-and-monkey shows, ventriloquists, balloon shows, freak shows, fire jug-gling, magnetism, comic speeches, mimics and many other international expressive forms.[53]

Such 'international expressive forms' appealed to a cosmopolitan pop-ulation that congregated in the main port cities. The European and Eurasian population in Batavia made up just 9 per cent of the total population of 115,000. The remainder comprised Malays, Indians, Chinese and Arabs.[54]

Bandmann companies visited the Dutch East Indies on eight sepa-rate occasions between 1906 and 1916, although not always at each of the main centres. In Medan on the island of Sumatra, whose European population numbered less than one thousand, they performed in the club rooms of the Witte Societeit (White Society), in Batavia in the old Schouwburg at Weltevreden and in Surabaya in the municipal theatre (Schouwburg).

---

[52] 'Bandmann's Exit', *South China Morning Post*, 17 March 1922, 6.
[53] Matthew Cohen and Laura Noszlopy, 'Introduction' to *Contemporary Southeast Asian Performance: Transnational Perspectives* (Cambridge: Cambridge Scholars Publishing, 2010), 7.
[54] Christopher Silver, *Planning the Megacity: Jakarta in the Twentieth Century* (London: Routledge, 2008), 38.

The critical reception in the Dutch East Indies differed significantly from that of the other ports of call, because here the genre of musical comedy encountered (in the Dutch-language press at least) a European cultural sensibility that had problems with Edwardian froth. The barriers were less linguistic than they were cultural and aesthetic. On their first visit to Surabaya from 16 to 26 July 1906, pre-publicity announced that synopses in Dutch would be distributed on the back of the programme notes.[55] Although advertised as a 'operagezelschap' (opera company), the press explained that 'real opera' would not be on offer, but rather 'merry spectacles' (the author uses the somewhat pejorative Dutch word *kijkstuk*), consisting of song, décor and costumes.[56] A try-out at the port of Semarang in the town's Rembrandt-Theater elicited despair from the local correspondent for the *Soerabaijasch handelsblad* – despair at the quality of the performers (except the 'low comedian' Harry Cole) and at the enthusiasm of the audiences, who evidently enjoyed the sold-out performances. He wrote, 'a definitely third, if not fourth-rate tarted-up operetta troupe, but it is a success, such as I have never seen in the Indies'. This led the reviewer into generalized cultural pessimism: 'They have to say goodbye to "art" in the Indies.'[57]

When the company finally arrived in Surabaya, the critical reception continued in a similar vein. The reviewer there wrote a lengthy article after the premiere of *The Runaway Girl* (a George Edwardes piece about a young English girl who joins a group of musicians in Italy who are really bandits). He puts the word 'opera' in inverted commas and warns the readers 'when going to the theatre to see Bandmann, think not of Art but of art', it being more 'circus' than 'opera', concluding that 'theatre for John Bull is on much the same level as golf, cricket and football'. Singing and comic turns remind him of a Rotterdam fair at four-thirty in the morning, but the applause is nevertheless 'dol' (enthusiastic). Like his colleague in Semarang, his philosophical mood is one of resignation: 'The philosopher analyses the motives and finds then that this applause is more a reflection of the spectators' merry mood than an appreciation of "art". He has to reconcile himself with everything on this earth, even with a jugged hare made from slender cats.'[58] The mixed metaphor of hares and cats presumably meant that the hybrid performance – consisting primarily of a mishmash of female bodies – offers a very meagre repast for the philosophically inclined spectator.

[55] *Soerabaijasch handelsblad*, 6 February 1906, 1.
[56] Ibid., 12 July 1906, 6.
[57] Ibid., 14 July 1906, 7.
[58] M. v. G. 'Het Bandmann Operageselschap', *Soerabaijasch handelsblad*, 17 July 1906, 1.

The debate continued a few days later with another extended essay from Semarang, where the 'correspondent' attempted to justify his dismissive assessment of the Bandmann company. The real source of chagrin was the poor attendance earlier in the year accorded to the great Dutch actor Louis Bouwmeester (1842–1925), who toured the East Indies with somewhat more demanding fare – Gerhart Hauptmann's *Fuhrmann Henschel*, a naturalistic drama ending in suicide, and *The Merchant of Venice*.[59]

Despite the critical sniping, the twelve performances in the Schouwburg from 26 June to 7 July 1906 were a popular success. Advertising for the nightly changing repertoire stressed the connection with the metropolitan centre: 'Great Gaiety Theatre London Success' (*The Runaway Girl*), 'The Present Rage of London' (*The Spring Chicken*), 'the beautiful Comic Opera *Florodora* from the Lyric Theatre London', 'The screamingly funny Musical Comedy *The Earl and the Girl* from the Adelphi and the Lyric Theatres London' and so on. The review after the first three performances was more balanced, recognizing that the combination of 'singing, dancing and a seemingly inexhaustible stock of costumes is completely in line with the theatrical expectations of a colonial audience', while at the time treading a fine line between providing 'innocent pleasure' and ignoring the actual demands of the local audience.[60]

However mixed the critical judgement, the popular (and presumably financial) success was undisputed, as the performances were largely sold out. In his review of the season, the journalist Hans van de Wal admitted that watching twelve performances back to back by the same performers with the same kind of music was a record for (and implicitly an imposition on) a colonial reporter. He struggled to assume an air of cultural relativism when assessing the overall impression and achievement. Citing Voltaire – every genre is permitted except a bad one – he opined that the company should be assessed on its own merits. While not demonstrating the top talent from London, the company was still good in its own particular genre of musical comedy. On not one single occasion did the performance falter, nor was the prompter seen or heard. The strengths lay in the female dancers, in the assured chorus singing, in the excellent ensemble, in the direction, in the acting and the wonderful costumes. Weaknesses could be found in the solo voices and the content of the operettas.[61]

---

[59] 'Brieven uit Semarang', *Soerabaijasch handelsblad*, 27 July 1906, 1.
[60] 'Het engelsche opera-gezelschap', *Bataviaasch nieuwsblad*, 2 July 1906, 4.
[61] Hans van de Wal, 'The Spring Chicken', *Bataviaasch nieuwsblad*, 9 July 1906, 4.

A special honour was accorded the company on their last night, with
the publication in the *Bataviaasch nieuwsblad* of a parody of a Bandmann
production, an aesthetic and social commentary on twelve evenings of
uninterrupted musical comedy. Entitled 'A Japanese Flirt', it was written by Edgar Blockhead with music by George Lovers Whim under the
musical direction of Edward Laughingstock. The action is set in Tokyo,
amongst English estate agents (Messrs Chicken, Sweetmouth, Ditto and
Smallhead) and the actresses of a Japanese opera company, Osaka Shiusu
Kaisja. The English gentlemen woo the Japanese dancers with promises
of champagne and flowers, but they are indifferent to such cheap allures,
much preferring diamonds. The 'play' ends in an ensemble chorus:

Men: Oh, oh, oh!	Girls: Ha ha ha
That is not nice	Isn't that nice?
Oh, Oh, Oh,	Ha, Ha, ha
Money gone, girls gone	Girls gone, money gone
Oh!	Ha!

Presumably, the parody references not just the content of the musical
plays but also the playing that went on between male Batavians and the
actresses of the company offstage.[62]

When the BOC returned in September 1908, the excitement in
Batavia was palpable as the Bandmann publicity machine went into
action, providing the local papers with advance copy. They were prom-
ised a comedian fresh from the Gaiety Theatre in London (Frank
Danby), and it went without saying that the 'men are handsome, and
the ladies above all charming'.[63]

The expectations were not entirely met. The local reviewer, Hans van
de Wal, explained to readers at great length once again that opera was
not be expected, the overall standard had not improved and the company was little more than a group of music hall performers compared
to London or Paris. But what could a colonial audience expect? They
could count themselves lucky to see European theatre at all (top-rate
European companies do not go out to the colonies), and the BOC does
not pretend to offer 'high art' nor even 'art'. They want nothing more
than to provide a good evening's entertainment. Bandmann's achievement is that his repertoire is up to date and therefore allows the colonial
audience to experience first-hand new works such as *The Merry Widow*,
which otherwise would only be available vicariously in newspapers and

---

[62] *Bataviaasch nieuwsblad*, 7 July 1906, 6. Translated from the Dutch by the author.
[63] *Bataviaasch nieuwsblad*, 8 September 1908, 2.

magazines. Van de Wal activates the colonial deprivation syndrome: *A Merry Widow manqué* is better than no *Merry Widow*.[64]

Although toleration of artistic deficiencies was generally recommended and practised, an attempt to play the musical comedy *Miss Hook of Holland*, complete with clogs, cheese and dikes before a largely Dutch audience, encountered mixed success with spectators, who were less than amused to see themselves caricatured in the manner of musical comedy. Although the piece had completed a successful run in London a year earlier, lines such as 'Ev'ry Dutchman when he wakes, a little piece of cheese he takes ...' had limited appeal, and the costumes fell well short on the verisimilitude front.[65]

Japan

Japan was a regular port of call for the Bandmann companies, which played there on average two times a year from 1906 to 1921. The foreign population of Japan was concentrated mainly in the two treaty ports of Yokohama and Kobe. A treaty port implied that Western foreigners enjoyed a certain degree of exterritoriality, although this status was removed after 1899. This meant that foreign residents established their clubs and places of worship and conviviality. In 1902, the foreign population of Yokohama, the largest of the foreign enclaves, excluding the Chinese, numbered 2,447, of whom roughly half were British.[66] Kobe had around 3,000 foreigners total, of whom two-thirds were Chinese.[67] The number of foreigners in Tokyo and Osaka was smaller still. The first Bandmann visits were centred, predictably, on Yokohama and Kobe, and only later did Tokyo become a regular part of the circuit. Yokohama boasted a European-style theatre, The Gaiety, which was built to host mainly amateur performances but provided basic amenities and could accommodate up to 500 spectators.[68] In Kobe, on the other hand, Bandmann performed in the local gymnasium. A major improvement occurred when the Imperial Theatre in Tokyo opened in 1911, providing Western-style performance facilities.

[64] Hans van de Wal, 'The Geisha', *Bataviaasch nieuwsblad*, 17 September 1908, 1.
[65] As usual, Hans van de Wal was not amused and bemoaned the eclectic settings and costumes: 'These Dutch peasants wore Norman bonnets and Swiss corsets.' *Bataviaasch nieuwsblad*, 21 September 1908, 4.
[66] *The Directory & Chronicle for China, Japan*, 612.
[67] Ibid., 647.
[68] The importance of the Gaiety Theatre, Yokohama, has been documented in great detail in Masumoto Masahiko, *Yokohama Geite-za*, 2nd ed. (Yokohama, 1986). It contains numerous references to Bandmann's visits. My thanks to Asumi Fujioka for providing me a copy of this book.

More than Tokyo, however, it was Yokohama that formed a nodal point on the international touring circuit with its ease of access as a port and its facilities.[69]

The tours were covered closely in the local English-language press. Japan had four to five newspapers, including a government-run daily, *The Japan Times*. Some Japanese papers also reported on the performances, especially once the companies visited Tokyo on a regular basis, where they performed to a largely Japanese public. Initially, the tours focused on Yokohama and Kobe, with their relatively large foreign populations but where a season would not last more than a week. Visits from the Bandmann companies invariably generated excitement, especially in Kobe, which saw itself as being 'badly treated by theatrical companies in the past'.[70] The first visit of the Bandmann Opera Company to that city was in May 1906 for a total of three nights after a somewhat longer sojourn in Yokohama. The BOC offered *The Earl and the Girl*, *Toreador* and *Lady Madcap*, all musical comedies, attended by 'one of the largest audiences ever assembled in the Kobe Gymnasium Hall'. The reviewer noted 'continuous laughter and applause' and that it was 'very rare that travelling companies make a stay at Kobe, or in Japan, for that matter'.[71]

If four nights in Kobe or a week in Yokohama was considered a good season (or four nights in the YMCA hall in Kanda), then it was logical that Bandmann needed to 'penetrate' the interior of the country, which implied almost entirely Japanese audiences. Charging prices of 2 or 3 yen (in 1910, 1 yen corresponded to US 50 cents) also meant that box office was limited, despite the mostly excellent houses and warm reception. As the Japanese began to build Western-style theatres (The Imperial in Osaka in 1910, the Yûrakuza and the Imperial in Tokyo), so too did these cities become attractive for the touring companies. In 1911, the BOC performed a three-night season at the Yûrakuza theatre. A year later, they returned for a longer season at the newly opened Imperial Theatre (Teikoku Gejiko) in Tokyo, which placed the company in full view of the Japanese theatre-going audience. While the Yokohama seasons had regularly attracted interested spectators from Tokyo, these were mainly theatre specialists who found the world of English musical comedy an exotically fascinating spectacle, although of limited artistic appeal.

---

[69] See Stanca Scholz-Cionca, 'Circulation', in Peter W. Marx, ed., *A Cultural History of Theatre in the Age of Empire*, Vol. 5 (London: Bloomsbury, 2017), 124.
[70] *The Japan Weekly Chronicle*, 7 September 1905, 299.
[71] *The Japan Weekly Chronicle*, 25 May 1906, 6333.

If Japan, perhaps more than any other Asian culture, epitomized the exotic for the European mind, so too did British musical comedy appear extremely strange to Japanese audiences. Whereas there had been a sustained effort on the part of Japanese intellectuals and theatre artists to indigenize Shakespeare and modern European drama (*shingeki*), Edwardian musical comedy, in the absence of any pre-existing literary translation, was a different beast. It could only be received on the basis of its performative spectacularity: the costumes, sets, dancing and singing. Texts were seldom if ever published, and then they provided little more than thin scaffolding (Fig. 3.6).

In an article entitled 'Foreign Music in Japan' published in 1910 in *The Times* by a Mrs J. M. S. Mollison, the author claimed that 'the Bandmann Opera Company played only once to a Japanese audience, the results did not justify a repetition'.[72] This was patently not the case, because Japan was a regular port of call for the Bandmann Opera Company, and the press reports were usually highly affirmative. Bandmann himself stated in several interviews that Japan was an important market. For example, in 1911 he claimed in an interview for the *Daily Mail* that 'the best supporters of English theatre companies in India, the Straits settlements, China, and Japan are native playgoers. Shakespeare, magic and musical comedy pay best.'[73] A year later, a Singapore paper reported, based on the previous tour:

He [Bandmann] is remarkably pleased at the success which attended his experiments in giving English opera at Osaka, and Kyoto, to Japanese audiences. He has the bill which was used to announce the Mousme at Osaka last July set up on a wall in his room, and it certainly does look incongruous to see the English print giving the title and the photograph showing the company followed by a mass of printing in Japanese characters.[74]

The reference here is to another musical comedy, *The Mousmé*, a 'musical play' by Robert Courtneidge with music by Lionel Monckton and Howard Talbot. Set in the then-recent Russo-Japanese War, this was a somewhat more serious treatment of Japanese culture than *The Mikado* or *The Geisha*, both of which Bandmann also performed. Nevertheless, it was still fraught with orientalist clichés and demeaning stereotypes. The spectacular visual elements of *The Mousmé* – the costumes, sets and scenic effects – caught the attention of the audiences and secured its popularity; the work's cultural superficiality did not appear to deter Japanese spectators.

---

[72] J. M. S. Mollison, 'Foreign Music in Japan', *The Times*, 19 July 1910, 72.
[73] 'Shakespeare in Far East', *Daily Mail*, 20 September 1911, 3.
[74] *The Singapore Free Press and Mercantile Advertiser*, 23 September 1912, 5.

Figure 3.6 Poster advertising the Bandmann Opera Company in Osaka, 1911. The Japanese text reads, from right to left, 'In the coming 6th month, 16, 17, 18, 19: every day. Admission every afternoon at 6 p.m. Programme changes daily. Large ensemble of the Bandmann Opera. Prices: chairs 5¥, balcony 3¥, 1st circle 2¥, 2nd circle 1¥, gallery 50 Sen.' (Houghton Library, Harvard University, MS Thr 1505.)

In July of 1912, the Bandmann Opera Company brought *The Mousmé* to Tokyo's Imperial Theatre for a week-long season, after it had performed at the Teikoku-za theatre in Osaka. There, the audiences that attended were almost entirely Japanese. According to a review from the *Straits Times*, the Japanese audience 'join[ed] lustily in the Banzai chorus, and call[ed] for its repetition half a dozen times'.[75] Another European reviewer present in Osaka also mentioned the enthusiasm for the 'Banzai' chorus but remarked on the 'generally indifferent manner of

---

[75] 'The Mousme in Japan', *The Straits Times*, 22 August 1912, 6. For an extended discussion of *The Mousmé*, see Henry Balme, 'Between Modernism and Japonism: *The Mousmé* and the Cultural Mobility of Musical Comedy', *Popular Entertainment Studies* 7(1–2) (2016): 6–20.

the Japanese section of the audience'.[76] It seems as though the Japanese audiences, although most did not understand the English, were receptive to *The Mousmé* and were not particularly disturbed by the orientalist connotations of the work. The production was also a great popular success in Tokyo: 'Night after night', the resident American theatre critic Zoe Kincaid Penlington, correspondent for *the Far East,* noted, 'there have been full houses made up largely of the Japanese, whose appreciation is but an evidence of the growing interest in what the Western stage has to offer'.[77] She was, however, scathing in her assessment of the production:

The piece was not only a threadbare version of its ancestor, the Mikado, of Gilbert and Sullivan fame, but a superficial acquaintance with real Japan would enable one to see how hopeless was the interpretation of local colour.... no attempt is made to make a thorough study of details [and] for the most part Japan is regarded as a place at the ends of the earth and looked at through a veil of mysticism ... [without] a genuine Japanese strain in the score.[78]

The argument could be made that musical comedies like *Peggy* and even *The Mousmé* represented advanced European modernity both in terms of the world(s) they represented – the contemporary, not the historical or mythological – and in the aesthetic means they employed. The narrativized variety form, with its singing, dancing and highly theatricalized female bodies, was clearly a novelty. Indeed, it did not take long before the Japanese themselves moved to imitate and adapt this form.

The Bandmann theatre impressed Japanese artists with its high standards of professionalism, pace of performance and a nightly changing repertoire, all of which placed huge demands on the performers. Just as the Japanese were absorbing the lessons of Western literary drama between Shakespeare and Ibsen, Bandmann arrived with a new type of Western theatre that exported and reinforced the Victorian division between art theatre and entertainment (the dominant theme of the theatre reform movement and most of George Bernard Shaw's theatre reviews). Even staunch advocates of modernist theatre (*shingeki*) such as Kaoru Osanai (1881–1928) were drawn to the performances of the Bandmann Opera Company. He recalled travelling to Yokohama daily

---

[76] 'An Anglo-Japanese Play in a Japanese Theatre: The Bandmann Opera Company in Osaka', *The Japan Weekly Chronicle*, 27 June 1912, 1141.
[77] Zoe Kincaid Penlington, 'The Stage', *The Far East*, 29 June 1912, 479. My special thanks to Stanca Scholz-Cionca for drawing my attention to Penlington and for providing material on Bandmann in Japan.
[78] Zoe Kincaid Penlington, 'The Stage', *The Far East*, 6 July 1912, 506.

from Tokyo just to see the performances: 'It was not in order to learn from their art, but rather to forget about the hardships of life. There at least there was freedom, a world free of constraint.'[79]

Japanologist Stanca Scholz-Cionca has argued that the sustained presence of the Bandmann companies in Japan was 'a ferment in the emergence of a modern entertainment culture that flourished during the whole [twentieth] century. One of its offspring [was] the all-female musical theatre, Takarazuka, [which] opened in 1914' and is now considered 'a classical genre'.[80] Indeed, it is probably no coincidence that the Japanese railway tycoon Kobayashi Ichizo founded his famous all-woman revue in Takarazuka near Osaka. There seems to be a direct connection between the disciplined respectability of the Takarasienne girls, the Gaiety girls and the Bandmann beauties. Another 'offspring' of the Bandmann presence was the emergence in Japan of a new genre, adapted from musical comedy. This innovation comprised popular works, called the Actress Plays (Teigeki Joyûgeki), that were performed in the Imperial Theatre, where Bandmann enjoyed his greatest triumphs in Japan, under the direction of Masuda Taro, director of the theatre, comedy author and admirer of Edwardian musical comedy.[81]

Although Bandmann visited over forty cities in the course of his career, the focus here has been on the most important from a network perspective. Most of the localities discussed were (and some still are) entrepôts, ports designed to enable the swift transhipment of goods with little to no impositions of taxes and tariffs. The Bandmann Circuit was structured around and along such centres, as it piggy-backed on the imperial trade routes that the British and other empires had already established. In contrast to most touring theatre, which viewed locality in terms of quick and transient profit, the Bandmann network engaged with locality. Its 'rhythms of return' recognized that long-term investment in theatrical infrastructure was more profitable in the long run. Of course, Bandmann was no philanthropist, although he frequently employed the convention of benefit performances to contribute to local philanthropic causes. He was a theatrical businessman for whom economics invariably trumped artistic considerations.

---

[79] Osanai Kaoru, 'Bandoman no tsuioku to inshô', *Engekironshû* 4 (1914): 407–11. Translation by Stanca Scholz-Cionca.

[80] Stanca Scholz-Cionca, 'Circulation', 133.

[81] See Ayumi Fujioka, 'Early 20th Century Transcultural Popular Entertainment in the British and Japanese Theatre: From Edwardian Musical Comedy to Teigeki Actress Plays', paper presented at the London Theatre Seminar, 2 February 2017 in the University of London Senate House. Fujioka argues that Masuda and an actress, Ritsuko Mori, both of whom had spent time in the UK, later contributed to the Teigeki Actress Plays, which enjoyed popularity between 1911 and 1929.

4   Repertoire and Publics

There is no demand for the Shakespearian drama
among the European community of Calcutta;
the frivolities of musical comedy alone spell
success to the manager from Home.[1]

The Friend of India

The Bandmann repertoire was highly varied and specialized, with each troupe representing a different genre: light opera, comedy/drama, variety. These catered in turn to pre-existing patterns of taste, derived mainly from English theatre-going practices. At the height of his activities, Bandmann had several companies moving around the globe in a rotating chain of changing genres and repertoires. Although the repertoire was derived from England and was therefore heavily influenced by local predilections, it was performed before astonishingly diverse audiences. Because of the generic breadth of the companies and the size of the repertoire – the Bandmann Opera Company had up to thirty works on offer – it could adapt to the diverse environments that were explored in Chapter 3.

The perpetuum mobile of the Bandmann rotation system meant not only theatrical trade on an almost non-stop basis, but also a spatial imaginary that connected points together stretching halfway around the globe. The itineraries themselves became ways of mapping a newly globalized world. They formed a structured route interconnecting distant towns and cities, which then became related to one another by virtue of sharing in the theatrical experiences provided by the companies. The newspaper reports demonstrate very clearly that the papers observed not just the latest theatrical fashions in London, but also the activities in the next colonial settlements. In many ways, the activities in Calcutta and Rangoon were more relevant to Singapore than London was. The newspapers quoted and reprinted from each other incessantly and constructed a kind of interrelated colonial public sphere independent of the metropolitan centre.

---

[1] Anon., 'Indian Theatres: The Alfred Theatrical Company', *The Friend of India*, 24 January 1907, 10.

The Bandmann companies performed around 250 different plays and programs of entertainment, including variety shows, on their circuit. On the basis of a representative sample of Bandmann's repertoire across the companies and venues, it is possible to gauge the changing tastes of his audiences.[2] Although his practice was to perform a selection of the latest London hits each year – hence the large number of titles – in practice he repeated particular works that proved crowd-pleasers between Malta and Manila. Amongst the top ten, we find in descending order the following: *Peggy, The Runaway Girl, Our Miss Gibbs, The Merry Widow, The Shop Girl, The Geisha, The Belle of New York, The Sign of the Cross, A Chinese Honeymoon, The Chocolate Soldier*. All but one – *The Sign of the Cross* – are musical comedies. Some, such as *The Geisha* and *The Runaway Girl*, date back to the 1890s, whereas *Peggy* (1911) and *Our Miss Gibbs* (1909) were produced in the decade before the First World War.

In an interview given in 1906, Bandmann described in detail his rotation system. He planned to keep companies going in regular rotation, working to and from London via the Mediterranean and Cairo to India and then moving on to the Far East and returning by the same route via Burma, Calcutta, Ceylon and Bombay. He also intended to have quick changes once the system became fully functional, so that during the next two years Calcutta would never be without theatrical entertainments:

[My dramatic repertoire company] will play a week's season, and that will carry us well on into January. In February my new musical comedy company arrives, and I shall open with them at the Theatre Royal on 1 February 1907, with an entirely new repertoire. I shall play in Calcutta seven weeks, with two changes a week... At the end of the seven weeks there will be another company on the road, and in May and June, 1907, you will have my Gilbert and Sullivan repertoire company. In July the dramatic company will be on its way back from the Far East, and will play in Calcutta for about a month, and in its turn make room for the musical comedy company. I shall probably reorganise and play the cold weather season with one of my companies in Calcutta.[3]

Although in reality the operation proved not quite as seamless as he envisaged, the rotation system was in fact implemented. A normal

---

[2] These results are based on a survey of 766 recorded performances stored in a database located on the website of the Centre for Global Theatre History, LMU Munich (www.theaterwissenschaft.uni-muenchen.de/forschung/gth/index.html). This represents only a partial record. An exhaustive list of all his performances along the circuit would be a formidable task and involve scouring newspapers in every city. This may be possible at a future date when sufficient newspapers have been digitalized.
[3] *Eastern Daily Mail and Straits Morning Advertiser*, 29 September 1906, 5.

sojourn in most cities comprised a week to ten days at most. A travelling company worked on the principle of structured circulation, selecting from a stock of productions depending on local conditions, predilections and the current state of the company. A repertoire could consist of up to three or four different works and genres performed in one locale over the course of a two-week run.

Genre and *repertoire* are key terms for understanding theatre as a mass medium in general and itinerant theatre in particular. During the course of the nineteenth century, the French term *répertoire* finds its way into most European languages but undergoes a shift in meaning from the early Victorian period, when it meant merely an actor's stock of roles, 'to denoting something beyond an individual's proprietorship, as in the repertoire of a theatre company or even a repertoire company'.[4] Tracy C. Davis argues that repertoire contributes not only to the formation of often mutually exclusive publics but also acts as a key factor in enabling 'intertheatrical' intelligibility. This refers to audiences' ability to establish interconnections between theatrical texts.[5]

A key component of such intelligibility was genre, because it determines on the level of production assumed patterns of taste; as a receptive category, genres are cognitive short-cuts that enable spectators to process the information-rich plethora of signs that any theatrical performance generates. Writers and producers, particularly in a commercially oriented theatrical culture (the norm in the long nineteenth century), utilized generic conventions to cater to assumed tastes and thereby minimize financial risk. The emergence and disappearance of specific genres can be seen as way to study the shifting cultural horizons of expectation.

The key concept to be explored in the context of Bandmann's touring is cultural differentiation. If we see the nineteenth century as a period in which different 'cultures' emerged – working class, lower, middle and upper, as well as different ethnic and religious groups coming into increased contact with one another – then it is logical that this differentiation would be reflected in the types of theatrical entertainment on offer. Across Europe, institutional changes wrought by new legislation

---

[4] Tracy C. Davis, *The Broadview Anthology of Nineteenth-Century British Performance* (Peterborough: Broadview Press, 2012), 13.

[5] The term was coined by theatre historian Jacky Bratton and refers to 'the mesh of connections between all kinds of theatre texts, and between texts and their users'. Jackie Bratton, *New Readings in Theatre History* (Cambridge: Cambridge University Press, 2003), 37. Cited in Davis, *Broadview Anthology of Nineteenth-Century British Performance*, 14.

moved to progressively deregulate theatre, which thereby enabled theatres to respond to the processes of cultural and class differentiation.
This led in turn to the 'variety principle', meaning on the one hand
that most evenings in the theatre consisted of a potpourri of different
genres and on the other the emergence of specialized theatres such as
music hall and vaudeville that created veritable industries centred on
one particular genre.

Playing a season, even in large cities such as Calcutta or Bombay,
meant performing a different show every night, as audiences would
only pay to see novelties. The long-run standard in metropolitan cities
was not an option on tour. Musical comedies were especially labour-
intensive, requiring not just performers with different vocal ranges but
also a relatively large chorus, musicians and a competent conductor.
A typical season in Singapore in 1912 included *The Mousmé*, *Peggy*,
The Count of Luxembourg, *The Belle of New York*, *The Girl in the Train*,
Gilbert and Sullivan's *The Gondoliers* and *Our Miss Gibbs*.[6] For the
slightly more discerning audience, the Comedy Company offered a
repertoire ranging from *Charley's Aunt* to Oscar Wilde's *The Woman
of No Importance*, while the Bandmann Dramatic Company had more
serious fare, such as *Trilby*, *East Lynne* and *The Prisoner of Zenda*. For
those determined to avoid any type of serious reflection, the Bandmann
Gaiety Company guaranteed a thought-free evening with a selection
of the 'Latest London Revues', including nightly programmes such as
'Frocks & Frills', 'All French' and 'Come Inside'.[7]

The troupes' repertoire changed considerably over the twenty-seven
years in which Bandmann managed companies. From the one-play
Manxman A and B companies of the mid-1890s, Bandmann expanded his
repertoire with the comedy companies which toured the Mediterranean
and Egypt in the late 1890s. By the time the company left Malta in late
December 1897 for Alexandria and Cairo after a ten-week season, it had
performed over twenty different works and had quite literally taken the
city by storm. Never before had Malta been exposed to such an extended
diet of English theatre ranging from older melodramas (*The Silver King*)
to popular hits (*Trilby*, *Lady Windermere's Fan*) and 'farcical' comedies. The musical comedies which would later come to dominate the
Bandmann Circuit were not yet on offer. The local newspapers struggled
to keep up with the rapidly changing repertoire and even politely suggested that instead of changing the bill nightly, the Malta public would

---

[6] Advertisement in the *The Singapore Free Press and Mercantile Advertiser*, 6 September
1912, 1.
[7] *The Straits Times*, 4 September 1915, 11.

appreciate repeat performances of some of the more popular plays. This intensity was superseded yet again on the later Far Eastern tours, where, to cite an extreme example, the Comedy Company played twenty-four plays in twenty-six nights during a season in Bombay in 1910.[8]

The plays that made up the offerings of 'dramatic' or 'comedy' companies of this period provide a glimpse of the late-Victorian and Edwardian English theatrical repertoire. While some titles are still familiar to the non-specialist, such as the cross-dressing farce *Charley's Aunt*, plays by Oscar Wilde or cinematic remake material like *The Prisoner of Zenda*, the genuine hardy annuals of the late nineteenth and early twentieth-century repertoire were melodramatic subjects, often adapted from novels. Three of these shall be described in more detail because of their persistent presence on the popular stage and because they featured consistently in the Bandmann repertoire from Gibraltar to Yokohama: *The Manxman*, *Trilby*, and *The Sign of the Cross*. They are linked by the fact that all three are adaptations from novels or vice versa, they conform to the mode of melodrama while moving into new social territory, and all were written in the mid-1890s, within a year of one another.

The play *The Manxman* was a dramatization of a novel by Hall Caine (1853–1931) by the actor-manager Wilson Barrett (1846–1904). Caine, a hugely successful novelist and exponent of popular melodrama, claimed that 'passion, … not fact, lies at the root of the novelist's art'.[9] Melodrama was the common 'mode' shared by novelists and playwrights alike, so adaptation between genres was common and often successful, as success in one genre reinforced interest in the other. Novel and play existed 'in a symbiotic but by no means simple relationship'.[10] This sometimes-complex relationship is evident in the adaptation of *The Manxman*, where Caine and Barrett had a major disagreement over form and content, so that novel and play differ considerably. As the title suggests, both novel and play are set on the Isle of Man. They relate the love triangle between the eligible girl, Kate Cregeen, and two friends – Philip Christian, well educated with good prospects, versus the illegitimate and almost-illiterate Manx-speaking Pete Quilliam. After Kate's father rejects Pete's request to marry his daughter, he goes to South Africa to seek his fortune in the Kimberley mines. Kate gradually falls in love with Philip, who becomes a lawyer and later a judge on the

---

[8] 'Mr. W. Henry Hargreaves', *The Era*, 23 April 1910, 13.
[9] Hall Caine, 'The New Watchwords of Fiction', *Contemporary Review* 57 (1890): 480. Cited in Mary Hammond, 'Hall Caine and the Melodrama on Page, Stage and Screen', *Nineteenth Century Theatre and Film* 31 (2004): 39–57, here 43.
[10] Hammond, 'Hall Caine', 49.

island. When, however, Pete returns to marry Kate, having made his fortune, a moral struggle ensues, with Kate torn between the two men. Although she marries Pete, she produces a child fathered by Philip and after many vicissitudes divorces Pete to marry Philip.

The disagreement between Caine and Barrett hinged on the two male figures. Whereas Caine in his novel concentrated on the unhappy love story of Philip, Wilson Barrett side-lined Philip by focusing on the lower-born character of Pete, his rags-to-riches story and marriage to Kate. Caine's novel was a bestseller, whereas Barrett's adaptation for the stage was only a moderate success on the London stage. In fact, many years later, Caine produced his own adaptation under the title *Pete: A Drama in Four Acts* (1908). Barrett's adaptation still enjoyed considerable popularity in the provinces where Bandmann toured with two *Manxman* companies (see Chapter 2). The speed with which Bandmann acquired the new play and assembled companies to perform it is remarkable. The London premiere of Wilson Barrett's adaption was in August/September 1894 (with Barrett in the role of Pete), in November 1894 Bandmann announced the formation of his *Manxman* company, and the first performances took place in December of that year. Bandmann himself played Pete throughout the 1890s, and the play remained in the repertoire of the international tours (see Fig. 4.1). In 1909, he also staged the new version under the title of *Pete*, which had had a successful London season with Matheson Lang in the title role. On the Bandmann Circuit, Henry Dallas played the part.[11]

The play *Trilby* was a stage adaptation of the eponymous novel by George Du Maurier, which was first published in 1894. Set in the artistic Bohemian quarter of the Paris in the 1850s, the story centres on three down-and-out British art students who make the most of their impecunious lifestyle by consorting with the shady musicians Svengali and Gecko but above all with the charming young model Trilby O'Ferrall. Trilby has a penchant for unusual attire (she wears a military uniform, goes barefoot and poses nude for the young art students), which also includes (in the stage version) a hat that still bears her name. Although tone-deaf, she becomes the willing medium of the musician and hypnotizer Svengali, who provides her with a divine singing voice so long as she submits to his hypnotic powers. During a performance, he denies her his power, she falters and Svengali dies of a heart attack. Trilby too is severely incapacitated and finally succumbs to illness, holding a picture of Svengali in her hand, which enables her to sing one last time.

---

[11] See 'Bandmann Dramatic Company: Successful Production at the Victoria', *The Straits Times*, 4 June 1909, 7.

Figure 4.1 Bandmann in the role of Pete Quilliam in *The Manxman*,
1895. (Helena Cowell Collection.)

The novel was one of the most successful books of the decade, the
American edition alone selling over 100,000 copies in the first few
months, while the English original went through numerous editions
in a few years. Apart from the famous hat associated with the title
figure, the character of Svengali also entered the English language as
a synonym for a sinister, mesmerizing figure (with fairly explicit anti-
Semitic connotations). Indeed, the second cinematic treatment of the
story, released in the United States in 1931, went by this name and not
the more jaunty Trilby.

The stage adaptation by the Anglo-American journalist and dramatist
Paul Potter premiered in the United States in March 1895, only months
after the novel's serialized publication in *Harper's Monthly*, where it was
seen by the actor-manager Herbert Beerbohm Tree. His London production in September of that year with himself as Svengali was one of the most

successful theatrical runs of the 1890s, with the royalties enabling Tree to build His Majesty's Theatre. The stage adaptation shifted the focus from the three bohemian students to a psychological study of Svengali's power over Trilby and his 'conversion' of her from a tone-deaf model to a star opera singer. The success of the London production inevitably spawned touring productions, including that of the various Bandmann companies. Like most popular plays of the time, *Trilby* divided critical opinion between outright rejection by a discerning modernist faction (including Beerbohm Tree's own half-brother Max Beerbohm) on the one hand and the almost-fanatical popular embrace of the work on the other. After seeing the American production, Max Beerbohm even advised his brother against buying the English rights – advice which the latter successfully ignored.[12] The modernist rejection remained, however, a very faint voice in a frenzy of fandom that extended to various characters, particularly the title figure, who generated a cult following. *The Era* surmised correctly after the premiere that the 'Trilby boom' was not going to be a 'passing craze'.[13]

Bandmann's production of the play is first mentioned in March 1896, only a few months after Beerbohm Tree's version at the Haymarket, when he launched the first of two *Trilby* companies.[14] The play was so dominant that a *Trilby* company or even two could tour this play exclusively. News that the Bandmann Repertoire Company was planning a visit to Egypt resounded as far away as Mexico, where the English-language *Mexican Herald* quipped, 'Egypt missed one plague in Pharaoh's time; it now comes along belated, for Maurice Bandmann is going to take a "Trilby" company to the Cairo and Alexandria theatres.'[15]

Initially, Gaston Mervale played the Jewish musician Svengali in the characteristic long beard popularized by Beerbohm Tree and Wilton Lackaye. Once Bandmann began touring two companies performing the play, he took over the role of Svengali in one of them. During the Maltese season the following year, his performance of Svengali was singled out: 'In "Trilby" Mr. Maurice Bandmann has shown himself to be an artist of whom any company might well be proud. Evidently Mr. Bandmann has made a peculiar study of the role of Svengali, which he has impersonated most admirably, to the minutest detail of speech, action and even costume.'[16] A review in Glasgow echoed this assessment with special mention of his Svengali as 'an excellent study'.[17] That

---

[12] See N. John Hall, *Max Beerbohm Caricatures* (New Haven: Yale University Press, 1997), 79.

[13] 'Trilby at the Haymarket', *The Era*, 2 November 1895, 11.

[14] *Sheffield Independent*, 21 March 1896, 11.

[15] *Mexican Herald*, 15 March 1899, n.p.

[16] Anonymous review, *The Malta Times and United Service Gazette*, 30 October 1897, 1.

[17] 'Glasgow', *The Stage Archive*, 16 February 1899, 3.

MR MAURICE BANDMANN, who ap-
pears to-night for the first time in
Buenos Aires, in the character of
Svengali, in «Trilby.»

Figure 4.2 Bandmann as Svengali, Buenos Aires, 1902. (*The Anglo-Argentine*, 24 May 1902, p. 679. Vanessa Lopez Family Archive.)

Bandmann himself played the star role was not without a special note, for, like Beerbohm Tree, his Jewish descent may also have added a particular *frisson*. Unlike Tree and Lackaye (and later John Barrymore in the film version), however, a rare photograph of Bandmann in a role in Buenos Aires (Fig. 4.2) suggests that he approached the part as a debonair gentleman rather than a wild-eyed Rasputin.[18]

---

[18] An English-language magazine noted, 'This is the part in which he himself considers that he made his best appearance on the English stage, and we have no doubt that he will meet with a flattering reception from a Buenos Aires audience, many of whom have their own conception of the evil genius of the heroine of the story.' *The Anglo-Argentine*, 24 May 1902, 679.

Another popular Bandmann vehicle was the role of Marcus Superbus in Wilson Barrett's 'toga play' *The Sign of the Cross*. Today a largely forgotten relation of *Ben Hur* and *Quo Vadis* in its day it was far more popular and, in theatre historian David Mayer's estimation, 'archetypal' of the genre.[19] However, like its better-known cinematic siblings, *The Sign of the Cross* (which also spawned two film versions) dealt with the theme of Christian persecution and martyrdom in the language of visual opulence. Set in Nero's decadent Rome, the central figure, Marcus Superbus, is a Roman rake redeemed by a Christian martyr, Mercia, who resists his lustful overtures and ultimately converts him to Christianity, thereby consigning Marcus to a certain death by lions. Conceived as an answer to the controversial 'divorce plays' of Arthur Wing Pinero and others (the main 'offender' being *The Second Mrs Tanqueray*), *The Sign of the Cross* was staggeringly successful, with an estimated 10,000 performances by the time of Barrett's death in 1904. During its London season in 1896–1897, it attracted 70,000 spectators per week.[20] One reason for the success lay in the unconditional endorsement provided by the church, which, much as with a late-medieval passion play, considered attendance to be almost on a par with a church service. It also conformed to the melodramatic mode of establishing clear binaries between good and bad, virtue and evil, and where nothing is left unsaid. Here the Romans are either cruel or immoral (or both), and the Christians invariably virtuous, kind and forgiving. The only character to cross the binary is Marcus himself, who, like Paulus, converts from persecutor to Christian believer thanks to the virtue (and physical attractions) of Mercia.

It is little wonder, then, that such a hot property should attract Bandmann in the mid-1890s as he was setting up his touring companies. However, there is no record that he performed it in Britain, presumably for copyright reasons, where Wilson Barrett toured it himself. Abroad, however, it became part of the dramatic repertoire. He tested it successfully in Malta, where local supernumeraries were recruited for the crowd scenes and clad in 'specially prepared wardrobes'.[21] Like all toga plays, *The Sign of the Cross* appealed because of its scenographic opulence and

---

[19] David Mayer and Katherine K. Preston, *Playing Out the Empire: Ben-Hur and Other Toga Plays and Films, 1883–1908: A Critical Anthology* (Oxford: Clarendon Press, 1994), 107.

[20] Mayer, *Playing Out the Empire*, 109.

[21] '"The Sign of the Cross" at the Manoel Theatre', *The Daily Malta Chronicle*, 29 November 1899, 2.

not just on account of its religious sentiments. Also, the road to redemption was a rocky one and required a detailed admonitory demonstration of sin in the form of Roman orgies and, more controversially, the extreme torture of a Christian boy. In the 1932 film version, Cecil B. de Mille famously included a scene where the Empress Poppaea bathes in asses' milk, naked girls are attacked by crocodiles, and an erotic 'Dance of the Naked Moon' is performed to make Mercia more amenable to Marcus Superbus' advances. It is remarkable, but not unusual, that touring companies would take on such works, with their huge demands on staging, costuming and manpower. It is perhaps little wonder that Bandmann's company could boast the transport of 'twelve tons of scenery'.[22] So popular was the genre that, later, Bandmann also toured a stage version of *Quo Vadis?*, the highly successful novel by Polish novelist Henryk Sienkiewicz.

Musical Comedies

Around 1900, Bandmann extended his repertoire to include musical comedy, by far the most popular genre of the late-Victorian and Edwardian periods. This coincided with the establishment of the Mediterranean and East Entertainment Syndicate Ltd and the partnership with Henry Dallas, who had already begun touring musical comedies to the East (see Chapter 2). Although Bandmann did not have any specialized musical training, and his background was more in drama through his parents, musical comedy came to be synonymous with his name through the Bandmann Opera Company, the most famous and popular of his various companies.

A form of musical entertainment that emerged in London's West End during the early 1890s, musical comedy was a genre located between operetta and variety that remained popular until the end of the First World War. This period is conventionally labelled the age of Edwardian musical comedy, borrowing its name from the eponymous era of British history (1901–1910). The figure who is unequivocally credited with having invented musical comedy is theatre manager and producer

---

[22] 'St John', *The New York Clipper*, 25 February 1905, 25.

George Edwardes (1855–1915). Over a career spanning almost thirty years, the tycoon established an entertainment empire in London's West End, where he owned and ran multiple theatres, including the Gaiety.[23] Employing a stable of writers and composers, he oversaw the production of over sixty works of musical comedy.

Despite the prominence and dominance of George Edwardes in the London theatre of the late-Victorian and the Edwardian periods, theatre historian Thomas Postlewait notes that 'with rare exceptions theatre historians have shown little interest in this popular form of entertainment'.[24] It is now being critically re-assessed for the importance it played in the globalization of theatre during the first decades of the twentieth century: musical comedy became a medium of extraordinary mobility, transmitted via the transnational travel and communication networks that had been put into place during the nineteenth century. Its shows, which originated in London, were dispersed to all four corners of the earth by itinerant theatrical troupes such as those of Bandmann.

Bandmann's turn to musical comedy needs to be examined as a means of connecting with culturally heterogeneous publics, many of whom did not speak English as a first language or did not have any command of English. The turn also needs to be seen in relation to intellectual property, as the choice of repertoire was determined as much by access to and control of copyright as by questions of popular taste. Bandmann traded in a wide variety of intellectual property, but the economic foundation of the Bandmann enterprise was a close cooperation with Edwardes and the Gaiety Company in London. Edwardes entered into an agreement with Bandmann around 1903, with the result that the latter obtained sole rights to the Gaiety plays for the British colonies and the 'Far East'.[25] Three years later, in 1906, he concluded a similar agreement with Helen D'Oyly Carte for 'rights of representation

[23] For a thorough account of British musical comedy and George Edwardes, see Kurt Gänzl, *The British Musical Theatre*, Vol. 1. (Basingstoke: Macmillan, 1986). For a critical reassessment of the link between musical comedy and modernity, see Len Platt, *Musical Comedy on the West End Stage, 1890–1939* (Basingstoke: Palgrave Macmillan, 2004).

[24] Thomas Postlewait, 'George Edwardes and Musical Comedy: The Transformation of London Theatre and Society, 1878–1914', in Tracy C. Davis and Peter Holland, eds., *The Performing Century: Nineteenth-Century Theatre's History* (Basingstoke: Palgrave Macmillan, 2007), 80–102, here 81.

[25] For a discussion of intellectual property in Edwardian theatre, especially with reference to George Edwardes and the Gaiety Theatre, see Tracy C. Davis, *Economics of the British Stage*, 350–3.

in the British Possessions in India, Ceylon, Burmah, Borneo, the Straits Settlements, China and the West Indies' for thirteen Gilbert and Sullivan operas. Initially for five years, it was renewed every five years, the last time in 1920.[26] The control and management of intellectual property was a highly territorial affair, as performance rights were assigned to people, usually agents, who represented countries and/or regions. Whereas in countries such the United States or Britain the rights holders could monitor their intellectual property themselves, this was not the case for the far-flung territories covered by the Bandmann Circuit. In his case, he both performed the properties and acted as an agent for them, collecting royalties where appropriate.

Losing the Plot

Musical comedies were not vehicles for profound treatments of pressing social or philosophical questions, although they certainly did deal with contemporary society – or at least a certain cross-section of it – from highly topical perspectives. Musical comedies were works in which the immediate present was represented through its fashions, behaviours and concerns. In Ben Macpherson's reading, they were centrally concerned with 'Britishness'.[27] The locales were equally of the time: fashionable department stores, seaside resorts, film studios and stock exchange floors pervade the stories of these works.

Peggy (1911) is a typical example of the genre. Written by British composer Leslie Stuart, with a book by George Grossmith Jr. and lyrics by C. H. Bovill, it opened on 4 March 1911 at the Gaiety Theatre, where it ran for a moderately successful 270 performances.[28] In a genre not renowned for verisimilitudinous plots, *Peggy* was even more plotless than most. In *Play Pictorial*, the richly illustrated magazine that accompanied and documented the Gaiety Theatre productions, editor B. W. Findon conceded, 'In the first place a musical comedy has no plot; and even if it had, to relate it would imply that a musical comedy should be taken seriously. And who wants to do that? Who goes to the Gaiety with even the slightest assumption of gravity?'[29]

---

[26] The D'Oyly Carte Archive, V&ATP, GB 71 THM/73/4/1.
[27] For a detailed analysis of both the topical concerns of musical comedies and their aesthetic forms, see Ben Macpherson, *Cultural Identity in British Musical Theatre, 1890–1939: Knowing One's Place* (London: Palgrave Macmillan, 2018).
[28] *'Peggy': New Musical Play in Two* Acts. Book by George Grossmith Jr. (founded on Xanroff and Guerin's 'L'Amorcage'). Lyrics by C. H. Bovill. Music by Leslie Stuart. Vocal score (London: Chappell & Co., 1911).
[29] *Play Pictorial*, January 1911, No. 18, 107.

The story begins in a hotel in London, where a pretty manicurist named Peggy Barrison is employed. She is engaged to a hairdresser at the hotel, Mr Albert Umbles, the obligatory comic role. Their relationship is less than passionate ('Peggy: What made you first think of proposing to me? Albert: Your mother').[30] However, a 'gentleman', the Hon. James Bendoyle, is also paying her attention with a view to matrimony, although Peggy does not care for him, so Bendoyle invents a plan to deceive her by having an impoverished but high-born acquaintance impersonate Umbles' millionaire uncle from Buenos Aires. In the second act, Umbles and Peggy leave for the French holiday resort Friville. Umbles loses his head over his sudden rise to fortune and begins to flirt with Polly Polino, a pretty French actress. The real uncle turns up and the scheme of Bendoyle comes to grief, but after various (mis)adventures, all ends happily.[31]

On the first Bandmann tour of the play, a reviewer in Singapore conceded that the plot mattered little and the succession of events was largely arbitrary:

If anyone took a fancy to play 'Peggy' backward, introducing the characters on the plage at Friville and leaving them in 'the lounge at the New Hotel, London,' it would not matter much. Plots and schemes of things and sequence of events are never very strong characteristics of Gaiety productions, and they are more noticeably lacking in 'Peggy' than in most. It has just enough thread of circumstances to legitimise the series of bright vaudeville turns of which it is composed, but not enough to make one care whether it ends happily or does not end at all.[32]

The key term here is 'bright vaudeville turns'. The plays, such as they are, provide a scaffolding for exhibiting the vaudeville or variety principle. The term *variety* can be seen as both an aesthetic principle and as a template for a whole 'variety' of related genres. An Edwardian musical comedy such as *Peggy* can therefore be seen as a kind of formalization and narrativization of the variety principle. It is largely a succession of song and dance acts interspersed with comic relief, usually provided by a central comic figure, in this case Alfred Umbles (Fig. 4.3). The vocal score lists twenty-one numbers. Singing and dancing and pretty girls form the dominant theatrical attraction.

---

[30] All quotations are from the typescript submitted to the Lord Chamberlain for licensing. 'Peggy'. Play. 2 Acts. Add. MS. 65917 N and LC Plays 1911/7. Lic. No. 998. The manuscript submitted to the Lord Chamberlain represents an earlier version; for example, the title figure is named Ella; here 22.
[31] *The Strait Times*, 11 March 1912, 8.
[32] *The Strait Times*, 12 March 1912, 9.

Figure 4.3 Bandmann Opera Company cast of *Peggy* at the Imperial Theatre, Tokyo, 1912. Bobby Roberts, second from left, in the role of Alfred Umbles. (Tsubouchi Memorial Theatre Museum, Waseda University, FH15303-01-263.)

At its height, shortly before the First World War, the Bandmann Opera Company had in its repertoire just under thirty musical comedies, and in some touring configurations, half a dozen plays, even revues. The Bandmann Musical Comedy Company that toured Egypt, Turkey and the Mediterranean in 1919 had a repertory of twenty-three musical comedies, two revues and one farce, and occasionally played vaudeville.[33] Normally, however, each genre was represented by a different, specialized company. A programme for the Japan tour in 1912 lists twenty-seven musical comedies and nine plays, the latter ranging from perennials such as *Trilby*, *The Sign of the Cross* and *The Manxman* to recent hits like *A Night Out*. On an earlier tour to the Americas that ended on the east coast of Canada, *The New York Clipper* noted a repertoire of 'something like forty plays and operas'.[34]

---

[33] 'Touring in Egypt', *The Stage Archive*, 17 April 1919, 8.
[34] 'St John', *The New York Clipper*, 25 February 1905, 25.

Revues and Variety

Edwardian musical comedy can be seen as form of structured variety show held together by a more-or-less plotted story. Bandmann also offered variety itself and its cognate forms, vaudeville, music hall and the revue. Occasionally the opera company performed variety evenings, because most of the performers had a background in music hall or vaudeville and could easily perform numbers for specially curated evenings. Variety genres are on the one hand specific to individual cultures – such as minstrel shows from the United States, music hall from England or cabaret in France – but they also achieved global impact as 'the variety show' as a format was adopted around the world, albeit under different names and in different regional inflections. Variety theatres sprang up in the 1890s and became integrated into a global economy of peripatetic artists and acts.

Bandmann's first attempt at variety was a Pierrot show in 1907 entitled the 'Bandmann Follies', which drew on accomplished performers from the Bandmann Opera Company. It was put together when the Bandmann Dallas Opera Co. broke up, and, not able to field a full musical comedy troupe, Bandmann took eight of his talented performers and created a vaudeville show.[35] Consisting of five men and three women, who remained on stage throughout the evening, they provided a potpourri of singing, dancing and ventriloquy, while Gordon Stamford, the pianist (and normally Bandmann's musical director), contributed humorous turns on the piano, demonstrating how to compose a waltz using just three notes. The latter also improvised around a newspaper advertisement on a suggestion from the audience. The sketches themselves ranged between folk songs such as 'Zuyder Zee' and more patriotic tunes and national dances.[36]

Bandmann entered the variety business on a large scale shortly before the First World War as the variety circuits expanded and began to dominate theatrical entertainment. As noted in Chapter 2, he formed partnerships with other circuits and floated a public company, Bandmann Variety Ltd. For a period, he renamed his Empire Theatre in Calcutta a 'Palace of Varieties' and targeted the local Indian audience. In 1913, he placed an advertisement in *The Era*: 'Mr. Maurice E. Bandmann has the pleasure in announcing that in addition to his Theatres and Touring Companies, arrangements have been concluded for a New Circuit of

---

[35] This is the gist of a letter from Bandmann published in *The Straits Times*; 'The Bandmann Follies Co.', *The Straits Times*, 10 April 1907, 7.

[36] The descriptions are based on performances given in Hong Kong and Singapore in April 1907. 'Bandmann's Follies', *The Straits Times*, 11 April 1907, 8; *The China Mail*, 19 April 1907, 5.

Variety Theatres in the above mentioned places, and is in a position to offer artistes engagements from three to eight months.'[37]

With its modular form, variety was an attractive proposition for both entrepreneur and performer, because it offered flexibility on both sides. The manager was not locked into delivering a particular show with all the accompanying problems of sickness, understudying, desertion, etc. An ailing or absent variety performer could simply be replaced by another at relatively short notice. The actual programme of a given evening was ultimately arbitrary. The performers – either individuals or smaller acts – could, as Bandmann advertised, join or leave a tour at different points: they could extend an Australian tour by joining the Bandmann Circuit through India and the Far East or vice versa.

Variety's problem was quality. Because of the pecuniary rewards, the form attracted a huge number of would-be comedians, tenors, magicians, ventriloquists, comediennes and contortionists (to name only some of the popular acts), but their abilities varied in the extreme. When Bandmann launched his first top-line variety company, the All-Red Circuit, in 1914 in collaboration with Harry Rickards of the Tivoli Circuit in Australia, the aim was to meet expectations generated by London programmes. In Bombay, it coincided with the opening of a new theatre, La Scala, which was actually the newly renovated (and still existing) Edward Theatre in the Kalbadevi quarter. The response was extremely positive, and the *Times of India* claimed it was 'one of the best vaudeville bills the Bombay theatregoers have had the pleasure of witnessing. At each performance last evening the theatre was packed to its utmost capacity ... if the Bandmann-Rickard people continue to put on such high-class programs as that last night, their success is assured.'[38] The evening featured as a star 'turn' Reynolds and Donegal, the world champion roller skaters and dancers who danced all the latest musical comedy hits. Lucille Savoy, billed as the Singing Venus, 'fairly brought down the house' with the combination of a pleasing voice and exterior plus the use of 'wonderful electrical and spectacular effects'. The 'brisk and lively' American musical duo Williams and Rankin performed on post horns and cornets. These various turns were interspersed with the latest London films.[39]

A year later, with the war intensifying, it became more difficult to field a programme featuring world-champion dancing roller skaters in Bombay. In June, the Excelsior advertised an evening consisting

[37] 'Bandmann's Eastern Variety Circuit', *The Era*, 25 January 1913, 18.
[38] 'La Scala', *The Times of India*, 4 April 1914, 12.
[39] Ibid.

(amongst other acts) of Miss Majorie Manners from the Duke of York's Theatre (a light opera performer who had come to prominence in *The Merry Widow*); Martin Rosse, a tenor from the Théâtre de la Monnaie, Brussels; *Locked in a Flat*, 'a screaming farce'; three Rosslyn Sisters in a musical sketch, 'Those Terrible Tomboys'; and the 'Great comedian and dancer', Mr Tom Payne, 'in new weird dances'. The live programme at 9:30 was preceded at 6:30 by a selection of short films, including newsreels. While most acts hailed from London, they were decidedly mid-range, plying their trade in the smaller suburban theatres. In many ways, such a programme harked back to the mixed evenings characteristic of most provincial theatres in England in the early and mid-nineteenth century, when farces, tragedies, melodramas and dancers could quite happily rub shoulders on one and the same evening.[40]

There was potentially no limit to variety. Any act within the bounds of propriety could be considered. Popular music was an obvious candidate, and research by Bradley Shope has shown that Bandmann was probably instrumental in brokering ragtime and jazz to Bombay audiences and through it to the wider Indian subcontinent. Ragtime featured prominently at the Royal Opera House in 1913 under Bandmann's banner. Shope reproduces an advertisement from the *Times of India* from 15 November 1913, which announces the appearance of the Bandmann Londoners 'in the latest Ragtime Revues' and a version of the hit show 'Hullo Ragtime' from the London Hippodrome.[41] In 1919, 'Bandmann probably booked the first shows including jazz aimed at large audiences, at least in Bombay'. He hired a jazz band off a docked ship, the *H.M.S. New Zealand*, and put them on at the Excelsior in April of that year.[42]

Shakespeare Abroad

In May 1911, while on one of his periodic trips to London to sign up new performers and acts, Maurice Bandmann gave an expansive interview to the newspaper *The Referee* in which he discussed the appeal of Shakespeare on his circuit:

How do I find the Indian audiences? Excellent. They roll up in shoals for anything good. We have educated the natives into playgoing. They have become especially fond of Shakespeare. In Calcutta and in Bombay they will pay

---

[40] For analysis of such a programme, see Christopher Balme, 'Repertoire and genre', in *A Cultural History of Theatre in the Age of Empire* (London: Bloomsbury, 2017), 187.

[41] Bradley G. Shope, *American Popular Music in Britain's Raj* (Rochester: University of Rochester Press, 2016), 7.

[42] Ibid., 47.

anything for seats, sometimes fifty rupees (about £3 6s. 8d.). And they always bring their 'Shakespeare' along, so as to follow the play. At first these natives were much surprised and annoyed at our necessary 'cuts.' When Shakespeare is given at the native theatres – as he often is now – he is always played entire. We are going to give the Indian and other natives a lot of Shakespeare presently. Mr. Matheson Lang and his wife, Miss Hutin Britton, and a company of twenty-five will open with me in Calcutta next year. Subsequently I take that company to China. I pick them up at Durban when they finish their South African tour.[43]

Bandmann's burden to tutor 'the natives' in the art of play-going was aimed less at acquainting them with the transcendental qualities of Shakespeare's plays than with entering into the oldest Western theatrical contract: paying an entry fee in exchange for entertainment. Far from needing such tutelage, the 'natives' had long since acquired the art of play-going in the Western sense, and this included a proclivity for Shakespeare. Bandmann did not tour a Shakespearean repertoire very often, which had less to do with local audiences than the European audiences on his ports of call.

The actor he mentions, Canadian-born Matheson Lang, was about to embark on a tour of South Africa, which, after Bandmann's intervention, was extended to include India and the Far East. The repertoire consisted initially of *Hamlet*, *The Taming of the Shrew* and three other successful, although today largely forgotten plays, *Bardelys the Magnificent*, *Sweet Nell of Drury Lane* and *The Passing of the Third Floor Back*. They soon added *The Merchant of Venice*. As Bandmann had predicted, the demand for Shakespeare was enormous. Whereas the troupe had played in South Africa to a predominantly white audience, in Bombay the situation was reversed. Crowds of Indian students poured into the newly opened Royal Opera House looking for tickets:

On the first night at the Bombay, although the house was sold out except for a few unreserved seats, at the time when the doors opened a mad dash was made for the pay box. The few remaining seats were sold in a few minutes, but this did not stop the rush. ... [T]he whole area was a mass of young students, waving money in the air and crying, 'I will pay thirty rupees for a stall' or 'Fifteen rupees for an Upper Circle'. In the end John [Holloway] had to call the police to clear the crowds so that those who had tickets could take their seats.[44]

---

[43] 'Mr. Maurice Bandmann. His Enterprises in the East: Shakespeare in India', *The Referee*, 28 May 1911, 6. In 1910, Bandmann had toured the actor Charles Vane with a selection of Shakespearean scenes but not a complete play.

[44] David Holloway, *Playing the Empire: The Acts of the Holloway Touring Theatre Company* (London: Harrap, 1979), 141.

Reviews of the production were, not surprisingly, very positive, because Lang's partner, John Holloway, had to write them himself, as all the local papers were too busy following the royal visit to India of George V and Queen Mary to provide a regular reviewer.[45]

From Bombay, the troupe moved to Calcutta, the headquarters of Bandmann's empire. Although having to play in severe climatic conditions, the performances were greeted with acclaim and full houses. *Othello* in particular, despite the fact that Lang's Othello makeup became streaky and wigs and beards became unglued, was hailed as a triumph:

Mr. Lang's 'Othello' must be seen to be appreciated. ... He invests it with a new pathos, and his portrayal of the agony of the noble Moor in the first grip of the suspicion implanted in his mind by Iago, in its rapid and terrible development, and in the supreme moments of its consummation and climax, is finer than any representation we had yet seen. ... Iago found a nice able interpreter in Mr. Charles Vane, and the hisses which greeted him towards the end of the performance reminded one piquantly of the Adelphi.[46]

The tour continued to Rangoon, where strange things happened. The scene between Hamlet and the ghost, staged to appear in a dim, grey cold light, was unexpectedly bathed in changing coloured lights. When the Burmese lighting operator was interrogated afterwards, the interpreter explained, 'Very long scene. Ghost talk very much. In our plays when an actor talks too much we throw coloured lights on him to divert the audience – why not?'[47] Shanghai was considered the highpoint of the tour. The company even rehearsed a new production of *Macbeth*, at the special request of the Shanghai Caledonian Society. The troupe continued to Manila for a fortnight's season. Then the whole route was played again in reverse via Singapore, Rangoon to India, with return seasons in Calcutta and Bombay and a final tour of South Africa (Fig. 4.4).

Theatre-going in general and Shakespeare in particular, was, as Bandmann mentioned, by no means the preserve of a colonial class. On the eve of the First World War, Shakespeare was an author who was not just being read and translated throughout the world but also performed in vernacular versions. Most importantly, the Shakespeare trade was not just confined to British actors. The latter arrived, in fact, at theatrical centres where performances of Shakespeare were already common.

---

[45] Ibid., 144.
[46] 'Mr. Lang's "Othello" – Saturday Night's Triumph', *The Empire*, 29 April 1912, 6.
[47] Matheson Lang, *Mr Wu Looks Back: Thoughts and Memories* (London: Stanley Paul, 1940), 102.

Figure 4.4 Mr Matheson Lang as Hamlet and Miss Hutin Briton as Ophelia, ca. 1912. (Private collection.)

In India, the Straits Settlements (Malaya and Singapore) and the Dutch East Indies, local troupes had already begun to stage Shakespeare in their own languages, the most prominent and successful being the versions of the Parsi theatre in India. The Parsi troupes, with their combination of mythological stories, singing and dancing, had already begun to stage Shakespeare and Indian mythological stories in the mid-nineteenth century using European staging techniques and technology. After amateur beginnings, this activity turned into large-scale commercial operations that toured large repertoires throughout the Indian subcontinent and beyond.

The Shakespearean tours of Matheson Lang and Allan Wilkie in 1911 and 1912 remained an anomaly when one reviews the normal repertoire of the colonial theatres. Ironically, Shakespearean adepts or addicts had a much better chance of seeing the Bard in an indigenous rather than a pukka-British version, albeit with dramaturgical and performative embellishments. It was the local, not the European, audiences that made Shakespearean productions commercially viable. Their enthusiasm and preparedness to pay black market prices for tickets ensured 'Lang houses' from Bombay to Shanghai.

Shakespeare was a tradable and profitable commodity, but from the point of view of entrepreneurs such as Bandmann, also a disputed one.

From an actor-network perspective and its application of the 'relation-ality of entities',[48] repertoire is one such entity or node in an inter-locking network or circuit. Bandmann officially called his operation a circuit, a perpetuum mobile of theatre troupes moving around the world in a carefully calibrated rotation system. Although Bandmann learned his trade performing Shakespeare with his mother and father, his network relied mainly on other theatrical genres. Shakespeare was in fact a risk, one which paid off, for him at least, but it is not one he often repeated.

Facsimile Aesthetics

The Bandmann repertoire was predicated on the prompt provision of near-exact copies of the latest London hits. Advertisements highlighted the aspect of reproduction and imitation: 'The company will reproduce among other latest London successes the following.'[49] The epithets 'fac-simile', 'reproduction', 'copy' or 'duplicate' were displayed as a badge of honour, a stamp of quality demonstrating the touring production's close affinity to the London originals. The practice of theatrical dupli-cation had both an economic and an aesthetic dimension. Tracy C. Davis has examined how the major London producers organized ways to maximize the economic life cycle of their theatrical commodities. She draws parallels between the rise of retail chains such as Woolworths and Marks & Spencer, so-called 'multiples', and the practice of the 'Savoy's simultaneous operation of several touring companies with the same interchangeable repertoire'.[50] Touring had for a long time enabled both small- and large-scale theatrical managements to derive more profit from the London capital investment. Often the actor would go on the road himself or herself, or the script would be sold for copycat productions. The Edwardian period saw, however, new developments that demanded greater artistic adherence to the visual imprint of the original. Sometimes the original production, complete with sets and costumes, would be sold on lock, stock and barrel. In the case of a genre like pantomime, even the *mise en scène* came to have a tradeable value – not just the script and score. By 1900, the established business model was the rapid exportation of a London hit to New York and even further afield while the original

[48] John Law, 'Actor Network Theory and Material Semiotics', 141.
[49] 'Theatrical Enterprise. Coming Bombay Season', *The Times of India*, 29 September 1911, 8.
[50] Tracy C. Davis, *Economics of the British Stage*, 341.

production was still running, since the markets were highly distinct and in no way in danger of cannibalizing one another. The practice of rapid export of a near facsimile was the basis of Bandmann's operations.

While the economic and business potential of multiple exploitation of the same commodity is clear, what was the aesthetic potential? What was the appeal of seeing an approximation of a London production, the theatrical equivalent of – to paraphrase Homi Bhabha's theory of colonial mimicry – the almost but not quite? There is no doubt that such approximations, the nearer the better, were demanded by colonial and indigenous audiences alike. On his tour of India, first under Elias Cohen's and then under Bandmann's management, Allan Wilkie proudly proclaimed that 'many of the scenes are facsimile reproductions of the "sets" used in the principle London Theatres'.[51] Sometimes a direct connection with the imperial centre could be made when actors reprised their roles from the London production, as in the tour of the Bandmann Comedy Company in 1909: 'Miss Lucy Beaumont and Mr. Douglas Vigors will be seen in Bombay in "The Night of the Party" in the parts which they took in the original production of the piece in London.'[52] In the case of amateur productions, Bandmann would sub-sell rights to the script and scenery of properties he controlled, as in the case of *The Geisha* in Bombay in 1915 or the highly popular Gilbert and Sullivan operas.[53]

The programme of the 1917 BOC season, including the newest addition, a production of the musical comedy *Toto* (1916) from the pen of Gladys B. Unger and with music by Archibald Joyce and Merlin Morgan, foregrounds reliance on the London originals.[54] While the scenery for all productions is promoted as 'entirely new and elaborate', it was specially painted 'from the original London models'. Similarly, the costumes were 'specially executed from original London and Paris models of the very latest fashions under the direct personal supervision of Mrs. BANDMANN' (see Fig. 4.5). The use of the stage as an *ersatz* fashion runway was a standard practice on the commercial

---

[51] 'Grand Opera House – Engagement of Mr. Allan Wilkie', *The Empire*, 2 September 1911, 4.

[52] 'Bandmann's Theatre: The Comedy Company's Visit', *The Times of India*, 13 April 1909, 4.

[53] 'Opera House Opens as Cinema', *The Times of India*, 13 December 1915, 11.

[54] *Toto* premiered at the Duke of York's on 19 April 1916 before transferring to the Apollo some months later. The book was a free adaptation of the French comedy *Les deux écoles* (1903) by Alfred Capus and provided a vehicle for Mabel Russell in the title role. *Pall Mall Gazette*, 20 April 1916, 8.

THE entirely new and elaborate scenery for all these productions has been specially painted by GEO. R. HEMSLEY & CO., London, from the original London models, kindly lent for this purpose by the various managements, and each production will be carried in its entirety.

THE entirely new and magnificent dresses have been specially executed in London from original London and Paris models of the very latest fashions under the direct personal supervision of Mrs. BANDMAN.

Figure 4.5 Programme note and photograph of *Toto*, Bandmann Opera Company season 1917. (Vanessa Lopez Family Archive.)

theatre of the time.[55] In both cases, the epithet 'original' refers not to the touring company's own artistic production but to its fidelity to a metropolitan origin.

[55] On this practice in the United States (but it applies equally to other metropolitan centres), see Marlis Schweitzer, *When Broadway Was the Runway: Theater, Fashion, and American Culture* (Philadelphia: University of Pennsylvania Press, 2009).

The insistence on imitation needs to be seen against the background of distance from the imperial centre and the experience of 'exile' in the colonies. For the colonials, theatre productions provided an approximation of an often sorely missed 'Home', where a visit to the theatre in London was usually a not-to-be-missed part of the itinerary. For the indigenous spectators, the productions offered a visual and acoustic experience of a metropolitan centre which was featured incessantly in the media they read, whether in English or local languages. There is no doubt that an aspect of colonial mimicry as a spectatorial practice was at play in the expectation of seeing copies of packaged duplicate productions. This expectation has remained remarkably robust, because it anticipates contemporary practices with mega-musicals where adherence to the original is both policed and marketed. It suggests, therefore, that this tendency towards standardization characteristic of contemporary globalization was already at play on the Bandmann Circuit.

Networked Publics and Colonial Spheres

The public for Bandmann's productions was heterogeneous in the extreme. While touring theatre was by definition subjected to different pressures than the more predictable matrices of metropolitan theatregoers, the difference between a tour through the English provinces and one that extended from Gibraltar to Yokohama cannot be emphasized enough. Although many of the ports of call had a core British audience, a number did not. In Malta, for example, the Bandmann companies attracted the local Maltese so that they could improve their English. As one journalist noted, 'a large number of the Maltese would patronize the excellent performances of the Comedy Company not only for amusement but to perfect the pronunciation of the spoken English language as in the metropolis'.[56]

Outside the metropolitan centres, touring companies needed to communicate with publics that were regionally circumscribed. The Bandmann Circuit benefitted from the existence of transregional colonial public spheres. Reports on Bandmann's activities invariably cite other news reports from centres along the circuit which indicate the existence of a chain of interlinking, networked publics that were not just focused on colonial locality and the metropolitan centre but also on

---

[56] '"David Garrick" at the Manoel Theatre', *The Malta Times and the United Service Gazette*, 23 October 1897, 1.

adjacent colonies, which created a sense of 'intertheatrical' intelligibility – that is, audiences' ability to establish interconnections between theatrical texts and performances. Although the term was coined to describe the dense theatrical culture of late nineteenth-century London theatre, it can also be applied to the colonial situation. A key component in such intelligibility was familiarity with repertoire, but media coverage played an equally important role. It may make more sense to speak of multiple public spheres marked by spatial contiguity and propinquity rather than a single, unified theatrical public sphere.[57] Although colonial publics certainly paid attention to what was going on at home, i.e. London or Paris, there also existed communities and networks of settlers, expatriates and indigenous elites that together – and sometimes opposed to one another – worked to establish institutions for the arts such as museums, theatres, orchestras and their attendant buildings, infrastructure and training institutions. Their endeavours were at once local and transnational as they sought to adapt metropolitan concepts and practices to local conditions.

Recent research shows that colonial public spheres were both connected to and independent of the imperial metropolitan centres. Tobias Becker has argued that professional itinerant theatre of the Bandmann kind as well as amateur dramatics constituted together a crucial institution of the colonial public sphere, providing not only a social space for the British diaspora but also a 'lifeline' to home: 'By watching theatrical performances either brought to them straight from London or which they staged themselves, colonial Britons felt in touch with the homeland.'[58] Yet, as Mark Frost argues, such colonial public spheres also had considerable non-European involvement:

The British Empire, as it spread out across the ocean space, functioned as a 'web' for information exchange that depended on oceanic communications. Especially after 1869, this web facilitated the emergence of a colonial public sphere that was 'transnational' (as it might be termed in modern parlance), one where non-Europeans played leading roles.[59]

Frost argues that these regionally organized public spheres sustained different networks of information exchange that complicate the usual colonizer/colonized binary. For a mobile theatre of the Bandmann kind,

[57] On the concept of the theatrical public sphere, see Christopher Balme, *The Theatrical Public Sphere* (Cambridge: Cambridge University Press, 2014).

[58] Tobias Becker, 'Entertaining the Empire: Theatrical Touring Companies and Amateur Dramatics in Colonial India', *The Historical Journal* 57 (2014): 699–725, 701.

[59] Mark Ravinder Frost, 'Maritime Networks and the Colonial Public Sphere, 1840–1920', *New Zealand Journal of Asian Studies* 6(2) (2004): 63–94, 66.

this web was held together by three main elements: advance agents, steamships and newspapers. The advance agents were employed by theatre managers to provide local newspapers with news of the company. They arrived ahead of the main company and coordinated both organization and publicity. The ships they arrived on contained also newspapers from other colonies, which provided a source of copy so that readers in Singapore or Hong Kong were able to peruse articles reprinted from the Bombay-based *Times of India* or the Calcutta *Statesman*. For example, in 1912, the *Straits Times* of Singapore reported on a successful performance of *The Mousmé* by the Bandmann Opera Company at the Imperial Theatre in Tokyo and Osaka:

> The Lord Chamberlain's refusal some time ago to sanction a revival of The Mikado at the Savoy will be recalled with a wondering smile when it is learned that The Mousme, with its treachery on the part of an officer of the Japanese army and its somewhat chaffing allusions to Japanese officialism generally, is being played in Japan with extraordinary success. A correspondent in Tokyo reports to the *Daily Chronicle* that the piece has been received with great enthusiasm at the Imperial Theatre there, and points out that The Mousme company enjoys the distinction of having been the first European theatrical company to perform on the stage of that house. In the theatre at Osaka, where the inhabitants are almost entirely Japanese, it was most warmly received, the audience joining lustily in the Banzai chorus, and calling for its repetition half a dozen times.[60]

The theatre-going public in Singapore had already seen the production a few months before. The report of the performances in Japan is mediated back to Singapore via a correspondent in Tokyo writing for the London *Daily Chronicle*. The article in turn references the scandal surrounding Gilbert and Sullivan's *Mikado*, which had been refused a licence in 1907 out of deference to the visiting Japanese prince.[61] Here we can observe an example of 'intertheatrical' intelligibility, as Singapore is connected not only to London but also Japan via a particular, in this case orientalist, theatre production. Theatrical news rubs shoulders indirectly with international politics.

Bandmann continually adjusted his repertoire and also calibrated individual productions to meet local requirements as they passed through a range of cultural contexts and zones. He needed to take account not only of differing cultural codes but also, it seems, the

---

[60] *The Straits Times*, 22 August 1912, 6. See also Chapter 3.
[61] The *Mikado* was actually banned in Japan shortly after its 1885 premiere. It was considered too disrespectful towards the emperor to be performed in Japan, and Japanese elites who saw it in European capitals were highly critical of the Chinese-sounding names of the lead characters and farcical depictions of Japan which seemed to confirm their view that Westerners could not distinguish between Japan and China.

excessively prudish sensibilities of English colonials not accustomed to the latest London theatrical fashions. Failure to do so meant not only box office disaster but on occasion direct political repercussions.

In a letter to the editor of the Karachi *Daily Gazette* written in 1920, a local theatre manager defended his employer, Maurice E. Bandmann, against savage criticism from a fellow colonial. 'I maintain', the manager wrote with barely concealed chagrin, 'that these plays are the dramatization of the local life of the world, Karachi exempted.'[62] The plays in question belonged, with one exception, to the category of light comedy. Nevertheless, they managed to engender a strong affective response on the part of a certain section of the colonial public. 'Moral rubbish' was one of the more restrained epithets bestowed on the repertoire of the Bandman Comedy Company that played a two-week season at the city's Palace Theatre. The author of the original article, a certain Mr M. de Pomeroy Webb, took extreme exception to most of the repertoire, but in particular to the comedy *The Naughty Wife* and the dramas *Mr Wu* and *The Voice from the Minaret*:

We all recognise the harm that has been done and is still being done, by the exhibition in India of cinema films wherein Europeans and Americans are represented as people whose chief aim in life is to break into a bank, or steal a plan of a mine, or destroy a factory or swindle one's neighbour, or do some other morally outrageous act by the aid of motorcars, wireless telegraphy, aeroplanes and all the other latest paraphernalia of modern science. We are not surprised if young boys from school are led astray, and the audience generally come to the conclusion that dishonesty and violence are the chief weapons of the white people who live in the East...White people are not philanderers, seducers and adulterers, nor is it in accordance with ordinary experience that such exceptional persons escape the penalties of their misdeeds, and are the centre of popular admiration and applause.[63]

For all the evident prudishness, such objections often revealed, however, a deeper anxiety focused on the mimetic power surrounding the depiction of Westerners as seemingly adulterous, criminal and impecunious before a 'native' public. This argument in fact gained in strength in the 1920s in response to the cinema and would lead eventually to a major enquiry into both the content and organization of the cinema industry in India.[64]

---

[62] 'Bandman "Rubbish" – Replies to Mr. Webb', *The Times of India*, 28 April 1920, 14.
[63] Ibid.
[64] We find, for example, the same arguments repeated in an article 'Films in India', *The Bioscope* (1920), 18d–18e. The vigorous public discussion resulted in a special enquiry into the Indian cinema industry and the need for censorship. A comprehensive *Report of The Indian Cinematograph Committee 1927–1928* was published in 1928 together with five volumes of 'evidence'.

Although theatrical managers such as Bandmann had no interest in alienating or scandalizing their publics, this happened repeatedly as the companies presented plays that had been approved by the Lord Chamberlain in London but still occasioned protest in the colonies. On one occasion, Bandmann was accused in Singapore of circumventing censorship by presenting Oscar Wilde's *Salome*, and in Bombay the controversial dancer Maud Allan performed her choreographic version of it, *The Vision of Salome*, at Bandmann's newly opened Royal Opera House. Both works had fallen foul of the censor back in England.[65] Apart from moral outrage, there remained the intractable problem of finding the right mix of works and genres for the colonial stage. In India, there was, as we have seen, little demand for Shakespearean drama among the European community, whereas performances of the Bard were overrun by Indian students willing to pay black-market prices to see Allan Wilkie or the Lang-Holloway company.

The question of scale was crucial for a commercial theatre enterprise. To maximize attendance, cultural sensibilities needed to be respected. It was not enough to differentiate between European and native, Hindu or Parsi; gender also needed to be taken into account. The introduction of Western-style theatre across the East posed new problems for accommodating men and women in the same public space. This was particularly pronounced in Muslim countries but by no means restricted to them. The solution to religious and cultural practices was the introduction of segregated and curtained-off sections in Western-style theatres. These sections were termed *zenana* and effectively extended the institution of women's quarters in private houses, common in both Muslim and Hindu communities in South Asia, to the public arena of theatre. In 1885, Daniel Bandmann described performing Shakespeare in Calcutta (after a successful season at the city's European Corinthian Theatre) for a few nights in the exclusively 'Hindu theatres': 'It was a sight of indescribable interest to behold three thousand black faces turned on the stage, and there were hundreds of their zenanas in the boxes, who could see us acting, though we could not see them.'[66] The audience was a mix of both Hindus and Muslims, as he later states, and in fact educated Muslims constituted an important part of the theatre-going public. The Star Theatre in Calcutta – another 'native theatre', as the English termed the houses that played in local languages – made

---

[65] 'Royal Opera House', *The Times of India*, 21 October 1913, 5.
[66] Daniel E. Bandmann, *An Actor's Tour; or, Seventy Thousand Miles with Shakespeare* (Boston: Cupples, Upham and Co., 1885), 142.

special allowance for this female public. When the actor Charles Vane toured India in 1909 under Bandmann's management, the newspaper publicity in the Bengali-owned, English-language paper *The Amrita Bazar Patrika* directly addressed the 'zenana ladies': 'A unique opportunity for one and all, and special for the student community and the Zenana ladies who have absolutely no chance of witnessing European artistes playing upon the stage.'[67]

In most of the cities comprising the Bandmann Circuit, the performances were frequented by, ethnically speaking, a broad cross-section of the population. This was certainly the case in India but also held true in Shanghai, where many Chinese people attended, and even more so in Singapore, where it was calculated that on one night of Matheson Lang's Shakespeare season, people from thirty different communities were present.[68] In Japan, the audiences were, except in Yokohama, primarily Japanese.

Although Bandmann's tours tended to follow the main settlements of the British Empire, where English was spoken or at least understood, he by no means restricted himself to the entrepôts of empire. As noted in Chapter 3, he regularly visited the Dutch East Indies, China and Japan, where the vast majority of spectators did not understand the English language well or even at all. This is where the genre of musical comedy appears to have had its greatest appeal. The fact that its dominant signs were music, song, dance and attractive (mainly female) bodies clothed in the latest fashions meant that European theatre could find a large audience that did not understand the language. For the performances of *Peggy* at the Imperial Theatre in Tokyo, a synopsis in Japanese was also provided in the programme – an unusual but obviously necessary measure to bridge the language gap. This may also have been a service provided by the Imperial Theatre to attract spectators. On Bandmann's first visit to Osaka and Kyoto in June 1912, a Japanese narrator was employed who stepped in front of the curtain before each act and explained the action 'in the familiar manner of cinematograph shows'.[69]

Musical comedy provided the core repertoire on the Bandmann Circuit. The diffusion of Edwardian musical comedy around the globe is one of the fascinating untold stories of theatre history. It has fallen through the cracks of established theatre historiography for the same reason that Bandmann has disappeared from the historical record.

---

[67] 'Amusements', *The Amrita Bazar Patrika*, 22 September 1909, 3.
[68] Holloway, *Playing the Empire*, 151.
[69] 'An Anglo-Japanese Play in a Japanese Theatre: The Bandmann Opera Company in Osaka', *The Japan Weekly Chronicle*, 27 June 1912, 1141.

Historiographically speaking, musical comedy is a marginalized genre, as it does not conform to the modernist paradigm in a formal sense. It occupied a clear position in what Thomas Postlewait has termed 'the oppositional narrative of the culture of commerce versus the culture of rebellion'.[70] Yet its content was, as we have argued, uncompromisingly modern in the way it represented topical concerns, the latest fashions and the new figure of the 'girl' as an independent subject. The unrelenting presentation of the genre through Bandmann's companies may also have left some legacy – for example, in the world of Bollywood. Although the latter normally traces its genealogy back to Parsi theatre, the predominance of singing and dancing in both musical comedy and Bollywood demonstrates parallels that are striking if difficult to connect in a direct casual sense.

Accounting for difference was the basis and bane of itinerant theatre as it moved through different zones of aesthetic appreciation. It would appear – to paraphrase H. L. Mencken's famous aphorism – that nobody ever went broke underestimating the taste of the colonial British public.[71] If the Bandmann Circuit was based on the concept of transporting facsimile productions of London musical comedies and other forms of entertainment around the British Empire and beyond, the question poses itself whether Bandmann and his kind were just a theatrical extension of British commerce and colonialism, detached from indigenous peoples and experiences? Yes and no. Bandmann purveyed a product designed for and tested in the metropolitan centre. Yet, there is no doubt that non-European audiences frequented the productions; in some cases they constituted a majority of the spectators. Indeed, non-European audiences were economically essential for the whole enterprise. The theatre-going public on the Bandmann Circuit was, in most cases, 'distributed' in a double sense: only a section of it corresponded to the 'implied spectators' for which the original productions had been conceived (very roughly a London metropolitan audience). It was also distributed in the sense of being dispersed over a large territory.[72] This state of dispersion marked the specific quality of touring theatre, but it was especially pronounced

[70] Postlewait, 'George Edwardes and Musical Comedy', 95.

[71] To H. L. Mencken, the famed US journalist and satirist, is attributed the saying 'No one in this world, so far as I know – and I have researched the records for years, and employed agents to help me – has ever lost money by underestimating the intelligence of the great masses of the plain people. Nor has anyone ever lost public office thereby.' It is often cited as 'No one ever went broke underestimating the intelligence of the American people', *The Yale Book of Quotations* (New Haven, 2006), 512.

[72] For the term 'distributed' in theatre and performance, see Christopher B. Balme, *The Theatrical Public Sphere*, Chapter 6.

on the Bandmann Circuit because of the astonishing geocultural and linguistic terrain covered by the troupes.

Whether colonial or local, we need to think of the relationship between Bandmann's repertoire and his publics in terms of 'rhythms of return': troupes sustained a culture of promise and expectation, they brought with them the excitement of London and the experience of their previous port of call and they carried messages to the next. Such visits were predicated on a delicate dialectic that balanced the strange and the familiar. An itinerant theatre company always brings with it a moment of the exotic and the incommensurable: it inserts itself into a patterned social fabric for a short period, bringing glamour and behaviours not fully controllable by the local environment. By virtue of its repetitive nature, however, the visits were also familiar and conformed to a broadly predictable pattern of events and behaviours. The repertoire of the Bandmann companies demanded from its performers remarkable flexibility, as up to thirty individual works could potentially be staged. Bandmann's companies were required to perform a different work every night, and the significant variations in audience, locale and physical performance conditions meant that companies had to have a much larger selection of works 'in stock' than they might actually show in any one place. The Bandmann Opera Company prided itself on presenting the latest hits from London: there existed a relentless pressure to produce and present novelty. But although last year's hits faded in favour against the lure of the latest musical comedy from the Gaiety Theatre, they still remained in the performance 'memory' of the company. Anxiety over audience taste and proclivities also underpinned Bandmann's operations. For this reason, light entertainment from London in facsimile productions remained the foundation of Bandmann's companies.

5   Transported Actors

> Insects abound. There are huge cockroaches (with wings), vast spiders, long-bodied winged ants, smaller-bodied wingless ants in myriads, white ants that eat your books and clothes, red ants that eat your food, black ants that eat you. There are scorpions, centipedes, lizards, hornets, mosquitoes, sandflies, flying beetles, dragon-flies, snakes, huge rats, and every description of crawling and creeping thing that it is possible to conceive.
>
> *The Stage Yearbook*[1]

Over the twenty-five years of his activities, Bandmann transported approximately 2,000 performers around the world on his circuit. The tours normally lasted between eighteen months and two years, so that members of the Bandmann Opera Company (the largest of his companies, with up to sixty people – actors, musicians, stage hands) were thrust together in situations of extreme propinquity. Bandmann calculated on forty-two weeks of work – i.e. nightly performances and daily rehearsals – and ten weeks of travel over the course of a year. Although provincial touring was part and parcel of the theatrical profession for most English actors (except for those who could make a steady living in the London theatres), touring abroad on the Bandmann Circuit was of a different category altogether. Performers needed to master up to twenty roles within an even larger repertoire, which could place huge strains on health and stamina, and the often tropical, but sometimes also extreme winterly, climatic conditions added additional duress to the bodies of the performers.

This chapter will examine what it meant to be a performer on the Bandmann Circuit. In addition to the material questions such as working conditions, pay and social interaction (love and marriage), it will

---

[1] 'Theatrical Touring in the Far East by One Who Has Tried It', *The Stage Yearbook* (1917), 41–8.

also examine the functions of the performers and other employees (advance and venue managers, musical directors) as parts of the theatrical network. In this chapter, the main approach will be actor-network theory (ANT). If we regard ANT as a form of ethnography in which processes and interconnections are observed using techniques such as participant observation and fieldwork, the question needs to be posed how we can obtain such access to the living material of the past, the actors in the actor network. Actors on tour are of double ethnographic interest: by travelling through many countries, they were in a situation of cross-cultural exchange, having embarked on a tour out of touristic curiosity as well as promises of economic reward. But actors themselves were objects of curiosity in the various cities they visited. This was especially true of the female members who engendered intense interest on the part of male spectators, which often translated into romantic entanglements and even marriage. While the former were part of the business, the latter were seen as potentially destabilizing and actively discouraged by the management.

Actor networks track connections, mainly with other networks. The following analysis will examine how the travelling actor 'connected' with the different cultures and countries. These connections took many forms, the most important being economic (labour and income), physical (mainly health) and affective. Occasionally there were juridical connections when performers sued their manager or vice versa. These cases were so frequent and often complex that they will be examined separately, in Chapter 6.

Economics and Labour

Bandmann's actors were for the most part of British origin and recruited in London on one of his regular trips home, with the help of his local representative. The English theatre industry produced a considerable amount of excess labour that he could draw upon. The attractions of the tour were twofold. Firstly, he paid relatively well, and he offered the guarantee of employment for periods of up to two years. This constituted a long interval of guaranteed earnings in an industry that was exceptionally fickle; a normal provincial tour might last eight months at most. The other attraction was touristic. Participation in a Bandmann tour meant that otherwise impecunious performers could literally see the world, or at least the colonized parts of it.

As touring gained in frequency (the Bandmann Circuit was only one, albeit the most extensive, opportunity for this kind of work), it became a component of the theatrical profession, an attractive option

for performers who could afford to be out of the country for long periods of time. In 1917, the *Stage Yearbook* published a detailed anonymous account entitled 'Theatrical Touring in the Far East by One Who
Has Tried It'.[2] Although the article does not reference actual tours or
managers by name, it contains a wealth of information on the route
Bandmann followed and can with a high degree of certainty be read as
a commentary on the Bandmann Circuit and its like:

> There can be few actors and actresses, I suppose, who do not feel something
> of a thrill when a Far Eastern tour is mooted or proposed. It is not given to
> everyone to explore the hidden mysteries of India, China, and old-world Japan,
> and to the inexperienced it must seem an exceptional privilege to be not only
> conveyed to these distant parts free of charge, but actually paid for going into
> the bargain. ('Theatrical Touring', 41)

The aim of the article is admonitory. It offers advice and warning to
prospective colleagues wishing to embark on such an adventure: of
the 'dangers, difficulties, and disappointments they will have to face'
as well as the benefits that may be gained. At the same time, it can
be read as a kind of self-ethnography of the 'theatrical tourist', as the
author terms himself (as well as his fellow thespian travellers). The
author hastens to add that he in no way intends to cast aspersions on
the reputation or integrity of the managers, but indirectly he does suggest that they wilfully or out of ignorance withhold information from
new employees. Rectifying this deficiency would help, he suggests,
ameliorate the atmosphere of such tours and the disgruntlement they
often engendered. The main topics of concern are money, conditions
of play (meaning work), health and sightseeing.

Money was of primary interest for the touring actor – not only the
making and saving of it, but also its protean permutations along the
tour. The author is blunt regarding the symbolic capital that an actor
might accrue by participating in a lengthy tour: 'London is his goal,
and every month spent in foreign countries is a month wasted so far as
building up a London reputation is concerned' ('Theatrical Touring', 43).
For this reason, salaries were relatively high, to offset the depletion of
reputation caused by absence from the metropolis. The economics
of touring, from the actor's perspective, comprised several questions:
the costs of accommodation, the incidental expenses, the vagaries of
money exchange and the downtime between performances.

[2] Ibid.

Accommodation inevitably meant staying in hotels, because rental accommodation would be too expensive and required furniture and servants. Bandmann claimed to cover hotel accommodation most of the time and therefore paid a proportionately lower salary. In an interview given to the *Daily Mail* in 1911, he described his conditions:

My engagements for musical comedy are for two years, and I buy each actor and actress a return ticket by P. and O. steamer available for that period. I pay all their travelling expenses from start to finish, and all their hotel bills and cab fares, so you see each individual who wishes to do so can save on the tour. There is much travelling but I calculate on getting forty-two acting weeks out of the year, allowing ten for travelling. The musical comedy company never breaks up. When one tour ends it begins another. There are sixty-five people in that organisation, and every year about twenty of them come home and I take out new people to replace them.[3]

A 1907 advertisement for Bandmann's Eastern Circuit stated, 'All salaries clear, as hotel expenses paid by Management from the time of leaving England until return'.[4] Although precluded by Bandmann, it was not uncommon for actors themselves to find and pay for their accommodations, a course recommended by the author of the *Stage Yearbook* article, because otherwise 'you are absolutely dependent on the manager's judgement and liberality' ('Theatrical Touring', 43). In such cases, a base salary of £8.00 per week needed to be calculated. The article assumes that the actor had to pay for the accommodation, but here practices diverged, with some managers covering expenses and others not doing so. The author gives the hotel rates as follows: in Bombay and Calcutta, a good hotel might cost 5–8 rupees per day (6s 8d–10s 8d). Seven days in a hotel would average at around 35 rupees (£2 10s) per week. Prices in Singapore were slightly higher, Hong Kong and Shanghai lower with Japan leading the list as the most expensive. Hotel accommodation included, however, all meals, baths and 'attendance' ('Theatrical Touring', 43).

Along with the basic needs of food and lodging came the incidental expenses of tipping, transport and drinks. The various servants required their small amounts ('the native domestic is not easily rebuffed'), which in the aggregate added to the overall expenses. The heat usually meant

[3] 'Shakespeare in Far East', *Daily Mail*, 20 September 1911, 3.
[4] *The Stage Archive*, 15 August 1907, 22.

that transportation was required – in India, gharries, and further East, rickshaws – in sum making a difference and eroding the budget. Finally, drinks (not part of the usual hotel offerings) could also add to expenses, because the theatrical tourist inevitably consorted with long-term residents who were 'habitually thirsty'. Bespoke white suits, although extremely cheap, were needed and could also be a burden on the budget.

Actors were always remunerated in the currency of the country they performed in, because the business model was predicated on a rapid turnover between box office receipts and running expenses: actors were effectively paid directly from box office takings, which in a number of cases meant non-payment and even the stranding of whole companies (see the example of Henry Dallas, described in Chapter 2, who abandoned his company and made off with the cashbox). The payment in local currency, so the 'Theatrical Touring' author's argument goes, leads to 'leakage' on the part of the unwary theatrical tourist. Although a weekly salary of £8 could translate to 120 rupees (at the official exchange rate of 1–15 rupees per pound sterling) and one rupee corresponded to roughly one shilling, in actual fact the value of one rupee was 1s 4d – resulting in an item costing one rupee actually costing 1s 4d. This same process of 'mental conversion' extended throughout the various ports of call, with varying degrees of pecuniary disadvantage for the unwitting theatrical tourist. The only answer was to think intrinsically in terms of the currency received and not through conversion – a somewhat daunting task on a tour which might visit a dozen different countries.

An additional difficulty was posed by the actual exchange rates and their often-severe fluctuations. While the pound-to-rupee rate remained relatively stable over the period in question, this stability referred mainly to conversion from pound to rupee but not necessarily the other way round. Although a gold sovereign would buy 15 rupees, 15 rupees at a money changer did not buy a sovereign, because of the volatile price of gold. As actors were paid in local currency, they were dependent on reconversion back to sterling by the time they returned to England. Another problem was convertibility between ports of call:

For every rupee you change into a Straits dollar the bank or money-changer is going to pocket a few cents. The same thing happens when you leave Singapore for Hong-Kong, again at Shanghai, again at Tientsin, Peking, Tokyo, Kobe or Yokohama. And all over again – reversed – on the return journey. Kindly imagine what this means, and decide what salary you are going to ask accordingly. ('Theatrical Touring', 45)

P.x O. ARABIA 1905

Figure 5.1 The Bandmann Opera Company relaxing on board the *P&O Arabia* en route to Bombay, 1905. Bandmann is seated fourth from the right. (Vanessa Lopez Family Archive.)

The only way to counteract this steady depletion was to change paper money into silver coinage. By transferring a Hong Kong $10 note into a Mexican silver dollar, which could be changed into smaller 'subsidiary' coins, a $1.50 profit could be made. Theoretically, one could convert a weekly salary of £8 into smaller silver coins and make a £2 profit; unfortunately, such coins had only limited utility as legal tender. In China, for example, each province had its own coinage. In sum, the movement between countries and currency posed a continual drain on the actor's income. From a network perspective, payment in the local currency meant a connection or 'edge' with the local economy. Because of the complexities of conversion, there was considerable incentive to spend the money where it was earned rather than save it. Cultural economics would regard this as contributing to the 'multiplier' or 'spillover' effects of theatrical activity. In this way, touring companies actually contributed to the local economies and did not just 'extract' from them.

A central cost factor was the travel itself, as it implied both expense and lack of income; except for occasional performances on board ships, travel time was invariably 'down time' (Fig. 5.1).[5] 'No play, no pay' was a basic

---

[5] Tracy C. Davis, *Economics of the British Stage*, 338.

principle of theatrical touring both at home and abroad. It was essential, therefore, for the prospective theatrical tourist to calculate the ratio of playing time versus non-playing time. Although ship travel included all food, it did not necessarily mean payment, despite Bandmann often mentioning that his contracts included payment while travelling. Travel could also create expenses such as drinks, tipping, porters, etc. Because particularly long journeys were involved in Eastern tours, this circumstance needed to be factored into the total of travel time and potential loss of income. For example, the journey between London and Bombay lasted on average sixteen days; a train journey from there to Calcutta, nearly two days; and the ship's passage onward to Rangoon, two to three days.

Health

Travelling and performing on the Bandmann Circuit inevitably meant exposure to health risks quite unlike those at home. The most common maladies were malaria, dysentery and various kinds of food-related disorders. The author of the *Stage Yearbook* article claims that there is no reason why the touring actor should suffer 'physical deterioration' when travelling in the East. The risks he lists are the same as those experienced today: water is taboo, fish to be largely avoided and 'salad eschewed altogether'. He is also dismissive of the need for inoculations against malaria, enteric fever, dysentery and plague: 'if you get a touch of fever, by all means take quinine – it is the only cure – but get your fever first' ('Theatrical Touring', 42). In the light of Bandmann's premature death after contracting enteric (typhus) in Egypt, or the sudden death of leading lady Florence Imeson, who died of enteric in Rangoon in April 1914 after a two-day illness, this is a somewhat cavalier recommendation, although the efficacy of inoculations at that time was still limited.[6]

It was of course not uncommon for actors to fall ill on such trips. Illness could be used to extract a release from a contract, as in the court case brought against Bandmann by a certain Miss Caird, who in 1906, after having toured in China, Singapore, Ceylon and other places, refused in Calcutta to accompany the troupe any further. In one account, Caird 'produced medical certificates from some Rangoon physicians that she suffered from Tubercular complaints and wanted to be immediately released'.[7] The case even generated controversy in the local papers. She argued that

---

[6] 'Death of Bandmann Opera Co. Actress', *Malaya Tribune*, 13 May 1914, 11. An obituary was published in the same paper on 13 May 1914, 9.
[7] Hemendranath Das Gupta, *The Indian Stage*, Vol. 4 (Calcutta: 1944), 216.

Bandmann refused to help her, saying, 'no work, no pay'. His case was that he was paying all her expenses although she was not working. Illness, especially if it befell leading actors or actresses, could have a deleterious effect on the whole company, because, unlike for long-run productions, talented understudies were not always available. For example, the production of *The Marriage Market* in Singapore in March 1914 attracted unusually harsh criticism because of the indisposition of Florence Imeson, the reviewer pointing out the lack of good understudies.[8]

The question of appropriate clothing was important, because a Bandmann tour covered the full gamut of climes, from the tropical to the sub-Arctic. India alone could provide extremes – from the chilly nights on the north Indian plains to the tropical temperatures of the south, with monsoon rain from June to August. The Bandmann companies were particularly renowned for playing in the hot season, when other troupes and segments of the colonial population fled the larger cities. Singapore and the Malay States provided a steady temperature of 90–97 °F in the shade during the day, 'cooling' to 88–90 °F at night. In China, temperatures also varied in the extreme, from the warmer temperatures in Hong Kong (which also has a cold-weather season) to Shanghai, Tientsin and Peking, which 'have a winter practically Arctic in its severity', with cold winds lasting well into March and April. Japan, on the other hand, matches closely 'our English climate', with much rain, snow in the winter 'and only at most three weeks or a month of anything like excessive warmth' ('Theatrical Touring', 42).

The recommendations for appropriate clothing are somewhat archaic and include a 'cholera belt', whose efficacy the author disputes.[9] Although a cholera belt was an excessive precaution, a topee 'should be rigorously worn in India as protection against the sun'. Protection against mosquitoes was equally necessary and required appropriate covering of exposed body parts, especially the ankles. In the category of inconvenient rather than dangerous were ailments such as prickly heat and boils, which meant that restraint should be exercised when imbibing lemon squashes, 'as the blood, already impoverished by innutritious food and excessive heat, is rendered poisonous and unhealthy by the infusion of acids'. The best remedy against chills, the principal danger for the theatrical tourist, was woollen undergarments followed by Indian gauze and aertex (made from woven cotton) ('Theatrical Touring', 42).

---

[8] 'Production of the Marriage Market', *The Straits Times*, 13 March 1914, 10.

[9] The cholera belt, a strip of flannel or wool worn around the abdomen, was first mooted in the early nineteenth century as a means to combat various tropical ailments such as cholera and dysentery amongst soldiers of the East India Company. It was based on the idea that these illnesses were caused by abdominal chills.

Working Conditions

Actors on the Bandmann Circuit did not just travel and tip, for they laboured as well, often under exceptionally difficult climatic and physical conditions. 'Labour' here means performing and rehearsing. The travelling actor could be regarded as the ultimate 'deterritorialized worker' in the Deleuzian formulation – although Deleuze and Guattari had a much more sedentary worker in mind than the peripatetic Bandmann actor travelling from port to port from Gibraltar to Tokyo.[10] If we follow the basic insight of ANT that connections or relations need to be 'performed' repeatedly to maintain the network, then the theatrical performances of Bandmann actors provide an almost tautological demonstration of this principle. Although the long maritime journeys 'out' appeared on the surface to offer potential for relaxation, in reality the company members were expected to learn their many parts and even perform. Adapted scores were provided at the beginning of the tour, and performers were required to learn a large number of roles. As we saw in Chapter 4, on repertoire, the Bandmann Opera Company disposed of a repertoire of nearly thirty musical comedies and up to a dozen plays. The rotation system meant that a complete company seldom started a tour in London and moved along the circuit in a linear fashion from Gibraltar to Tokyo. The preferred practice was that new performers were continually recruited and transported out to join the larger company to replenish vacancies. Favourite relay points were Bombay and Colombo. On the journey out, singers might be expected to give concerts. The musical comedy actress Hettie Muret, who sued Bandmann for breach of contract (see Chapter 6), gave concerts in Port Said, Aden and Colombo before joining the company in Bangalore, where she commenced rehearsals. Only there did the musical director decide that she was unsuited for the parts and should be dismissed, which then led to a court case that she won.

When the company was performing, rehearsals were conducted daily from 10:30 a.m. to 12:45 p.m., followed by evening performances starting, depending on the location, between 8:00 and 9:30 in the evening and lasting until nearly midnight. Sometimes matinees were given as well, and these might begin as late as 5:00 p.m.[11] The gruelling working conditions under which particularly the leading performers laboured is

---

[10] For the term 'deterritorialized worker', see Gilles Deleuze and Félix Guattari, *Anti-Oedipus: Capitalism and Schizophrenia*, trans. R. Hurley, M. Seem and H. R. Lane (London: Athlone Press, 1984), 245.
[11] On rehearsal practices, see 'Touring in Egypt', *The Stage Archive*, 17 April 1919, 8.

enumerated in great detail in the trial of Corlass (Georgina 'Georgie' Major) versus Bandmann (see Chapter 6), in which Bandmann was sued for breach of contract. On an earlier tour, which began in December 1906 in Bombay and lasted nineteen months, Corlass's salary was £8 a week and the repertoire comprised twenty-one plays. During this time, she regularly fainted on stage in public and had to be carried off.[12]

The stress suffered by Corlass was partially due to her specialization as a soubrette, a generic role required in every musical comedy, which meant almost continuous presence on stage. While this was strenuous enough in a long-run system, the Bandmann repertoire required nightly changes of repertoire. The range of performers and musicians travelling in one company can be gauged by the regular advertisements Bandmann published in the trade press. For his ill-fated Mediterranean and East Entertainment Syndicate, he required the following:

First-class Comedian (must be Small, Sing and Dance essential); first-class Soubrette (must be Young, Pretty, and good Dancer); Aristocratic Old Lady (must be good Contralto), Musical Director, two tenor choristers, two bass choristers, two more first-class acrobatic dancers (must be Young, Pretty, and thoroughly Trained and Experienced).

Another advertisement for the same tour sought, in addition to the foregoing, a 'first-class Young and Attractive Juvenile Leading Lady, a Versatile Leading Man, a Refined Principal Eccentric Comedian, a Young Character Actress, and a Responsible Lady and Gentleman'.[13] Apart from the somewhat oxymoronic 'refined eccentric comedian', these job descriptions comprised fairly standard role types around which the repertoire was structured. Musical and dramatic comedies were usually written with such roles in mind. To these roles could be added the normal operatic vocal categories of baritone, soprano and chorus, for which Bandmann also advertised.

Apart from the chorus girls he recruited from the vast supply of theatrical labour available in London, Bandmann also needed well-known performers as attractions. Sometimes he would promote and manage stars such as Ada Reeve, who toured India under his management, but they were not available for the Bandmann Opera Company (also known as the BOC) or the Bandmann Comedy Company. For these

---

[12] 'A Theatrical Suit', *The Amrita Bazar Patrika*, 14 February 1913, 7.
[13] *The Era*, 15 September 1900, 23.

companies, he sometimes employed understudies from the successful London productions of George Edwardes. Although not as well known, they were familiar with the repertoire and could be promoted as London stars 'by association'. As one Hong Kong paper reported, 'He had been fortunate in securing Miss Gertie Millar's understudy, Miss Connie Leon, who had been "lent" to Mr. Bandmann by Mr. Edwardes. She was undoubtedly a great actress, so the people of Hongkong have something in the way of a treat to look forward to.'[14] While Gertie Millar certainly was a big star, there is no record that Connie Leon achieved the same recognition (although much later in life she went on to have a career as a film actress in Hollywood playing bit parts).

As we have seen from the calculation of touring expenses, the financial rewards varied considerably. At the top was Bandmann the entrepreneur, who carried the risk and profit in equal measure. A post-mortem court case brought by his estranged wife calculated that after 1913 he had an average annual income of £3,000 (of which she claimed an allowance of £1,000). Put in relation to other annual incomes of the time – for example, for professions such as judge, general or doctor – this meant that Bandmann was a wealthy man and commanded an income three times higher than that of his best-paid performers.[15]

The human capital contained in the companies – i.e. the performers, conductors and stage managers, all of whom had to be paid – constituted the principal expense. Their remuneration varied from that of top-billing performers, who could command up to £25 per week, to that of chorus girls, who were paid around £5 per week (which was still higher than in London or provincial centres). These figures need to be seen in relation to other occupations in 1920, at which time the average wage for a bricklayer was 40s, i.e. £2 per week.[16] Records kept by one of Bandmann's managers, Gibraltar-born Stephen Lopez, give an indication of salaries paid in the period 1919–1920. Lopez managed the Bandmann Varieties Co. after the First World War and kept detailed notes of salary payments while stationed in Alexandria, where the

---

[14] 'New Theatre for Hong Kong: Mr. Maurice Bandmann's Views', *South China Morning Post*, 17 January 1910, 4.

[15] In 1910, the average annual income of a general practitioner was £600–£700, while a principal medical officer could earn up to £1,000. A member of parliament received an annual salary of £400 in 1911. For these figures, see R. M. Titmuss, 'Health', in Morris Ginsberg, ed., *Law and Opinion in England in the 20th Century* (Berkeley: University of California Press, 1959), 299–318, here 311.

[16] See *Hansard*, 30 July 1925, Vol. 187, cc671, for a list of average earnings in 1920 and 1925.

troupe performed at the Alhambra Theatre and were paid in Egyptian piastres.[17] The salary ranged from £12 per week at the top down to £5, with the average salary around £8.

These figures show that the range was considerably less than in London, where for instance a star such as Ellen Terry could earn a staggering £200 a week in the 1890s.[18] Such disparities in earnings still characterize the economics of the performing arts today.[19] Touring only attracted top stars if they were billed as solo acts and could either take a large share of the box office or were paid a large set fee. Gaiety Theatre and music-hall star Ada Reeve reputedly earned £5,000 for a nine-week tour of South Africa, before going on tour to India with Bandmann (with whom she then had an acrimonious court case; see Chapter 6).[20] These were exceptions, however. Reeve was a top-line star and not to be compared with the members of the BOC. In a similar league was Shakespearean actor Matheson Lang, who toured his own company under Bandmann's management. The top salary was Lang's, at £30 a week; his wife and business partner John Holloway each received £15. The salaries went down from there, to £5 a week for small parts.

The exigencies of touring, exacerbated by frequent bouts of illness, meant that performers had to understudy roles and intervene at short notice, which resulted in chain reactions moving through the company. An example was recorded in Shanghai, where Georgie Corlass's 'indisposition' shortly before a performance of *The Runaway Girl* resulted in three role changes with only a few hours' notice: 'Her part was taken by Miss Norah Morra at very short notice, and Miss Elsie Probyn was called upon to take the part of Alice in her place ... Few would have known that Miss Morra had had to take the part of Winifred Grey so suddenly as she certainly acted as though she had filled the role many times before.'[21]

Although the companies were overwhelmingly British in composition, the Bandmann Opera Company also comprised Indian musicians (see Fig. 5.2) and the occasional local performer. Examples include

---

[17] Source: Vanessa Lopez Family Archive. The exchange rate was approximately 100pt per £1. See 'Notes on Currency' in the front matter.
[18] Tracy C. Davis, *Actresses as Working Women: Their Social Identity in Victorian Culture* (London: Routledge, 1991), 24.
[19] See here Sherwin Rosen, 'The Economics of Superstars', *American Economic Review* 71(5) (1981): 845–58.
[20] 'Millions for Music-Hall Favourites', *Weekly Sun* (Singapore), 17 February 1912, 8.
[21] 'The Bandmann Company at the Astor Gardens', *The North-China Herald*, 15 June 1906, 625.

Figure 5.2 The Bandmann Opera Company, with Indian musicians in the back row, Calcutta, 1913. (Tsubouchi Memorial Theatre Museum, Waseda University, FA1-06740.)

that of the famous Anglo-Indian Indian film star Patience Cooper from Calcutta, who began her career as a locally recruited chorus girl. Employment of local musicians was quite common, since the larger theatres all had resident orchestras, while the larger centres often disposed of municipal orchestras, usually under European conductors.[22] The opera company often employed Filipino musicians who elicited considerable admiration, as evidenced by one review from Japan of *The Country Girl*: 'The high finish of the performance was enhanced by the delicate and well-modulated tones of the Filipino orchestra.'[23] Other sources suggest that musicians were drawn from Goa, where, like Manila, the Portuguese had established strong traditions of church and orchestral music.[24]

Bandmann also made use of unpaid or very lowly paid local extras, who were recruited on-site to fill in the crowd scenes, following the practice common amongst provincial companies of hiring enthusiastic home-town amateurs. What they lacked in stagecraft, they made up for in numbers, especially in the toga plays. A former police inspector, Maurice Springfield, who worked for twenty-eight years in Shanghai,

[22] For a discussion of municipal orchestras, see MeLê Yamomo, *Theatre and Music in Manila and the Asia Pacific, 1869–1946* (London: Palgrave Macmillan, 2018).
[23] *The Japan Weekly Chronicle*, 12 September 1913, 337.
[24] See 'The Indian Stage: A Chat with Mr. Twinning', *The Sketch*, 8 April 1896, 476–7.

recalled performing in a number of Bandmann productions, including most of the Gilbert and Sullivan operas, the words and music having been learned through the local Amateur Dramatic Club:

Those of us who had a yearning for the stage were well catered for. The professional side offered 'going on' parts in crowd scenes with the touring companies, brought out from England by Maurice Bandmann, who usually arrived in Shanghai with a very meagre handful of chorus girls, following a season in India and various ports en route for Japan. Marriage and concubinage invariably played havoc with these companies.[25]

Affective Affinities: Bandmann's Brides

The depletion of chorus girls while touring was a continual theme in press coverage of Bandmann's companies. Like the borrowing that took place with other aspects of musical comedy, Bandmann replicated George Edwardes' Gaiety Girls on his extended tours, and his group became known as Bandmann's Beauties. In 1906, a Singapore paper announced the arrival of 'Bandmann's Brilliant Bevy of Beauty'.[26] A few years later, a columnist from Singapore noted a pattern being repeated with the departure of the much-loved troupe: 'More broken hearts. Great loss. The Bandmann girls gone. Give me back my diamond? Nothing doing.'[27]

It is clear that Bandmann's 'girls' or 'beauties' provided a major attraction in male-dominated colonial societies. A key component of the Edwardian musical was the exhibition of the female body within the bounds regulated by censorship and the generally agreed-on rules of propriety. A musical comedy usually required two or three prominent female roles plus a chorus of young singers and dancers. Musical comedy, especially of the George Edwardes variety, focused on 'the girl' – the young, unmarried, often working woman, who was usually led to matrimony in the final act. Over a dozen works featured a 'girl' in their titles, and the Gaiety Girls (the chorus of Edwardian comedy) were an established feature of the Gaiety Theatre. Marketed as respectable and marriageable, they functioned as living mannequins, visual vehicles of the latest fashions. Len Platt has argued that the focus on

---

[25] Maurice Springfield, *Hunting Opium and Other Scents* (Suffolk: Norfolk and Suffolk Publicity Services, 1966), 35.

[26] '"Lady Madcap" Visits Singapore. Bandmann's Brilliant Bevy of Beauty: A Volatile Vaudeville', *Eastern Daily Mail and Straits Morning Advertiser*, 16 February 1906, 2.

[27] *Weekly Sun* (Singapore), 8 April 1911, 5.

female figures in Edwardian comedy was a means to stage femininity as a spectacle, but within conventions of 'respectable voyeurism'. At the same time, this foregrounding of young women was also a sign of musical comedy's investment in modernity.[28]

That the girls were a major attraction of the company cannot be doubted; in fact, their corporeal allures far outweighed the intellectual appeal of the pieces presented. A satirical poem published in the *Rangoon Gazette* entreated Bandmann to spare the local public any serious drama. Entitled 'Advice to Mr. Maurice Bandmann', the poem was prefaced by the admonition 'Rangoon audiences do not care for serious musical and dramatic Art. What they appreciate is something "light and leggy".'

> We do not want superb technique.
> Give us instead a farce each week
> With maidens frisky;
> quip, innuendo, jest, lampoon
> And – if you want to draw Rangoon –
> jokes that are risky.
>
> Give us the merry whirling dance
> the postcards smile, the audacious glance,
> Of Flo and Peggy.
> Give us a little jeu d'esprit.
> Bother the art – just let it be
> Both light and leggy!
>
> (G. R. in *Rangoon Gazette*)[29]

Since Bandmann's Beauties were certainly leggy, if not light, the poem should perhaps be read with the irony with which it was intended.

Shortly before his death, Bandmann gave an interview in which he calculated that he had transported roughly one thousand girls around the world, insisting that, following the Gaiety model of respectability, they had always been screened for good character. There had been inevitable losses due to marriage, which he estimated at around 20 per cent per tour.[30] Cast depletion through marriage was a continual

[28] Len Platt, *Musical Comedy on the West End Stage, 1890–1939* (Basingstoke: Palgrave Macmillan, 2004), 25.

[29] Letter to *Rangoon Gazette*, reprinted in *The Singapore Free Press and Mercantile Advertiser*, 7 May 1912, 4.

[30] 'Bandmann's Casualty List', *The Singapore Free Press and Mercantile Advertiser*, 21 May 1921, 12.

problem for the touring manager that featured in the press throughout the period. An article in *The Playgoer* of 1904 referred to a recent Bandmann world tour, although without mentioning him by name:

The English Stage as a matrimonial market has its advantages, but the actress who stays in England does not get a tithe of the chances that those who go touring abroad do. This is amusingly illustrated by the woes of a well-known theatrical manager who has just returned from an eighteen-months' tour with a Comic Opera Company. He left London with some thirty-five ladies, chorus and principals. At Gibraltar his troubles began – two of them got married and left without giving him notice. At Cairo he lost another in the same way. At Bombay he missed one of his chorus in the first scene, and on going behind to demand where she was, had her pointed out to him sitting in a box – the damsel had been married that morning, and had come round to see her friends play. So they kept leaving. He lost another at Calcutta, another at the Cape, and two at Valparaiso, until at last, not being able to replace the deserters, his company was reduced to nearly half its original strength. The manager did not intend to be a matrimonial agent, and he is just now drawing up a new and more stringent contract for his next company to sign – and hoping for the best.[31]

In fact, after this particular tour, Bandmann's contracts did contain a penalty clause for marriage, which the yearning husbands were often only too happy to pay.

A tongue-in-cheek article published in the *Malaya Tribune* in 1921 suggested that Bandmann should be placed alongside the great colonizers of history such as Robert Owen (founder of the utopian New Harmony colony in Indiana) or Captain John Smith (of Pocahontas fame) and that the city of Calcutta should honour him with a statue in a public square: 'For Mr. Bandman is the greatest little bride-bringer that has ever favoured the East. Since 1899 when he first took his first musical comedy company to India, he has imported a fruit crop of nearly a hundred percent peaches that on the average has lasted only about long enough for the basket to be passed around.'[32] Bandmann claimed that the girls often wed colonels, men in high government positions and extremely wealthy businessmen. '"Do any of them marry millionaires?" We enquired, getting excited. "Some of them," said Mr. Bandmann, "One of our girls married a Dutchman who assayed about eighteen millions … Yes some of them do well for working girls."' In the same interview, he further claimed that in Calcutta there was a whole colony of Bandmann brides, because most of the marriages took place there, although there had also been desertions in Hong Kong and Shanghai.[33]

---

[31] *The Playgoer* (1903–1904).
[32] 'Bandman Brides: Matrimonial Casualties in the East', *Malaya Tribune*, 20 September 1921, 8.
[33] Ibid.

Bandmann maintained that the supply of potential performers far outweighed the demand. For a company of thirty, he could choose from up to a thousand applicants: 'My American assistant in London sorts them out through the year, eliminates the pigeon-toed and the others of the unfit and then leaves the final choice to me.' After completion of the pre-selection process, auditions were held to test singing and dancing abilities, followed by a personal interview in which 'manners' were observed: 'We pick girls for three things – voice, looks, and gentility, the greatest of these is gentility ... The other two are also necessary but we wouldn't take Venus de Milo herself if she chewed gum and hashed her grammar.'[34] Although the contracts were supposed to hinder the matrimonial depredations of his companies, Bandmann admitted that he had not yet managed to collect a single fine. Marriages had taken place not only in the Far East but also in Egypt and South America and across nationalities.

In one of the many obituaries published on Bandmann's death, the writer wistfully noted:

One of the difficulties of our theatrical manager bringing out companies of good looking artists, both musical and comedy, is the danger of losing them through marriage. In the seventeen years that he has been furnishing entertainment for the public in the East Mr. Bandman has lost many of the members of his company that way. Many of his old artistes now happily married in India, Burma and other parts of the East will receive the news of his death with great regret. So will everyone who remembers how much Mr. Bandman did to make time pass pleasantly for those whose lives have had to be lived here.[35]

Leaving aside the obvious sexism of the language employed to describe the colonial theatrical marriage market (fruit crop, peaches) and the overall tongue-in-cheek tone of the articles and interviews, the picture evoked is one of theatrical touring as a highly attractive alternative for the working girls of the Edwardian chorus. Apart from the marriage market, the relatively good salaries and the opportunity to see the world made a Bandmann tour an attractive possibility within the wider ambit of professional theatre.

Bandmann's insistence on 'gentility' references a widely held prejudice that theatrical companies were hotbeds of promiscuity since they moved quite literally outside the normal frameworks of respectable society. It was a highly anomalous situation for between forty and sixty people to travel and live together for up to two years. It was perhaps inevitable that such situations of extreme propinquity led to sexual

[34] Ibid.
[35] *The Straits Times*, 23 March 1922, 11.

peccadilloes and even more serious disputes. A spectacular example of impropriety on tour led to a much-publicized divorce case reported in the English papers – the misdemeanours committed in India, the evidence given in Cairo and the case adjudicated in London.

The suit concerned a Mrs Dora Phoebe Charles with the stage name Dora Dolaro, who pleaded for a divorce from Henry Wolseley Charles, a music-hall artist, on the grounds of his cruelty and adultery with a Mrs Molly Manolesque, also known as Molly Leicester. In January 1916, after being married for less than a year, the couple left for Calcutta with a touring company called The Scamps, under Bandmann's management, which during the course of the tour was renamed the Bandmann and Charles Touring Company. The journey included Japan, China, India and the Malay States. The Scamps was a vaudeville, or Pierrot, company which had achieved a certain amount of success during a London season at the Strand Theatre. According to testimony, the respondent, Henry Charles (the company's director), became acquainted with Mrs Molly Manolesque, who had attached herself to the company as a chorus girl, 'and especially to the respondent, who was susceptible to feminine charms'. Mrs Manolesque was described as a 'flashily dressed woman of prepossessing appearance'. The respondent's contact with her was so obnoxious that Mrs Charles was unable to stay under the same roof. She could not leave the company, however, as she was under contract. Despite her errant husband being the manager, she arranged 'to get Mrs. Manolesque left behind' when the company departed India for Egypt. Mr Charles then booked his mistress a passage to Egypt by the next boat and on arrival introduced her to people as Mrs Charles in the presence of all, including the real Mrs Charles. According to the court plea, her husband's conduct seriously injured her health and amounted to legal cruelty. The evidence taken on commission in Cairo included a number of eyewitness accounts of the adultery:

One witness swore that the respondent said to him that when he met Mrs. Manolesque at Simla, 'our eyes met, and I said to myself, "that woman is going to change my life."' ... [F]urther evidence was read. It was that the respondent and the woman were seen in bed together, through shutters which were not properly closed, and that 'Molly Lester's "glad eye" was noticeable, even in Simla'.[36]

Needless to say, the judge – who observed that 'The Tramps' would have been a better name for the troupe – pronounced a decree *nisi* with costs. While this kind of behaviour may have been extreme, it was seldom associated, at least in the divorce court, with the companies that Bandmann himself directly controlled. Perhaps his insistence on 'gentility' bore fruit.

[36] 'An Actress's Divorce Suit: Charles v. Charles', *The Times*, 7 March 1919, 2.

Most performers only signed up for one or two tours, while some made it the centre of their professional life and toured repeatedly. It is not possible to calculate how many performers were involved on the Bandmann Circuit over the roughly twenty years of its operation, but the number is probably close to two thousand. If we take Bandmann's 'one thousand girls' as an orientation, we can easily double that number by accounting for an equal number of male performers. The cast photographs show roughly an equal number of men and women. Because of the extended nature of the tours, which lasted up to two years, they appealed to young, unmarried performers, although sometimes married couples were also engaged. Professional marriages were not uncommon in the entertainment business.

Actors and Managers

Bandmann's touring model came under pressure during the First World War, as it became increasingly difficult to recruit men who were fit for military service. As the war progressed, questions were asked along the circuit about why seemingly able-bodied men were on stage when there was war to be fought. The discussion in Singapore in 1917 was particularly severe, and a letter to the editor of the *Straits Times* posed this question:

There appear to be a certain number of men of military age in the Bandman company, and they appear to be British subjects. They appear, further, to be in good health. If they have been exempted from military service for good reasons, there is nothing more to be said, but, if they have not been exempted, is that right to be flocking to their performances and that's giving them the means of keeping out of the reach of the conscription law?[37]

Bandmann's representative, Roy Smith, replied immediately, pointing out that four members of the opera company had been exempted the previous October as physically unfit and over military age. Of the others, one was an American, three had been rejected in England in 1915 as unfit, one had been discharged from the Royal Engineers at Gibraltar for 'incurable defective eyes' and one, 'which is myself, has been twice rejected in India with a weak heart and general debility'. Smith also pointed out that the Bandmann companies had a 'Roll of Honour' – i.e. a list of twenty-three men serving – prominently posted at the Empire Theatre in Calcutta. Notwithstanding Roy Smith's spirited rejoinder, the criticism took its toll: a few days later, the *Ceylon Observer* reported that a member of the company had been

---

[37] *The Straits Times*, 10 February 1917, 8.

found dead on the railway line at Johore Bahru – a Mr Jack Harper, who had been exempted from military service on account of wounds received in the Boer War. He had been 'mentally affected by recent criticisms in Singapore regarding the Bandman Company and man power'.[38]

Although there was considerable fluctuation in the companies (Bandmann replaced about twenty performers a year in the BOC alone), he also managed to forge robust long-term relationships with many actors and staff. Blanche Forsythe (1873–1953) was a leading lady and a member of Bandmann's companies from the mid-1890s until around 1905, first appearing in provincial companies in 1891. She toured in the 1890s with Bandmann's *Manxman* company, playing Kate Cregeen as well as the title role in *Trilby*, which she helped popularize (Fig. 5.3). She toured extensively around the Mediterranean, South America, Canada and the Far East and also became the main shareholder in Bandmann's Mediterranean Syndicate (see Chapter 2). Later, she became an accomplished silent-film actress and involved herself in the Actor's Association, to whose first board, presided over by Herbert Beerbohm Tree, she was elected in 1910.[39] In the same year, she was praised as 'England's greatest emotional actress', on the screening of the film *East Lynne*.[40] Forsythe was an exceptionally versatile leading lady, as she had to be in the extensive Bandmann repertoire. She possessed a finely modulated voice that prompted a reviewer during the first Maltese tour to remark that she acted as model for the local audience to improve their pronunciation: 'We are sure those who listen to Miss Forsythe's elocution, will never permit anyone to remark in their presence that the English language is either harsh or monotonous.'[41]

Another mainstay of the Bandmann Opera Company was the comic actor Harry Cole (1869–1929). Like the soubrette, the principal comedian was an established part of the musical comedy genre. Together with his wife, Cole joined Bandmann on his first Indian tour in 1900–1901 and remained a loyal member for two decades. Born in Greenwich, he began performing in suburban theatres until he was discovered by William Greet and made appearances in musical comedy. A West End run in the 'military comic opera' *The Dandy Fifth* – in which he became known for the role of Sergeant Milligan and his rendition of the song 'A Little British Army Goes a Damned Long Way' – brought

[38] 'Bandman Opera Co. Player Killed', *Ceylon Observer*, 27 February 1917, 349.
[39] *The Era*, 31 December 1910, 23.
[40] *Burnley News*, 3 December 1913, 3.
[41] '"David Garrick" at the Manoel Theatre', *The Malta Times and the United Service Gazette*, 23 October 1897, 1.

Figure 5.3 Blanche Forsythe in the role of Trilby, ca. 1896. (Helena Cowell Collection.)

him to Bandmann's attention. He was a favourite along the circuit. On his final performance in Calcutta during his first Bandmann season in 1901, Cole was carried on the shoulders of spectators, who 'cheered him and his talented wife'.[42] He performed all the principal comic roles in the musical comedies, often opposite the soubrette and comedienne Georgie Corlass. Cole retired from the Bandmann Circuit around 1920 and returned to provincial touring in West End revues.[43]

The BOC did not just consist of performers but also of approximately fifteen backstage staff, many of whom remained connected with Bandmann throughout his career and even after his death. A programme from Yokohama in 1911 lists the following functions and people (Table 5.1):

[42] 'The Bandmann Company', *The Statesman*, 10 March 1901, 3.
[43] 'Obituary Mr. Harry Cole', *The Stage*, 11 April 1929, 17.

Table 5.1 *List of Bandmann Opera Company backstage staff, 1911*

Proprietor and Manager	Mr Maurice E. Bandmann
General Manager, Musical and Stage Director	Mr Warwick Major
Sub-Musical Conductor	Mr H. Weil
Secretary and Treasurer	Mr Roy H. Smith
Assistant Secretary	Mr H. von Boch
Stage Manager	Mr Will Smith
Librarian and Perruquier	Mr W. J. Baker
Assistant Stage Manager	Mr F Norman, Mr Percy Haydn
Master Carpenter	Mr Stephen Lopez
Stage Carpenter	Mr H. Strouth
Machinist	Mr J. Hackett
Scenic Artists	Mr F. Roult, Mr H. Lee
Wardrobe Mistress	Mrs M. Hamilton

Source: Theatre programme, Yokohama. Vanessa Lopez Family Archive.

Warwick Major features here in more than one function – as general manager as well as musical and stage director – because he was an experienced, multi-talented figure. Major began touring with the Carl Rosa Opera Company in the early 1890s and quickly graduated to running small theatre companies, including one starring Lily Bandmann. He joined Maurice Bandmann around 1903 and became musical director of the BOC, while also carrying out other functions. He married the soubrette Georgie Corlass and managed a theatre in Colombo and a touring company starring his wife before returning to Bandmann a few years later. On the latter's death, Major was effectively second in command and assumed a managerial role. Later in the decade, he returned to Britain, where he became active in theatre management in the provinces. Like Major, Roy H. Smith, here secretary and treasurer, later became one of Bandmann's managers, a role he too continued in Britain after Bandmann's death. James McGrath first appeared as a performer in the Bandmann Opera Company, but after Bandmann's death, he established a touring company in Bombay (see Chapter 2). Likewise, David Forbes Russell (1892–1969) joined the Bandmann Comedy Company in 1920 and then set up his own company, touring initially under the management of the Bandmann Eastern Circuit and then, according to his obituary, on his own until 1930.[44]

[44] 'Obituary: David Forbes Russell', *The Stage Archive*, 13 November 1969, 23.

Figure 5.4 Bandmann with his managers, ca. 1918. Left middle, Stephen Lopez; left front, Roy H. Smith. (Vanessa Lopez Family Archive.)

An important figure is the erstwhile master carpenter Stephen Lopez (1877–1953). Lopez, who came from a Gibraltese family, joined the company in his home country around 1900 as a stage carpenter and worked his way up to advance agent and finally company manager; he managed the Comedy Company and variety troupes. After Bandmann's death, he remained in India with his wife, Bessie Webb (also a performer), and continued to work for Bandmann Varieties until the late 1920s, before becoming an independent manager based in Calcutta, where he became a tour manager for emerging Indian dancers such as Uday Shankar and Menaka (see Chapter 8), both of whom toured extensively in Europe as well as India.

The fact that Bandmann posed with his managers (Fig. 5.4) is testimony to the importance he accorded them. They formed crucial nodes in the heterophilic network of the Bandmann Circuit, because they not only had to manage the venues he leased but also to supervise the touring companies when Bandmann himself was absent. Apart from the practicalities of programming, they dealt with the local presses, writing copy and providing pre-publicity. They also worked as theatre directors in the sense of staging plays. In a business with high turnover of personnel, they remained for the most part remarkably loyal.

Conclusion

The actor networks of the various Bandmann companies were sustained by 'edges' with many other networks. The most important of these was the British theatre industry itself, which produced a surplus of labour in all the many subcategories of theatrical production: actors, singers and dancers, conductors and musicians, but also stage managers and the various backstage support staff. In addition, Bandmann needed venue managers for his many leased theatres and advance agents to oil the publicity machine at the next port of call. Some of the performers and backstage staff worked their way up to be managers and agents within the Bandmann companies. They in turn made use of the existing networks to set up their own companies in the East. James McGrath's Bombay-based venture into theatrical touring in 1924 would have been inconceivable without the existing networks established by his former employer. The same holds true for Stephen Lopez's managerial career post-1922.

The estimated 20 per cent 'casualty rate' caused by girls marrying local men provided affective ties to the various locales along the circuit. Both the local press and Bandmann himself emphasized the positive rather than the negative effects: the infusion of 'new blood' in male-centred colonial societies and the guarantee of future audiences, as the former performers could be relied on to bring friends to performances. Most, however, returned home, which was usually Britain, where performers continued to ply their trade in the provincial theatres. Their names appear in connection with pantomimes, variety shows and, after the Second World War, weekly repertory at the holiday camps.[45] Here, the achievements on the Bandmann Circuit lived on in the realm of theatrical anecdote.

[45] Ibid.

6   Contested Contracts

According to actor-network theorist Bruno Latour, the function of law is to 'circulate throughout the landscape to associate entities *in a legal way*'.[1] The key term here is 'association': the law *links* other entities and makes them part of a social network. Law and society theorists Ewick and Silbey formulate a similar perspective when they suggest that law can be studied as a *social* phenomenon, in the sense that 'legality is an emergent feature of social relations rather than an external apparatus acting upon social life'.[2] This means that we can study law and legality not so much in terms of its 'inner logic' (Latour), which is the work of the legal system itself, but rather as a powerful force linking and regulating individuals and groups in situations of productive and occasionally disruptive relationships. This is nowhere more applicable than in the itinerant theatre of the Bandmann kind. Law and litigation played an important but paradoxical role in both holding the circulation of theatre together and threatening to destabilize it as disputes erupted with almost predictable regularity. Enacted in the public 'theatre' of courts and trials, these disagreements impacted not only on labour relations, but also on the 'intimate relations' of marriage and reproduction; they affected artistic production and were influenced by cultural differences and media reporting. Maurice E. Bandmann's many and often highly publicized court cases generated a secondary stage, as it were, where his artists had additional appearances. In ANT terms, the stage and the courts thus became linked, acting on one another in a mutually reinforcing activity that, as I shall argue, ultimately strengthened the network.

---

[1] Latour, *Reassembling the Social*, 239.
[2] Patricia Ewick and Susan S. Silbey, *The Common Place of Law: Stories from Everyday Life, Language and Legal Discourse* (Chicago: University of Chicago Press, 1998), 17.

The legal disputes centred on two main kinds of breaches: copyright and labour contracts. Both elements constituted crucial assets in the Bandmann Circuit. Copyright protected the network's intellectual property, whereas contracts regulated the deployment of human capital. Both needed to be protected against infringement, and both had to be adjudicated under legal conditions of 'extraterritoriality'. The special situation of transnational legal proceedings meant that a double mobility was at play: the transferral of English law to another legal system constituted a form of legal mimicry, where the law was almost the same but not quite. Also, the circumstance that misdemeanours or contractual breaches often occurred in places other than where a case was being heard created an additional level of complexity. Itinerant theatre therefore implicitly challenged the legal principles of *lex loci* and *lex fori*, which refer to the arbitration of laws of another jurisdiction.[3] Extraterritoriality was both the literal and metaphorical situation of the Bandmann Circuit.

Apart from performing the law, the trials themselves provided an additional theatrical dimension to the circuit. They were reported in almost real time, with the press providing the next day verbatim transcripts of exchanges in the courtroom. When famous actors appeared in court, like Allan Wilkie, Georgie Corlass or Bandmann himself, then these trials offered not just spectacle but also extra publicity for the circuit.

Enforcing 'Playright'

Theatrical copyright, understood here as the rights pertaining to a written or composed play or opera, evolved gradually over the course of the nineteenth century. Because of the mobility of theatrical business, it soon tested the boundaries of national law. With the establishment of dramatic copyright in 1833 in England and its extension in the Copyright Act of 1842, the law distinguished between copyright *in sensu stricto* (the rights of the author) and the right to license dramatic works for performance – the more important provision in the light of multiple productions and performances of the same work.

---

[3] *Lex loci*, which is more commonly used under the term *lex loci contractus*, refers specifically to the law of the place (usually district or country) where a contract is made. *Lex fori* refers to the principle that the executions of judgements are to be regulated solely and exclusively by the laws of the place where the action is instituted. See *Collins Dictionary of Law*, s.v. 'Lex loci' and 'lex fori'. Retrieved 20 March 2018 from legal-dictionary.thefreedictionary.com/lex+fori (last accessed 2 April 2019).

The 1842 Act remained in force with several alterations until the wide-ranging Copyright Act of 1911, which incorporated the provisions of the 1908 revision of the Berne Convention and extended British copyright law throughout the British Empire. The first Berne Convention of 1887 was a milestone as an attempt to implement copyright law on an international level to provide protection to the authors of the signatory countries. The isolationist United States, however, was not a signatory to the Berne Convention, nor to its subsequent revisions, and this left it isolated from any international agreement for the reciprocal granting of copyright protection.

The right to perform a 'dramatic piece' was known quite literally as 'playright' in English law, as opposed to 'copyright', which pertained to printing a work.[4] The distinction, however, did not extend to international law, which preferred the more general term of 'copyright'. Because plays were frequently not printed, playright dated from the time of first representation, i.e. public performance. This was a major difference to the United States, which did not consider an unpublished play to be protected by copyright in the same sense as a published work.[5] A number of countries on the Bandmann Circuit remained outside the copyright union in 1908 (i.e. signatories to the Berne Convention) and included most Latin American countries, Egypt, China, the Dutch East Indies (via Holland) and Turkey. Japan was inside the union.

The first performance (representation) of a play in any British possession secured statutory protection throughout the empire and the countries of the copyright union. Copyright or playright did not, however, extend to novels which could be freely adapted for the stage. As Bernard Weller complained in his lengthy disquisition, 'How to Protect a Play', written for the trade magazine *The Stage* in 1908, 'there is in the United Kingdom no recognition of playright in a novel. Provided none of the dialogue is used, a playwright is free to make a dramatic piece out of a published novel though the public odium attaching to this course … is now so strong that few managers of position would care to lend themselves to presenting a piece derived in this way.'[6] Right from his very first managerial undertakings, Bandmann was involved in the intricacies and contradictions of 'playrighting'. In his *Trilby* company (see Chapter 4), he had already exploited the discrepancies existing

---

[4] See Bernard Weller, 'How to Protect a Play', in *The Stage Yearbook* (1908), 35–44, here 36.
[5] Ibid., 39.
[6] Ibid., 42.

between the United Kingdom and the United States. Capitalizing on a gap in international copyright law, Bandmann had obtained the rights to the earlier American version, which he began to tour in April 1896 despite legal opposition from Herbert Beerbohm Tree, who first performed an adaptation of the novel in England. Bandmann stated in an interview, 'my counsel was of the opinion that the American version was absolutely free, as England was not within the jurisdiction of the international copyright law as regards plays produced in the States. "Trilby," as you know, was produced in America long before we had it in England, and it created quite a furore across the water.'[7]

In practice, respect for copy- or playright on the international circuit was enforced less by the authors or their agents than by the owners of the subsidiary rights who had a vested interest in preventing competitors from exploiting valuable properties for which they had paid fees. In 1901, a dispute erupted in Calcutta between two theatre managers, John Gunn and Henry Dallas, the latter Bandmann's soon-to-be partner, as both were playing in Calcutta musical comedies from the George Edwardes stable. Both had applied to and obtained performance rights from Edwardes but for different times. Perceiving an overlap, Gunn slapped an injunction on Dallas, which the latter ignored. Edwardes, acting through solicitors, supported the claim which Dallas sought to test in court.[8]

Two years later, Bandmann ran into similar trouble when touring the eastern states of Canada. The *New York Herald* reported that news of Bandmann performing George Edwardes' comic operas (*The Chinese Honeymoon*, *Florodora* and *The Silver Slipper*) in Québec had reached the ears of the Shubert Brothers, who immediately dispatched a lawyer to enforce their rights over their properties.[9] Although Bandmann had already entered into an agreement with Edwardes over these properties, Québec seems to have been disputed territory. Calcutta, however, was firmly under Bandmann's control, so when a certain Fred Ellis and the Lyric Opera Company advertised performances of *The Cingalee*, *The Orchid* and *The Geisha* at the Grand Opera House, Bandmann applied for and was granted an injunction by the Calcutta High Court.[10]

---

[7] *The Chronicle* (Leigh), 31 July 1896, 5. Reprinted from *The Nottingham Argus and Independent*, 17 July 1896.

[8] 'Theatrical Imbroglio: Gunn Versus Dallas', *The Singapore Free Press and Mercantile Advertiser*, 15 November 1901, 3.

[9] *New York Herald*, 3 September 1903. Press clipping, n.p.

[10] Hemendra Nath Das Gupta, *The Indian Stage*, Vol. 4 (Calcutta: Metropolitan Printing & Publishing House, 1944), 215–16.

Despite the complex and changing stipulations of international copyright law, there is clear evidence that writers, composers and their agents were determined to enforce provisions even across great distances. An example of this can be seen in an exchange between Bandmann and the Society of Authors, which represented, among other dramatists, George Bernard Shaw. In 1912, Shaw complained to G. Herbert Thring, the society's secretary, that unlicensed performances of *Candida* had taken place at the Royal Opera House, Bombay, Bandmann's newly opened theatre there. He demanded a fine of twenty-five guineas for the infringement, to which Bandmann replied that 'getting the ordinary fees' of three guineas per performance was more realistic. Bandmann explained that the culprit was actor-manager Allan Wilkie, who was touring India under his own steam, and he made a counterproposal:

If Mr. Shaw desires it, I will write to my people in India and try to collect the fees. I am afraid this will be somewhat difficult in the case of this company, as I understand they are at present somewhere in the North West of India. I note what you say re Mr. Shaw's insistency, and of course quite agree with him, but to enforce compensation in a country like India is a far more difficult task I am afraid than what Mr. Shaw imagines, and also a very expensive proceeding. 'Prevention is very much better than Cure' in matters of this sort out East, and if your society could make up their mind to appoint me as their representative, I would then be in a position to instruct the agents which I have in every town of any importance in India and the Far East to act accordingly, and I think your society would find that illicit performances of their plays would be put a stop to.[11]

Bandmann's 'agents' were the managers of the various theatres he owned or leased. In this proposal, Bandmann drew attention to how his circuit, although principally designed to facilitate the movement of theatrical productions, could also be refashioned for other purposes. Once the network was in place, it could be assigned multiple functions. While copyright and protection of authorial intellectual property existed in principle, its actualization was dependent on a functioning system of agents. Shaw remained sceptical, however, remarking to Thring, 'I wonder has B[andmann] really any agents, and, if so, what they do!'[12]

Shaw continued his pursuit of Wilkie for several months by trying to urge the society to act for him and other injured authors (including Pinero). Thring was reluctant to get the society involved, presumably because the considerable legal fees involved would have been disproportionate to the potential returns from performances in India.

---

[11] Letter to G. Herbert Thring, 16 May 1912, British Library, Add 56627.
[12] Shaw to Thring, 19 May 1912, British Library, Add 56627.

For Shaw, Wilkie was an 'Indian Pirate', and he was prepared to invest his own money in an attempt to 'lock up' Calcutta:

We must go ahead at any cost against this Indian Pirate. If we could get a judgement against him in Calcutta he would have to give in, because I presume we could in any case attack his salary and come down on his personal belongings even if he tried to dodge us in the way you suggest. If the Society won't risk the money I must risk it myself.[13]

Finally, he let it go and a year later wrote a mildly admonitory postcard to Wilkie's wife for performing *Candida* without permission: 'A youth spent in piracy may be a spirited beginning of a career of legitimate enterprise ...'[14] Shortly after this exchange, Wilkie began touring under Bandmann's management, so he came under his direct supervision.

Despite a brief exchange of letters and telegrams, the Society of Authors did not appoint Bandmann as their representative, but the proposal with its reference to 'agents...in every town of any importance in India and the Far East' represents the formation of an actor network in embryonic form. It also sheds light on the networked nature of theatrical business. The imagined or actual passage of theatrical intellectual property around the globe with Bandmann and his 'representatives' as translational mediators illustrates a web of connectivity linking Bandmann, Shaw, the Society of Authors, putative agents and the Bandmann theatres as conduits for the commercial transaction. The enabling technological 'mediators' are the telegraph and postal systems, without which the whole system of monitoring would have been almost impossible.

Despite his frequent presence in court, Bandmann was seldom involved in actual copyright disputes, which suggests that after the passing of the Copyright Act of 1911, the legal situation had become clearer, and the will of rights holders to prosecute their rights even in far-flung imperial dominions had made itself known. The agreement with George Edwardes certainly made things clear for Bandmann's most lucrative theatrical properties, the musical comedies, for which he diligently kept accounts and remitted royalties back to London.[15]

---

[13] Shaw to Thring, 10 September 1912, British Library, Add 56627.
[14] Postcard in the possession of Lisa Warrington, given to her by Wilkie's son; cited in an email communication to the author, 31 August 2011.
[15] See Tracy C. Davis, *Economics of the British Stage*, 351; and Chapter 2 of this book.

Breaches of Contract

If the regulation of copyright law on the Bandmann Circuit attained a certain equilibrium after 1911, the same could not be said about the contracts with his performers and the companies he managed. The rules of contract were crucial, and they differed considerably. The importation of one legal system to another cultural context was an integral part of the colonial project, which had to govern subjects beholden to completely heterogeneous understandings of the law, often determined by religious beliefs and long-standing practices. Recent research into law and colonial rule in India has highlighted the attempts by the colonial regime after 1857, when the British government assumed direct control, to extend the application of English law. In this regime of governmentality, the authority of legal discourse was employed, in the words of historian Preeti Nijhar, 'as a means of structuring power relations'.[16] It affected the relations between colonial subjects and rulers as well as more broadly those between indigenous and European interactions, wherein racial anxieties, fears of miscegenation and outright revolt found expression in laws specific not just to a country but even to particular regions. The imposition and absorption of the English legal system in India, for example, has been described as an example of cultural hegemony, because the latter 'requires that the subordinates be accomplices in perpetuating the symbolic structures that uphold existing inequalities'.[17] The term 'negotiated hegemony' has also been used, meaning that 'the subordinated groupings can play an active part in adjudicating the character of the dominant value system'.[18]

The actual introduction of English law to India well predates 1857, because its first application was to commercial activity under the East India Company. As early as 1753, mayoral courts were established in Madras, Bombay and Calcutta next to or above the courts of the East India Company. This period saw the categorization and division of Indian subjects into 'the two monolithic categories of "Hindu" and "Muslim": Hindus were to be governed by Hindu law, and Muslims by Muslims law.'[19] The development of the English legal system has been

---

[16] Preeti Nijhar, *Law and Imperialism: Criminality and Constitution in Colonial India and Victorian England*, Empires in Perspective, Vol. 10 (London: Pickering & Chatto, 2009), 19.

[17] Douglas E. Haynes, *Rhetoric and Ritual in Colonial India: The Shaping of a Public Culture in Surat City, 1852–1928* (Berkeley: University of California Press, 1991), 14.

[18] Ibid.

[19] Sandra Den Otter, 'Law, Authority, and Colonial Rule', in Douglas M. Peers and Nandini Gooptu, eds., *India and the British Empire* (Oxford: Oxford University Press, 2012), 173.

described as being complicit in shaping India 'as an agglomeration of communities, with religion and caste forming the primary building blocks of Indian society' and leading to a consolidation of a hitherto more flexible caste system.[20] The caste system will not feature in the following discussion, as the legal disputes in question were between Europeans in transit, whose arguments, however, were often adjudicated in Indian courts presided over by both English and Indian judges and often argued by Indian legal counsel. The interest here is more on theatrical than cultural questions, but the former were discussed outside the cultural matrix in which the contracts were initially enacted. Contracts signed in England were often disputed before a colonial court.

An important step in the establishment of English law for the pursuit of capitalism in India was the 1872 Indian Evidence Act and the Indian Contract Act. In the words of historian Ritu Birla, 'These measures standardized rules of evidence and defined the rules of contract as well as the competency to contract, establishing the figure of the rational contracting subject as legal subject.'[21] This law was not a simple transfer of English jurisdiction to India; it was something new, almost but not quite, and it stood in a subordinate relationship to its English progenitor. And it was, as we shall see, of some consequence whether the 'rational contracting subject' was English or foreign.

Most of the legal disputes brought by or against Bandmann involved contracts, the breaches thereof, and attempts to enforce their observance. This is not surprising in light of the commercial nature of Mr Bandmann's theatrical enterprises. Contracts and contract law lie at the heart of commercial relations, and they are already well defined in Roman law, which forms the foundation of English common law. The new early-modern model of theatre was founded on two interconnected principles: the joint-stock company and contracts. The joint-stock company, with its idea of shared risk and pooled capital, became the fundamental organizational form for professional theatre in Europe until well into the twentieth century. Contracts and the expectation that they will be enforced by courts of law constitute the institutional framework within which capitalism and free trade function and flourish.

Bandmann's regular appearances in court to either prosecute or defend himself against actors regarding breaches of contract need to be seen in terms of a disciplinary regime. The contract was the device by which obedience to the exacting demands of prolonged touring

[20] Ibid., 8.
[21] Ritu Birla, *Law, Culture, and Market Governance in Late Colonial India* (Durham: Duke University Press, 2009), 35–6.

was enforced. In 1903, he was awarded damages by the Westminster County Court against two ballet dancers for breaking their contract, which required them 'to go with a touring company round the world'.[22] Evidently, the girls got cold feet at the last moment and literally jumped ship, which did not prevent Bandmann from exacting from them his dues.

A more serious case, with the opposite consequences, was that brought by Miss Hettie Muret (aka Torrianno) against Bandmann for breach of contract at the Bombay High Court in February 1910. The two-day trial was reported at length by *The Stage* in London because of its wider implications for touring artists.[23] Muret had had extensive experience in musical comedy before she joined the Bandmann Opera Company through a London agency in August 1909 for an eighteen-month tour of India and the East. She had appeared in a number of productions in London, including at the Gaiety Theatre of George Edwardes. She played the leading soprano part in *The Catch of the Season* and had been a mermaid in *Peter Pan*. Bandmann initially offered her £8 a week for the duration of the tour, which she refused, so he included the possibility of a 5 per cent benefit in every place where they played for more than a fortnight. This meant she would potentially have benefits at six different theatres, amounting to around £3 a week in addition to her salary. She left England on 3 September 1909 with members of the company. She performed in concerts at Port Said, Aden and Colombo. During rehearsals for *The Arcadians* at Bangalore and Pune, she was heavily criticized by the musical director and stage manager, Warwick Major. 'It's a waste of time rehearsing with Miss Muret', he told Bandmann. The latter informed her that he had been instructed by his musical director that she was incompetent and could neither properly sing nor act. At Bombay, he terminated the agreement and requested that she return to England; he would pay her a passage back and two weeks' salary of £16. She refused and remained in Bombay to prosecute a case against him for breach of contract.

In contention was the agreement, which was in the form of a letter from Bandmann to Muret, in which it was expressly agreed that 'this engagement is for the whole run of the tour – not to exceed eighteen months. I alone have the right to terminate the same, but only subject to the rules and regulations on the back hereof.' The 'rules on the back'

---

[22] Reported in the *Manawatu Standard* (New Zealand), 17 September 1903, 7 (Papers Past).
[23] See 'An Indian Engagement. Action against Mr. Maurice Bandmann', *The Stage*, 17 March 1910, 15. All quotations are from this article.

stated that two weeks' notice for the termination of the agreement could be given but that this did not include short breaks in the tour nor holiday periods such as Easter, Christmas vacation, late arrival of steamers, etc. Counsel for Muret argued that these clauses only gave Bandmann the right to terminate the whole tour and thus the engagements of all the artists; it did not give him the right to terminate the contract of a particular individual. Bandmann's lawyer argued precisely the opposite: that he was entitled to put an end to the engagement of any artist at a fortnight's notice. Because the agreement was with the plaintiff only, it could not be applied to any other person. Therefore, the damages could only be assessed on the grounds of loss of salary that the plaintiff would have earned.

Under cross-examination, Bandmann explained how the termination of contract came about and that he paid her one night's salary for each of the concerts she had sung. He had no recollection of having stated that the 5 per cent benefits would amount to £2 or £3 a week. He also claimed that he provided most of the stage clothes for the artists (in her evidence, Muret stated that she had spent £100 on clothing for the tour). The plaintiff's lawyer asked Bandmann whether he was satisfied with her singing when he heard her in London, to which he replied, 'I was not thoroughly satisfied with her voice, but I was satisfied with her experience.' Bandmann did, however, accept responsibility for letters sent to Muret by his solicitors in which he threatened criminal proceedings for slander. Although she had not apologized for the alleged slanderous statements, he had not prosecuted her.

COUNSEL: Now be honest, do you intend to prosecute?
BANDMANN: I suppose so.
COUNSEL: When?
BANDMANN: After this case, I think.

In his judgement, the High Court judge summarized the case according to three main questions: firstly, whether Bandmann was within his rights to dismiss the plaintiff at his pleasure; secondly, if the dismissal was justifiable on account of the plaintiff's incompetence; and thirdly, whether the defendant, Bandmann, was entitled to make a counterclaim against Muret for damages for an alleged slander. The latter two claims, incompetence and slander, had been withdrawn, but the judge criticized Bandmann in that they had been brought at all, because this meant that they were touched on during the proceedings. He was particularly severe in his criticism of the alleged slander, which he interpreted as an attempt to intimidate Muret so that she would withdraw her claim for damages: 'an attempt was made in that letter to terrorize the plaintiff, a lonely and friendless lady in India, seeking in a court of justice, redress for damages done to her professional reputation'.

On the first and most important point, the claim for damages for breach of contract, the judge was equally severe in his judgement of Bandmann's arguments. The agreement was perfectly clear, in that Muret bound herself to join Bandmann's company for a period of eighteen months. Less clear were the provisions to protect the manager of the company through a clause that provided for two weeks' notice to terminate the agreement. The judge interpreted this as referring to the whole tour and company, and certainly not to a specific individual, because then 'he or she was to be at the mercy of the manager'. If that was the meaning of the clause, then the judge did not believe any manager would be able to induce any actor or actress to join a company under such conditions, as it would confer upon a manager arbitrary powers. The clause only empowered a manager to terminate the whole tour but not individual engagements.

In consequence of this ruling, the judge awarded damages of £600 in respect to income lost, four months' residence in Bombay and a passage home. He also noted that he would have dearly liked the assistance of a jury in assessing damages, but in India 'judges were deprived of the assistance of a jury in cases like this'. The judgement was an unequivocal ruling in favour of an individual actress against a theatre manager and for this reason was of some consequence because it provided a precedent for future cases of this kind. While an actor or actress could be dismissed on grounds of incompetence, this could not be an arbitrary whim but had to be clearly justified.

Another unsuccessful case concerned the variety star Ada Reeve, who was under an eight-month contract with Bandmann to tour Egypt, India, Ceylon and the Far East between 1916 and 1917. In Calcutta, she broke her ankle and dislocated her hip while fleeing from a 'rat as big as a rabbit' and was unable to finish the tour.[24] While convalescing (or probably before the accident), she received an offer from Bandmann's erstwhile partner Hugh McIntosh of the Tivoli Circuit for an Australian tour. She terminated the contract herself after performing for a further three weeks, initially sitting in a chair. This moved Bandmann to sue

---

[24] Ada Reeve, *Take It for a Fact: A Record of My Seventy-Five Years on the Stage* (London: Heinemann, 1954), 169–70.

her for damages amounting to Rs. 50,000 (£5,000) and breach of contract. Bandmann's application was ultimately dismissed on the grounds that the moment she became incapacitated through the accident from carrying out the terms of her engagement, the contract automatically terminated. Although he appealed the decision, this too was rejected.[25] The *Bandmann* v. *Reeves* case points to the differential power at play in such contracts. Aided by the accident, Reeves was able to end the contract of her own volition, as a more lucrative contract was on offer in Australia, where she had a huge following. The earning power there exceeded by far the possibilities offered in Ceylon or further along the Far Eastern rim of the Bandmann Circuit.

Cohen v. Wilkie: *Theatre in the High Court*

By 1911, Bandmann, who now controlled two theatres in Calcutta, had a new competitor on the European theatre scene in the city. A local Jewish businessman, Elias Moses Cohen, had rebuilt the old wooden Opera House and renamed it the Grand Opera House, although its repertoire was directed more at the lower end of the theatrical hierarchy: vaudeville, not grand opera, was his main focus. In 1912, Bandmann had formed a partnership with the Shakespearean actor Matheson Lang for a tour in India (see Chapter 4). Following and probably in direct competition with Bandmann's business model, Cohen had contracted the actor Allan Wilkie to appear in the Grand Opera House and in other theatres in India with a programme of plays. Despite much pre-performance puff claiming great achievements for and with Shakespeare at home, prior to his tour, Allan Wilkie had been a small-time actor-manager eking out a meagre living playing the English provinces with a repertoire of Shakespeare and contemporary melodramas. When Wilkie arrived in India, two months before Matheson Lang, local audiences had had a long and intensive acquaintance with different versions of the Bard, mainly of the Parsi Indian variety. There had not been, however, much *pukka*-English Shakespeare immediately prior to Wilkie's visit. There existed, indeed, the perception, as noted in Chapter 4, that colonial audiences were averse to demanding plays.

Cohen was evidently of the opinion that modern comedies should be the mainstay. Wilkie offered instead Shakespeare, classics such as Sheridan plus an assortment of contemporary dramas. Cohen agreed to

[25] See 'Calcutta Theatrical Suit', *The Amrita Bazar Patrika*, 3 March 1917, 7; and 'Sequel to Theatrical Suit: Fresh Evidence on Commission', *The Amrita Bazar Patrika*, 13 March 1917, 7.

Mr. ALLAN WILKIE as " Shylock."
SPEIGHT, PHOTO., KETTERING.

Figure 6.1 Allan Wilkie as Shylock, ca. 1906. (Private collection.)

pay Wilkie and his company £300 per week while in Calcutta and £200 when in other towns in India – the same salary that Bandmann was paying Matheson Lang. The Allan Wilkie company opened in Calcutta with its 'lucky mascot', *The Merchant of Venice*, in October 1911, with Wilkie as Shylock, the role he was most famous for and which he reportedly played over 1,500 times in the course of his career (Fig. 6.1). The tour organized in partnership with Cohen consisted of three-and-a-half weeks in Calcutta, a two-week season in Bombay, followed by a return season in Calcutta for four-and-a-half weeks, and two weeks in Rangoon and Madras before finishing in Colombo. The contractual arrangement with Cohen expired after the Colombo season. After that, Wilkie was supposed to return to England. Instead, he entered into an arrangement with Bandmann to play his theatres in Calcutta and in smaller towns. Cohen slapped an injunction on Wilkie to prevent him from appearing in Calcutta or elsewhere in India. The widely reported trial took place in the Calcutta High Court on 11 March 1912 – on the same night Wilkie was programmed to appear in Bandmann's Empire Theatre.

All trials are dramas, and prominent ones were often reported verbatim in local newspapers, with the dialogue written by the courtroom. When a prominent actor famous for playing Shylock is himself placed on trial by a Jewish businessman for breach of contract, then the connections were almost too thick to be missed. Cohen sued Wilkie for breach of contract, claiming Rs. 35,000 (£2,300) as damages. It was countered by a cross-suit from Wilkie for Rs. 5,000 (£330) as damages for breach of the same contract.[26] Two Bengali lawyers, B. L. Mitter and D. N. Bose, appeared for Cohen; two English lawyers, Pugh and Pearson, represented Wilkie. Judge Fletcher presided. The following analysis is based on testimony recorded verbatim in several newspapers.[27]

Wilkie stated that after the 17 February 1912, his performances were under his own management. He had an arrangement with Bandmann by which he played at Bandmann's theatres and took a portion of the receipts. Cross-examined by Mr Mitter, Wilkie affirmed that Cohen had paid him a total of Rs. 55,951 out of a total gross receipt of Rs. 76,100.

MR MITTER:	Mr Cohen gave you to understand what sort of plays the Calcutta theatre-going public would like?
WILKIE:	Yes.
MR MITTER:	He gave you a list of a number of plays of modern comedies?
WILKIE:	I sent him a list of plays I proposed to produce which did not include modern plays, and he did not object to it.
...	

---

[26] In the cross-suit, Wilkie claimed breach of contract and Rs. 2,250 in respect of four days – in Calcutta, Rangoon, Madras and Colombo – during which he gave no performances owing to Mr Cohen's fault. He claimed an additional Rs. 1,281 in respect of carting and transhipment charges as well as 50 per cent of the gross receipts. Wilkie asserted that Cohen failed to make any arrangements for the company to play in an Indian theatre, and hence the company were idle. Cited in 'Theatrical Dispute: Mr. Allan Wilkie in Court', *The Amrita Bazar Patrika*, 12 July 1912, 10.

[27] The transcript is taken from a Calcutta newspaper report: 'Theatrical Dispute – Mr Allan Wilkie in the Box', *The Englishman*, 11 July 1912, 19. It has been cross-checked with an almost identical report in the *Amrita Bazar Patrika*, 12 July 1912, 10.

MR JUSTICE FLETCHER:	Is it your point that the Calcutta public will not go to see Shakespeare plays?
MR MITTER:	They like modern comedies. Your production of 'Rob Roy' was a failure in Calcutta?
WILKIE:	I don't admit that.
MR MITTER:	Not dramatically but financially?
WILKIE:	Financially it stood fifth in a list of eighteen plays.
MR JUSTICE FLETCHER:	What play stood first?
MR MITTER:	'The Merchant of Venice'.

Much more was discussed besides, including Judge Fletcher's experience as an amateur actor, the difficulty of obtaining rights for *The Three Musketeers* and the provision of weapons for Wilkie's production of *Rob Roy*. The relevance to the case was not always entirely apparent, but each example provided levity for the courtroom audience.

Justice Fletcher passed judgement the same day. At stake was Clause 9 in the contract, which stated explicitly, 'The said Allan Wilkie undertakes not to play at any other theatre in Calcutta, or in any other town under his own or under any other management until after the termination of the tour and the return of himself and the company to England in pursuance of the agreement.'[28] Judge Fletcher conceded that under English law the principle of *lex loci contractus* meant that this clause would unequivocally justify Cohen's request for an injunction. 'But in India', Fletcher argued, implicitly applying *lex fori*, Indian law applies and 'Section 27 of the Contract Act clearly provides that a contract in respect of trade by which a man is restrained from exercising his lawful profession, trade or business, is void. … It seems to me that this Clause 9 in the contract is under the terms of Section 27 of the Indian Contract Act void as being in restraint of trade.'[29] The suit was dismissed with costs (for Cohen), and Wilkie performed the same night at Bandmann's Empire Theatre.[30]

The trial is of interest beyond its specific ruling and the fact that Judge Fletcher had the best one-liners and continually belittled the plaint, if not the plaintiff. From the beginning, it was clear that Elias Cohen was not going to get his pound of flesh. More important for the global theatre business was the central legal, and political, principle 'void as

---

[28] Justice Fletcher, 'E. M. D. Cohen vs Allan Wilkie on 11 March 1912', Calcutta High Court, http://indiankanoon.org/doc/1026435/ (last accessed 6 August 2019).
[29] Ibid.
[30] *The Straits Times*, 20 March 1912, 6.

being in restraint of trade'. Nothing – not even a binding contract that was unequivocal under English law – would permit an Indian-Jewish entrepreneur from preventing a British actor-manager from exercising his trade. For free trade was the very foundation of an empire designed to permit goods, people and services to move around its dominions unencumbered by restrictions.[31]

A Theatrical Suit: *Corlass v. Bandmann*

On 13 February 1913, a trial began at the Calcutta High Court in which the actress Georgiana Major (Corlass) brought a suit against Bandmann to recover Rs. 18,000 for alleged wrongful dismissal. Corlass had entered into an agreement by which she was engaged as principal soubrette. That arrangement was agreed at Colombo on 30 March 1912 and continued until 11 December of that year, when she was dismissed – in her eyes wrongfully. The terms of the contract stipulated that she was to receive £20 a week while she was actually performing, as well as first-class hotel accommodation and first-class railway fares. The contract was for nineteen months. On 3 December 1912, a rehearsal had been called at Calcutta in which she was asked to perform the part of Ilka in the operetta *Nightbirds*. She refused, claiming that the part was outside her vocal range. The stage manager, Fred Coyne, suspended her from rehearsals, and after some negotiation with Bandmann, she was formally dismissed.

Theatrical business practices were examined in excruciating detail in the ensuing trial, which took place two months later over a six-day period and included in addition a preliminary hearing (a judicial curtain-raiser in which Bandmann tried unsuccessfully to force the plaintiff, Corlass, to provide security for costs). The newspaper reports note that the court was always crowded, as Corlass (a darling of the Calcutta theatre), her husband, Warwick Major, Bandmann's employees and a variety of musical experts gave extensive testimony. Inordinate amounts of time were spent defining the vocal limitations of a soubrette, the practice of transposition and the cutting of parts, as well as defining the genre of *Nightbirds* and enumerating the extremely taxing conditions under which leading performers were expected to labour.

---

[31] In fact, differences between countries were considered a problem for the British Empire, because, as an article in the *Friend of India* in 1907 pointed out, there existed in the British Empire no fewer than '22 different systems of company law, contained in 145 Acts, Laws and Ordinances for India and the Colonies of Canada, Australia, New Zealand and South Africa'. The author calls for new rules to standardize the floating and regulation of joint-stock companies to better enable imperial trade. 'The Empire's Company Laws', *The Friend of India*, 15 August 1907, 6.

Figure 6.2 Georgie Corlass. (Billy Rose Theatre Division, New York Public Library.)

The plaintiff, Mrs Georgiana Major, was known under the stage name Georgie Corlass (Fig. 6.2). She had begun performing some sixteen years earlier, in 1897, in a children's opera company known as Battersby's Opera Company, where she was cast as a soubrette. She then switched to straight drama, and, after touring in England, began performing pantomime. She played in both drama and pantomime until September 1904, when she received an offer from Bandmann and started at £5 per week under a contract to tour the West Indies, Gibraltar, Malta, Cairo, India and the Far East. She signed up for a second tour, joining the company in December 1906 in Bombay for a tour which was to last nineteen months. During the first tour, she met her (later) husband, Warwick Major, Bandmann's musical and stage director. During these two tours, she worked her way up to be the principal soubrette and attained a significant following on the Bandmann Circuit. Her performances invariably garnered positive notices.

At the same time, the constant touring of a repertoire that comprised twenty to twenty-five works, mostly musical comedy, took a toll on her health. The court heard that on the second tour she would frequently faint on stage and have to be carried off. She then returned to England for five months for complete rest. Eventually, she returned to the tour in July 1910 to join her husband's new company in Karachi, playing for another five months. She then settled in Colombo, where Warwick Major managed the Public Hall, the main venue for touring companies. Warwick Major continued to work for Bandmann on a contract basis at this time but no longer toured with the latter's companies. From their base in Colombo, the couple began to plan independent tours for Corlass. It was in this situation of semi-retirement and freelance work that Bandmann approached her in March 1912 in Colombo because he was in a fix. His leading lady and principal soubrette, Florence Beech, had suffered a serious accident in Singapore and was unable to complete her contract. As the company was due to perform in Calcutta, where Corlass was extremely popular, Bandmann was willing to make financial concessions beyond the normal range.

The Contract

On the contractual level, the issue was whether Bandmann could compel Corlass to perform a role outside her vocal range. In the first contract signed in 1904, there was a clause in the agreement which declared that she was to play not only the part of a soubrette but 'any part that was cast'. The Colombo contract appears to have been more general – so general, in fact, that Corlass and her husband insisted that additional notes be appended. These concerned regular nights off and a stipulation as to the parts she was to play.

The dismissal revolved around Corlass's refusal to play the part of Ilka in *Nightbirds*, an adaptation of the famous Johann Strauss operetta *Die Fledermaus*. This new version by Gladys B. Unger (book) and Arthur Anderson (lyrics) had premiered just a year before at the Lyric Theatre in London in December 1911. Although some of the characters were renamed (Ilka is the maid Adele), others retained their original names (such as Countess Rosalinda, the other major soprano role). More importantly, the music remained the same. Both Adele/Ilka and Rosalinda are extremely demanding soprano roles, which enabled the operetta to find a place in the standard repertoire of most opera houses. Both parts are considered prime prima donna material and have attracted star sopranos such as Edita Gruberova and Kiri Te Kanawa.

The court needed to clarify a number of theatre-related questions: what is a soubrette? What could be reasonably expected of such a performer in vocal terms? Was *Nightbirds* really a musical comedy? What were the actual stipulations of the contract? Could she have rendered the part if it had been transposed or adapted to suit her voice? Because much of the testimony was of a technical-music nature, the musical (in)competence of judge and counsel were first ascertained in light-hearted banter:

Counsel believed his Lordship was a bit of a musical expert and that would render his task somewhat less difficult.

MR JUSTICE CHAUDHURI:	Not at all.
MR NORTON:	Well Mr Garth [counsel for Bandmann] is. Therefore we are on equal terms.[32]

Norton, counsel for Corlass, the plaintiff, first defined the current understanding of a soubrette. He argued that originally it meant a light, bright, sparkling part by a pretty woman who was able to display before an audience 'the charming grace of a pretty French maid'. In that part, there was little or no music. Over time, music was introduced which required that the soubrette performer do a considerable amount of singing and dancing. A soubrette consisted of really two distinct and separate ideas. The first was the acting, secondary was the music. The soubrette was called upon to sing if she could, 'to warble if she could not'. The real qualification of a soubrette, even in musical comedy, lay in her power to charm her audience by her person, her tone and gesture, her face, her figure, her general make-up, her voice and her power to fascinate the audience; the question of singing was a subsidiary matter.

Because the focus of the soubrette was on acting and dancing, it was unrealistic to expect Corlass to sing the part of Ilka, Norton argued. *Nightbirds* was, he claimed, not musical comedy at all:

The quality of the music never was intended to be within the range, the voice and the abilities of a soubrette. The music of the 'Nightbirds' was really opera music, probably halfway between grand Opera and musical comedy, but certainly not musical comedy. It required a specially trained technique and vocalisation and it was childish to suggest that any member of Mr Bandmann's company was competent to render that music, either as it was rendered in London or at all.[33]

[32] *The Amrita Bazar Patrika*, 14 February, 1913, 7.
[33] Ibid.

The part of Ilka had been played in the London production by Muriel George, who, while not an opera singer, probably had more formal vocal training than Corlass.[34] The sheet music identifies Ilka as a 'parlourmaid',[35] and in the course of the trial it was reported by Bandmann's counsel that George had been asked to relinquish the role because she refused to play it as 'a low comedy part'.[36] The reference here is to a widely reported suit for damages brought by Muriel George against the producer of *Nightbirds*, Michael George Faraday, which came to court in November 1912, one month before Corlass was dismissed. Faraday became dissatisfied with the way George was rendering the part of Ilka and made use of a clause in the agreement to 'retire' the actress. He had offered to her £80 in compensation, which she refused. A letter from Faraday to George was read out in court in which he stated, 'I wish you would appreciate that yours is the only low comedy part among the women.' He asked her to accentuate her lines in the first act so that all in the house, besides those in the stalls, could hear. This he knew she could do. He was afraid, he went on, that she resented playing the part as he wanted. The letter in which the plaintiff was dismissed began, 'Dear Miss George, – I am very sorry to have to write this letter. Sentiment, unfortunately, cannot enter into business matters.' Faraday went on to say that he had to make a change in the part of Ilka because of the tastes of the patrons of his theatre and that George would not suffer any financial loss. Finally, George won her suit because the 'retirement' clause Faraday applied was designed to allow managers to close their theatres for alteration or summer recesses without having to recompense performers, but not as a means for summary dismissal.[37]

The reason for Corlass's dismissal was, however, an artistic one – or, as Faraday saw it in the George case, a 'business' question. Was the part of Ilka being performed in the right way? George, with her background in both variety (she was a member of The Follies company) and classical singing, clearly saw it as a more elevated role than the 'low comedy' that Faraday claimed the patrons of the Lyric Theatre demanded. Corlass, on the other hand, who could have performed the role 'low' with ease,

---

34 Muriel George (1883–1965) was initially a variety performer and later became known as a character actress in films. Her father, Robert George, taught singing at the Royal Academy of Music. See her unpublished autobiography, www.murielgeorge.info/index/view/story/memoirs/id/13 (last accessed 2 April 2019).

35 *Nightbirds: A Musical Comedy in Three Acts.* Libretto by Gladys Unger, lyrics by Arthur Anderson, composed by Johann Strauss. London: Cranz & Co., n.d.

36 'A Theatrical Suit', *The Amrita Bazar Patrika*, 18 February 1913, 4.

37 'Actress' Tears: Miss Muriel George and the "Nightbirds"', *The Evening Telegraph and Post*, 15 November 1912, 4.

baulked at the vocal demands of the part. The fact that George had successfully sued the producer may have encouraged Corlass to do the same. The connection between the two trials was made explicit during the cross-examination of Warwick Major on the vocal demands of the role of Ilka: 'I made inquiries and was told it was a soprano part. Miss George is my informant.' Musical experts further corroborated the heavy demands of the part. The opera singer Alex Marsh ('I am the original impersonator in nearly every town in England of Wolfram in Tannhäuser') stated unequivocally that the part required a 'prima donna soprano – a very highly trained voice', and, knowing Corlass's voice, it was quite impossible for her to sing it.[38] Charles E. Richardson, bandmaster of the King's Own regiment based in Calcutta, was also called as an expert witness. He had seen Muriel George in the original London production and confirmed that a soubrette could not perform the part.

Throughout the testimony, attention returned repeatedly to the 'Laughing Song' in the second act. This was deemed by far the most difficult section. In her testimony, Corlass detailed the extreme demands the role represented (Fig. 6.3):

[On 3 December 1912] I was first called upon to attend a rehearsal of the 'Night Birds' in connection with Ilka's part. I tried to sing a portion of the music. I did not try the heavy songs in the second act. Ilka has a lot to do in the first act. My song in the second act begins at page 83 (*shown a book*). I could not sing the song. I listened to it very attentively. The songs from pages 83 to 85 (*shown a book*) do not, in my opinion, fall within the definition of soubrette music. It is beyond my scope vocally. At page 85 the song goes up to 'C' in alto and to 'D' in alto and then a fearful trill in 'G'. There is a shake on 'F' sharp for two bars at the bottom of page 85.[39] [emphasis added]

Corlass's evidence, buttressed by the visual proof of the score itself, emphasizes the act of 'shown a book'. Although it is not entirely clear to whom the showing is addressed, presumably the judge, the exhibition of the score provides incontrovertible proof of the impossible demands placed on Corlass. Like O. J. Simpson's (or somebody else's) bloody glove, the score becomes, as it were, an exhibit. Its demonstration underlines the performative nature of evidence itself. It is an unusual moment in the trial where the rhetorical understanding of *evidentia*, making something vividly manifest, conjoins with the referential notion of legal proof.[40]

---

[38] 'A Theatrical Suit', *The Amrita Bazar Patrika*, 18 February 1913, 4.

[39] 'A Theatrical Suit', *The Amrita Bazar Patrika*, 14 February 1913, 7.

[40] On the concept of *evidentia*, see Heike Roms, 'Mind the Gaps: Evidencing Performance and Performing Evidence in Performance Art History', in Claire Cochrane and Jo Robinson, eds., *Theatre History and Historiography: Ethics, Evidence and Truth* (Basingstoke: Palgrave Macmillan, 2016), 163–81.

Figure 6.3 Original score of *Nightbirds*, p. 85. 'The Laughing Song' with the 'fearful trill in "G"' and 'shake on "F" sharp' marked. (Private collection.)

Although the proof could only really be in the singing (or not, as the case may be), Corlass restricted her testimony to visual, even philological, demonstration.

A central point of contention revolved around whether Corlass over-reacted when she refused to sing the demanding arias. The defence argued that Bandmann's musical director had offered to transpose the song, yet Corlass did not accept the offer. Charles E. Richardson, the Kings Own bandmaster, testified that in the performances he witnessed in Calcutta, *Nightbirds* had been extensively altered and thus did not do justice to the music as written. The musical quality he compared to an 'excellent curry made out of a leg of mutton…It had some flavour of mutton about it.' Much had been cut, and sections were spoken instead of sung; ultimately, 'it was much beyond the capacity of the Company'. The opera singer Alex Marsh considered the version of *Nightbirds* given in Calcutta to border on deceit on account of the many cuts and altera-tions compared to the London original.[41]

Fred Coyne, producer and stage manager for Bandmann, described the practice and rationale behind the cutting of scores. The first step was to adjust the works 'to avoid unnecessary orchestry [*sic*]'.[42] In the case of *Nightbirds*, these emendations were carried out early, because the cut scores had to be sent to England in time to catch the new company mem-bers before they embarked on the passage out to India – the idea being that the new members could familiarize themselves with the scores before their arrival in Bombay for rehearsals and first performances. Coyne confirmed that the cuts included the first song of Ilka and the duet between Ilka and the countess in the first act but claimed that the cuts were for dramatic and not for musical reasons. The second act, however, remained intact, while all of Ilka's musical parts in the third act were removed. Coyne claimed that in the light of this usual practice of cutting, adaptation and transpos-ing songs to a lower key, Corlass could easily have coped with the role. While Corlass could or would not sing the song as it was composed, the song was evidently rendered by her understudy, Moyna Hill, in a fashion befitting her voice: she 'laughed the Laughing Song' rather than sang it.

Moyna Hill, the understudy, was also called. She stated that she was a soubrette and that her voice 'goes up to "A" with comfort and I can go up to "B"'. Norton, counsel for Corlass, retorted, 'Miss Corlass has the same voice. She can take "A" and also "B" but she prefers to take "tea" (laughter).'[43] In fact, Norton's attack on Moyna Hill was more serious.

[41] 'A Theatrical Suit', *The Amrita Bazar Patrika*, 18 February 1913, 4.
[42] 'A Theatrical Suit', *The Amrita Bazar Patrika*, 19 February 1913, 4.
[43] 'A Theatrical Suit', *The Amrita Bazar Patrika*, 22 February 1913, 4.

In his closing remarks, he intimated that Corlass's dismissal was also motivated by pecuniary considerations. He argued that Bandmann had by December acquired in Hill a much cheaper soubrette (at £6 a week) and that he was looking for an opportunity to rid himself of the financial burden of Corlass, who was costing the company more than four times as much.[44] What was not explicitly stated but may have been insinuated was that Bandmann's relationship to Hill was more than just professional: in September of the same year, they married, so by this time, their liaison was well known. Norton also attacked Bandmann directly, accusing him of cowardice: 'Mr. Bandmann did not go into the witness box. This gentleman who came here and perorated through two Counsel had not the physical or moral courage to go into the witness-box.'[45] Norton argued that, in the final analysis, the case came down to the contract, the written document signed in Colombo, which placed the onus on Bandmann to justify his dismissal of Corlass.

In his judgement, Mr Justice Chaudhuri admonished witnesses for both the plaintiff and the defendant, ruling that a certain amount of oral evidence was hardly admissible on account of influence. Finally, he accepted the claim of wrongful dismissal and awarded Corlass damages in the amount of Rs. 7,500, or £500.[46] His criticisms of the various witnesses, especially those for Bandmann, convey the impression that there had been a great amount of mutual corroboration among them before they gave testimony.

The trial gives insight into the inner workings of a travelling opera company, especially the exigencies of performing metropolitan successes with much reduced financial and vocal capacity. In London, works were performed as long-run productions; on the Bandmann Circuit, they were rotated in a repertoire system. The latter produced stresses on both performers and management. The extended trial in Calcutta documents a potential breaking point in the system, when a key performer refused her labour, arguing that unfair and contractually illegitimate demands had been placed on her. Recourse to the courts meant that employees could and did find justice. For Bandmann, the courts were a vehicle to enforce his regime; for Corlass, they provided a means to obtain some kind of recompense for losses in income. There was, however, much more at stake than just the adjudication of

---

[44] This argument is made explicit in the English press: 'A Calcutta Case: Corlass v. Bandmann', *The Stage Archive*, 20 March 1913, 24.

[45] 'Calcutta Theatrical case', *The Amrita Bazar Patrika*, 25 February 1913, 4.

[46] 'A Theatrical Suit', *The Amrita Bazar Patrika*, 4 March 1913, 7.

a contract: the Bandmann theatre itself was on public display as many of its most important members – a star and minor performers, stage managers, musical directors – gave testimony before a packed courthouse. That such a trial was not just a local affair can be seen through various interconnections with London, where the trial was reported by the trade press and a related case, the dismissal of Muriel George in the same part, was related back to Calcutta.

The connectivity linking different parts of the network was made manifest in the trial, which went on for six days and was reported in *extensio* and verbatim in the Calcutta press and beyond. The actual testimony given at the trial makes clear that the specific case linked together a whole matrix of elements – the press, shipping, the contract itself (which bound the performers to the enterprise) and the wider theatrical business – because the Calcutta ruling could, like the earlier case involving Hettie Muret, establish a precedent for future contractual arrangements. There were also affective drivers at work, including the usual tensions between cast members, management and even legal counsel. Norton's personal attack on Bandmann bordered on character assassination. Also in play was the sphere of exigency, where illnesses and accidents could weaken the network as much as the economic constraints of touring musical comedies in cheap fit-up versions. On the level of performance, the trial highlighted the singing voice and its limitations, including the conventions and constraints of the theatrical system of type parts (in this case the soubrette). It also demonstrated how the physical materials of performance circulated around the network: the scores that were transported from London to Calcutta, adapted there to suit the exigencies of the touring company and then sent back to London for the new company about to embark.

Contract by Cable

The reliance of the Bandmann theatrical network on telegraphic communication can hardly be over-estimated. It was second only to the shipping network in importance for the smooth functioning of the circuit. The close connection between cable networks and trade routes has often been noted, and the Bandmann Circuit is no exception. Its trajectories map almost exactly onto the cable networks established by both private companies and governments (with the former carrying by far the lion's share of investment). The convergence between cable networks and trade routes was remarked on by the British government in 1911:

> The routes of the cables to British Colonies and Protectorates follow the main trade routes across the Atlantic to North and South America, along the Mediterranean and Red Sea to Bombay, and down the west coast of Africa as far as Sierra Leone, and most of the main trade routes and main cables converge alike on main centres of commerce, many of which are naval bases ... while others, such as those to the West Indies, between India and Singapore and Hong Kong, though they cross or pass near important trade routes, do not follow their course.[47]

The trade and cable routes from India eastwards certainly 'passed near' one another – in fact, they converged in many places, especially at those cities boasting theatres.

Most theatrical business of the itinerant kind was concluded by telegraphic communication. This ensured rapidity and flexibility, as the travelling companies were often afflicted by circumstances beyond their control. Normally, a company would cable ahead to a theatre to book a season. There seems to have been a kind of tacit agreement that extenuating circumstances, such as storms or changes in shipping timetables, could lead to an annulment of the agreement with only minor costs for the theatrical company. Short-term changes in plans or a no-show at short notice could, however, lead to litigation for damages.

A case in point, which also involved a Bandmann company, albeit indirectly, was a three-day trial conducted at the US court in Shanghai in January 1913 between the Arcade Amusement Company of Tientsin and the Hughes Musical Company, a small American troupe. The special extraterritorial status of the Western settlements in Shanghai also extended to the judiciary. Westerners were exempt from Chinese jurisdiction so that a defendant could be sued in the court of his own nationality, a rule which was also extended in favour of a plaintiff of other foreign nationality.[48] Thus, the United States installed a higher court there. The trial in question was presided over by Rufus H. Thayer, a federal appointee.

---

[47] National Archives, London, CAB 16/14, 'Standing Sub-committee of the Committee of Imperial Defence. Submarine Cable Communication in Time of War. Report with Table and Appendices', December 1911, 6. Cited in Roland Wenzlhuemer, *Connecting the Nineteenth-Century World: The Telegraph and Globalization* (Cambridge: Cambridge University Press, 2013), 130.

[48] See F. E. Hinckley, 'Extraterritoriality in China', *The Annals of the American Academy of Political and Social Science*, China: Social and Economic Conditions, Vol. 39 (1912): 97–108.

The case concerned the cancellation of a seven-night season at the Arcade Theatre, a variety hall located in Tientsin's French Concession, by the American company at very short notice. Thereupon, the theatre management sued the theatre company for damages calculated at exactly $3,663. The latter had cabled the theatre from Manila in mid-April 1912 to arrange to perform at the theatre starting on 8 May. The agreement was concluded by telegram on 25 April, only two weeks before the season was due to commence. The contract provided for the typical profit-share arrangement whereby the host theatre covered local expenses (mainly publicity) and retained 40 per cent of box office, while the visiting company received the remaining 60 per cent of proceeds. On 6 May, two nights before they were due to open, the Hughes Company telegraphed from Shanghai that they were unable to arrive in time and cancelled the contract. The defendant argued that it was physically impossible for the company to reach Tientsin by the agreed date. Arrangements were made by cable from Manila, and the journey to Shanghai by way of Hong Kong took seven or eight days. In May 1912, transportation from Shanghai to Tientsin was by means of small steamships of limited passenger accommodation sailing at irregular intervals. These constraints were well known to the plaintiff, while the defendant and the company were 'strangers to the Orient and were unacquainted with conditions of travel between Shanghai and Tientsin'. It was impossible for the defendant to know or learn at Manila the sailing dates or passenger accommodation of steam ships sailing from Shanghai to Tientsin in the month following. So the argument went.

Apart from the logistical difficulties of arranging speedy transportation for a twenty-three-strong company in 'oriental territories', Hughes claimed that it was an *implied term and condition* of the agreement made by cable that it should only be effective provided it were possible for the company to reach Tientsin in time to open the performance on the agreed day, 8 May. In fact, the case for the defence rested mainly on this principle: that it was an implied condition of such agreements, and a 'usage and custom of the theatrical business known to and contemplated by said parties' that if either party 'by reason of sickness, accident, or any other unforeseen event, or by reason of any occurrence or circumstances beyond the control' should be unable to meet their engagement, then the company should not be held liable for any damages beyond out-of-pocket expenses incurred by other party.[49]

---

[49] 'U.S. Court for China', *The North-China Herald*, 18 January 1913, 204–7, 205.

The case for the plaintiff argued and provided proof that far from being a logistical impossibility, it would have been quite feasible to reach Tientsin from Shanghai by the agreed date. Furthermore, he produced booking figures for the Bandmann Opera Company and the Allan Wilkie Company, which occupied the theatre after the aborted season, to demonstrate the scale of the putative losses. The latter were vigorously contested by the defence lawyer, who remarked, 'a Chinese boy with a blue pencil might have marked these up'.[50] He reiterated the principle that 'it was the custom in the United States not to hold theatrical company liable for non-fulfilment of an agreement through unforeseen circumstances, and he submitted that such usage applied in that court'.

In his ruling, the presiding judge, Rufus M. Thayer, said it seemed clear that a contract was made 'as a result of telegraphic negotiations between the parties … [and] in the circumstances in which the contract was made no comparison could be made between it and the written form of contract', even though the latter may have contained paragraphs where the parties themselves agreed that in the event of failure to fulfil the contract through some unexpected cause no damages should be suffered on that account. People were free, he argued, to make such an agreement if they wished, and 'it may be that that was a customary form of agreement among theatrical parties in making an engagement of this character'. Whatever the specific practices, it was essential that parties entering into a contract did so in good faith, and 'one of them failing to fulfil the contract could not be given relief because that party had not found it convenient to perform its part of the contract'.[51] He awarded the plaintiff $725 and costs, substantially less than the $3,663.20 claimed.

Conclusion

An American theatre company was prosecuted by a theatre owned by an Indian proprietor located in the French concession of a Chinese city that was largely controlled by foreign powers. The case was in turn heard before a US court located in Shanghai. The contract had been concluded by telegram from Manila with the brevity usual for the medium. In the end, the judge applied US law. Such multiple connections are perhaps extreme but ultimately not untypical for the globalized theatre trade. A tension is apparent between the ephemerality of performance in an extraterritorial mode and the inherent territorial nature of the legal system.

[50] Ibid., 206.
[51] Ibid.

Court hearings and trials provide insight into the networked character of the itinerant theatre trade. They highlight points of tension and even weakness in the network: the dependence on shipping and telegraphic communication, the reliance on performers vocal abilities, their willingness to work under extreme conditions. These cases also demonstrate the fragility of the theatrical contract in situations of extraterritoriality. Contracts concluded in one country could not necessarily be enforced in another. The 'letter of the law' varied in significant ways between England and its far-flung colonies, even though they had legal systems predicated on English law. It could be argued that Bandmann's often failed attempts to sue his own performers threw into relief a weak link in the network of itinerant touring over so many disparate jurisdictions. The role of law and litigation is paradoxical, because while contracts and their legal enforcement provide the foundation for commercial theatre (no contract, no commerce), the frequent disputes in which the theatre manager Bandmann regularly lost his cases suggest that it may have had a destabilizing effect on the whole business model.

7   Infrastructure: From Theatre to Cinema

Throughout his career, Bandmann worked tirelessly to buy, build or improve theatres along his circuit. He frequently complained about the substandard venues his companies were required to perform in: very often they were public halls, school gymnasiums or rough theatres consisting of little more than a stage and an auditorium. These endeavours were motivated not only by practical and pecuniary considerations – the bigger and better the theatre, the greater the potential revenue – but also, as we have seen in Chapter 3, as a means to form deeper relationships with the localities where he operated. We have defined as examples of micropolitics both the lobbying and the networks of local relationships he formed. While leasing a theatre already involved numerous relationships with municipal authorities, local businesses and potential users of the venue, building a new one expanded the network by multiple ties. In the logic of network analysis, this meant a multiplication of potential nodes and edges. It involved connections with architects, engineers and above all local partners who provided the necessary capital. It could also mean conflict and strife as cultural taboos and sensitivities were infringed upon. Theatrical infrastructure also needs to be understood in its broadest sense, because very early in his career, Bandmann explored the possibilities of the cinematic medium. He understood theatre in its original sense as a *theatron*, a place to watch. Whether it was live or cinematic entertainment depended entirely on strategic opportunity. In fact, many of the major building projects Bandmann was associated with were ultimately converted into cinemas, a purpose he had already designed them for.

In India, the theatrical infrastructure that Bandmann planned or constructed (there was a great deal more planning than actual construction) followed in the wake of theatre-building that had largely been initiated by the Parsis and their successful attempts to instigate proscenium theatre on the European model. It was most obvious in Bombay, where there had been a tradition of theatre-building going back to the early part of the nineteenth century, when in 1839 the first purpose-built theatre was constructed on Grant Road, to be followed by others.[1] In Calcutta, the situation was similar, although the first purpose-built theatre houses dated back even earlier. Bandmann's two Indian theatres, the Empire in Calcutta and the Royal Opera House in Bombay, should be seen, then, as a step towards a greater *embourgeoisement* of the medium, designed to cater for both colonial and elite Indian publics.

When Maurice Bandmann embarked on his first tour to India in 1900, he was confronted by extremely poor theatrical infrastructure. On subsequent visits, he continually criticized the lack of adequate performance venues. In Bombay, visiting companies were usually confined to the Novelty, a corrugated-iron structure notorious for its discomfort. In 1905 on his first tour back in the city, he complained, 'It is discreditable to a city of the magnitude and importance of Bombay, that it has no better accommodation to offer theatrical companies than a crude and wholly inadequate structure of wood and corrugated iron.'[2] The town hall in Singapore he described as 'a caricature of a theatre,'[3] while the public hall in Colombo was so poorly equipped and patronized that its manager was 'doubtful if Bandmann would send any more troupes'.[4] Each complaint (and there were many more) was a prelude to campaigns to renovate or build new theatres in these cities, a pattern he repeated along his circuit. Using his advance agents, he would often begin a newspaper campaign to sound out public opinion and also scout for possible partners. Although it was relatively easy to lease a theatre, building one was quite a different matter. For this he needed economically well-endowed local partners who were not only interested in theatre but had the necessary capital to finance such a building.

By 1907, he had established his headquarters in Calcutta as the lessee of a local theatre, the Royal, and here he began his first construction, the Empire. His partner was the Armenian jeweller and real estate developer Arratoon Stephen (1861–1927; see also Chapter 2). The Empire in Calcutta was built extremely quickly over a nine-month period. The foundation stone was laid on 28 April 1908 in a public ceremony widely reported by the press in India and beyond. It utilized the 'the latest designs' and made use of the cantilever principle for the roof construction,

---

[1] See Kathryn Hansen, 'Parsi Theatre and the City: Locations, Patrons, Audiences', *Sarai Reader* (2002), 40–9.

[2] 'The Theatre in Bombay', *The Times of India,* 23 May 1905, 4.

[3] 'A Chat with Mr. Bandmann', *Eastern Daily Mail and Straits Morning Advertiser,* 17 February 1906, 3.

[4] 'Melville's Notes from Ceylon', *The New York Dramatic Mirror,* 15 June 1907, 17.

Figure 7.1 Interior of the Empire Theatre. (*The Era*, 3 December 1908, 3. Newspaper Image © The British Library Board. All rights reserved. With thanks to the British Newspaper Archive, www.britishnewspaperarchive.co.uk)

which obviated the need for supporting pillars. A special feature was the attention to comfort and coolness. The theatre was designed and built by a local company, Macintosh, Burn and Company, and comprised four tiers – 500 seats in the stalls, 260 in the circle, 450 in the balcony and the gallery (Fig. 7.1). In addition, there were eighteen private and twelve proscenium boxes. It boasted 'crush rooms, loungers, and cloakrooms, and it is possible in 24 hours to transform the place into the finest ball-room in the East or a skating rink'.[5] The ceremony was presided over by local businessman and freemason Sir Charles Allen, who, after providing an extensive history of theatre in Calcutta, noted, 'anyone who could chain and entertain Calcutta residents and enable them to forget the disadvantages of the climate even for a brief space was entitled to their hearty gratitude'.[6]

[5] *The Empire*, 29 April 1908, 3.
[6] 'Empire Theatre – Laying of Foundation-Stone – Sir. Ch. Allen's Speech – A Brilliant Gathering', *The Indian Daily News*, 29 April 1908, 5.

Seven months later, on 3 December, the newspaper *The Empire* announced the opening of the theatre, which had been completed in record time:

It is a magnificent structure without and a surprise within, and it can be said safely that there is no playhouse in the East that can approach it for luxury and up-to-date-ness. The stage, a model of his Majesty's, is by Frank Matcham, the architect of the Hippodrome and the Colosseum. It is 40' × 64', of teak, and the whole of the centre slides away, giving every facility for scenery schemes and trapdoor effects.[7]

To underline the new theatre's metropolitan pedigree, the article stressed that in the following year the ceiling would be covered by paintings, and a motto borrowed from the Haymarket in London, *summa ars est celare artem* (the summit of art is to conceal art), would be placed in gold lettering over the proscenium. The theatre seated 1,300, and major features included ninety-one fans – some placed on columns so as not to obstruct sightlines, the others hanging – which addressed a major problem of theatre-going in the tropics: ventilation. The colour scheme favoured white and gold highlighted by red-velvet upholstery. A special feature was a twelve-foot-thick concrete roof as opposed to the usual corrugated-iron roofing employed in Indian theatres. It was also equipped with electricity rather than gas.

With this theatre, invariably advertised as 'the premier theatre of the East', Bandmann established his credentials as a major player with local interests and proved that he was not just an itinerant theatre-manager. As well as leasing the Theatre Royal and co-owning the Empire, Bandmann attempted to secure a monopoly on European entertainment in the city by also bidding for the lease of the Opera House in Lindsay Street, in which he was ultimately unsuccessful.[8] By 1909 his interests in Calcutta included proprietorship or joint proprietorship of the Empire, the Theatre Royal, the Albany Hotel and the Empire Rink and Hippodrome.[9] With these acquisitions, he extended his control over the local entertainment scene, at least that directed at European residents.

Once the building was finished, it had to be operated at a profit. Although as half-owner he did not have to pay rent, he was responsible for the programming. He was also co-proprietor with Stephen of

---

[7] 'The "Empire" Theatre', *The Empire*, 3 December 1908, 3.
[8] 'Theatre Deal: Mr. Bandmann Bids for the Opera House', *The Empire*, 19 October 1907, 3.
[9] Advertisement in *The Era*, 1 May 1909, 20.

the older Theatre Royal. For this reason, he regularly advertised in the trade papers in London, such as *The Era* and *The Stage*, extolling the virtues of the new and old buildings. The Theatre Royal was praised as the 'largest stage in the East', holding at ordinary prices £250, whereas the new Empire's holding capacity exceeded 'at ordinary prices more than any other theatre in India or the Far East'. Both theatres provided a resident scenic artist, full orchestra and permanent staff.[10] While the Theatre Royal was eventually demolished, the Empire became Bandmann's headquarters in India, and indeed of all his operations. It was for at least a decade truly the premier theatre in Asia, although it was soon rivalled by his own Royal Opera House in Bombay and the Imperial Theatre in Tokyo. Nevertheless, the Empire established itself as the place for social gatherings, especially for the Calcutta elite. In the highly stratified colonial society, theatres were places where all races could meet and mingle, provided they could afford a ticket. The social prestige accorded to the Empire and Bandmann's companies can be seen by the first-anniversary celebrations in December 1909, when the wealthy jewellery firm Rai Bedree Dass Bahadur and Sons reportedly placed fifty lakhs' worth of jewels at his disposal to display in the coronation scene of the musical comedy *The King of Cadonia*. Florence Beech, playing Princess Marie, was burdened with upwards of forty lakhs, whereas James McGrath in the title role was 'covered with jewels, one star ornament he will wear being worth more than five lacs of rupees … This, it is claimed, will be the most elaborate display made on any stage, not only in India, but throughout the world.'[11] Quite apart from being an excessive exercise in product placement, this display demonstrates the theatre's function as a locale of high social status. By this time, Bandmann, according to the American impresario Michael B. Leavitt (1843–1935), who toured India in 1904 and 1905 with the hypnotizers Lee and Zancig, 'practically [had] a monopoly of the show business in Calcutta'.[12] Although he was disparaging about Bandmann's 'second hand, inferior companies' and the Empire in particular – 'the acoustics are bad, and few people, beyond the first six rows of the stalls can hear what is being said on stage' – he was disparaging about most theatrical enterprises except his own.[13]

---

[10] See, for example, the advertisement in *The Era,* 8 May 1909, 20.
[11] *Homeward Mail*, 18 December 1909, 1602.
[12] M. B. Leavitt, *Fifty Years in Theatrical Management* (New York: Broadway Publishing Co., 1912), 676.
[13] Ibid., 671. Leavitt was mainly disappointed about the lack of sufficient spectators in India to guarantee an American-style long run.

As we have seen in Chapter 2, Bandmann invested heavily in the variety business from late 1913, establishing a new company, Bandmann Varieties Ltd, as a key player in the global All-Red Circuit. He renamed the Empire 'Palace of Varieties' and addressed Indian audiences more energetically than ever before. His advertisements in the English-language Bengali newspaper *The Amrita Bazar Patrika*, whose readership was largely the educated Bengali elite, emphasized the provision of *zenana* sections in his Empire Theatre. An advertisement from October 1914 shows that after Bandmann had renamed his flagship theatre and was showing a mixture of films and live acts, the advertising specifically targeted Indian audiences by framing the theatre as a 'House for refined Vaudeville'. The matinee at 6 p.m. was 'specially organised for the Indian gentlemen', and an additional note emphasizes the 'Special Arrangement for Zenana Ladies', which was a deliberate attempt to attract higher-class Muslim spectators in particular by providing segregated seating (see also Chapter 4).[14]

The Empire remained his headquarters until his death in 1922. He leased the building to his own company, Bandman Varieties Ltd, which actually owed him money on his death. His associates continued to operate the theatre for some years before it was finally sold, converted into a cinema and renamed the Roxy in the 1930s. It still operates under that name as a single-screen cinema. The characteristic 'tower' is still visible, and the basic concrete shell of the original theatre remains (Fig. 7.2).

Bombay: Royal Opera House

After the tribulations caused by the 'errant theatre' scandal in Bombay, discussed in Chapter 3, Bandmann relocated his activities to another area of the city. He first erected Bandmann's Hippodrome, which was also known simply as Bandmann's Theatre, on the Maidan as a provisional structure made of corrugated iron. It hosted his companies and other troupes until a more permanent home could be built. Opening on 25 September 1908 with a performance of Somerset Maugham's hit comedy *Lady Frederick*, the somewhat-drab exterior of Bandmann's Theatre belied a pleasing and comfortable interior, as discovered by a reviewer for the *Times of India* who was sceptical of Bandmann's venture to build a 'tin' theatre. He reported, 'The seating accommodation is arranged in rows right across the theatre, rising in the usual tiers from front to back, with a couple of small boxes near the stage. The

---

[14] 'Amusements', *The Amrita Bazar Patrika*, 5 April 1914, 3.

Figure 7.2 The Roxy Cinema, formerly the Empire Theatre, 2013. The original tower is still visible. (Author's collection.)

nakedness of the walls and roof is concealed with red material and electric lights and fans light the place very prettily and keep one pleasantly cool.'[15] This 'tin' theatre remained Bandmann's centre of operations until his most ambitious theatre construction, the Royal Opera House, was opened in 1911.

Undeterred by local opposition, Bandmann secured, together with his business partner, the Parsi coal merchant J. F. Karaka, a section on the corner of New Queen's Road and Matthew Road in March 1909 and set about constructing another theatre on the lines of the Empire, but even larger and more luxurious. The site was located at the northern end of Back Bay and Chowpatty beach, near the Malabar Hills and

---

[15] 'Lady Frederick: The Bandmann Company', *The Times of India*, 28 September 1908, 4.

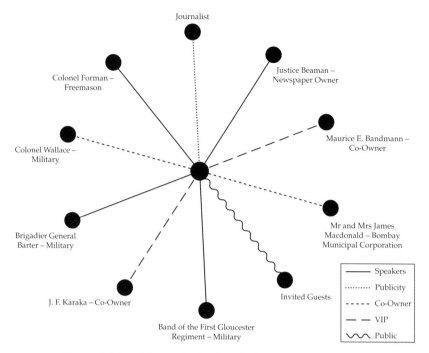

Figure 7.3 Participants in the foundation-stone ceremony of the Royal Opera House, 1909, represented as a network with the ceremony forming the central (ego) node.

Grant Road, the original centre of 'native' theatre. When the foundation stone was laid in July 1909, the goal was, on the one hand, 'to form a permanent home in Bombay for Mr Maurice E. Bandmann's companies',[16] but on the other also to provide 'a link in the chain of theatres managed by Mr Bandmann in the Mediterranean, the Far East, Ceylon, Calcutta, etc'.[17] The double goal of permanence and linking encapsulates the multivalent dynamics of theatrical circuitry of the Bandmann kind.

The laying of the foundation stone on 10 July 1909 was itself a theatrical ceremony, which Bandmann used to politically validate his undertaking. As argued in Chapter 3, such ceremonies can be seen as performative proof of underlying micropolitical networks (Fig. 7.3). Six hundred invitations were issued and leading Bombay dignitaries

---

[16] 'New Bombay Theatre', *The Times of India*, 10 July 1909, 7.
[17] *The Stage Archive*, 5 August 1909, 17.

enlisted: Justice Frank Beaman, a judge of the Bombay High Court, presided, and General Barter, the commander of the Bombay Brigade, the resident garrison, performed the actual laying of the stone. A notable presence was Colonel R. H. Forman, best known in Bombay as a Grandmaster of All Scottish Freemasonry in India, as well as an officer of the Army Medical Services.[18] The band of the First Gloucester regiment provided a programme of music ranging from Greig's *Peer Gynt Suite* to a selection of tunes from *The Girls of Gottenberg*.[19] At this point, the project was still entitled the Grand Opera House, or simply 'Bandmann's new theatre'. The ceremony was a major social event, and the *Times of India* reported on it at length, including verbatim transcripts of the speeches and an image of the building's proposed grand exterior.

Bandmann himself was not present for the celebration, as he was back in London recruiting new actors, but he directed activities through his local manager. In the publicity material and copy provided to the local newspapers, he emphasized the new building's place in his network. For example, the size of the stage (60' × 36') corresponded to 'the standard dimensions used by Mr Bandmann in all his theatres in the East so as to make the scenery carried about easily interchangeable – and large enough for the reproduction of great scenic effects'.[20] The longest speech was delivered by his partner, the Parsi coal merchant J. F. Karaka, who enumerated in detail the architectural innovations: 'The theatre will boast special features embracing all the most modern ideas in the construction of play houses and will, we hope, compare very favourably with the most popular of the London places of amusement... [I]t will add to the number of palatial buildings which grace this great city.' Ultimately, the theatre should provide an attractive venue for 'high class European companies' throughout the year, who tended to avoid Bombay because of its lack of modern theatre houses. Karaka emphasized that the architectural structure reflected and protected the highly stratified composition of audiences in a colonial city: 'The upper tiers will be reached by two separate staircases located in the towers, so that each class of ticket holder will have its own particular entrance and exit.'

---

[18] Freemasonry is often considered the prototypical social network; see Niall Ferguson, *The Square and the Tower: Networks and Power, from the Freemasons to Facebook* (New York: Penguin, 2018), esp. chapter 20.

[19] 'New Bombay Theatre', *The Times of India*, 10 July 1909, 7.

[20] *The Times of India*, 12 July 1909, 5. All quotations from the speeches are from this article, which was widely reprinted. Versions of it appeared also in London in *The Era* (7 August 1909) and in *The Stage* (5 August 1909).

Justice Beaman's speech was remarkable for its almost self-deprecating honesty. Beaman, who was born in 1858 in India and spent his whole professional life there, was also a director of the *Bombay Gazette*, Bombay's oldest English-language newspaper. In many ways, he was representative of the ruling colonial class, in that he had, he admitted, 'a Catholic ignorance of his subject ... [and] Bandmann had bidden him there that night, so to speak, to give his blessing to the undertaking'. Although he was clearly unimpressed by the theatre that was normally on offer, he articulated the hopes attached to the enterprise by the city's cultural elite: 'of bringing within their reach a higher class of drama and opera than they had yet been familiar with. Mr. Maurice Bandmann's was a name which had long been familiar to the playgoing public of the East ... a name to conjure with'. Beaman recalled the visits of Daniel Bandmann and expressed his admiration for the younger Bandmann's perseverance, 'and he hoped that a large measure of pecuniary as well as artistic success might crown his latest enterprise'. Beaman's speech was also notable for its self-reflexive tone as he alluded ironically to reasons behind Bandmann's invitation to him to speak: 'he would be doing himself an injustice if he did not grasp it [the invitation] and once again appear prominently before what he hoped was an appreciative public besides adding a new zest to the reading of his daily paper'.

Brigadier-General Barter, CVO, CB, who performed the actual laying of the stone, struck a less sceptical note and expressed his conviction that the erection of such a building 'devoted to lyric and dramatic art in a place where *none existed before* must have its effect on the refinement and culture of the people' (emphasis added).[21] Considering that the new theatre was situated within a stone's throw of the vibrant theatre quarter on Grant Road, dominated mainly by Parsi, Marathi and Gujarati theatres, the statement documents the entrenched cultural dichotomy between the English and the Indian theatre-going publics.[22] In his speech, Barter made repeated reference to Bandmann but none to Karaka, who despite his physical presence as co-owner and main financial backer, was elided discursively from proceedings. The list of speakers and notables demonstrates Bandmann's efforts to secure the project micropolitically as well as financially. The overwhelming presence of the military, the judiciary and the local press at the ceremony underscores the deeper network that

---

[21] Ibid.

[22] On the development of Indian theatres in Bombay, see Kathryn Hansen, 'Parsi Theatre and the City, 40–9.

such a project required. This support was doubly necessary because local opposition to the theatre had also been voiced, which, although not on the same scale as the 'errant theatre' controversy, reflected cultural opposition to theatre in principle: 'the grounds of objection are that property in the neighbourhood will be depreciated in value by the erection of the theatre because of the presence of large crowds and of undesirables such as Pansupariwallas [*paan* vendors] and orange sellers who will be found near the building before and after the performances!' Although the *Times of India* dismissed such objections as 'too ridiculous to deserve serious comment', they are still indicative of political opposition.

No doubt following Bandmann's instructions, the *Times of India* predicted that the new theatre would be ready by the following February. If the construction of the Empire in Calcutta was the model, then this was a realistic schedule. The prognosis proved overly optimistic, however. Work dragged on for another two years. One problem was an evident lack of theatrical fittings of the luxurious kind. In June 1910, an advertisement appeared in the *British Architect* asking for possible suppliers of 'CHAIRS and other FURNITURE, decorative iron fittings, and decorative materials, for stage, ceiling, and entrances, as well as electric fittings, dados, pavement, wall papers, and window glasses'.[23] In July 1911, although a long way from completion, the theatre had an improvised pre-opening with a demonstration of Kinemacolor, the 'new system of colour cinematography whereby the actual colours are photographed instead of the films being painted', that Bandmann was promoting in his theatres when no companies were present.[24] A special effort was made to mark the coronation of George V and to keep the theatre in the public eye. The new technology was staged in the bare concrete hull of the building, whose walls were draped with curtains, carpets laid on the bare earth and makeshift seating organized.

In September 1911, the *Times of India* announced that the theatre is 'now nearing completion' and described the projected offerings as well as the facilities, including ventilation by the 'exhaust fan principle'.[25] In some ways the building was never really completed, as additions to the decorations continued over several years. The name was changed from 'Grand' to 'Royal' Opera House to commemorate the 1911 Durbar,

---

[23] *The British Architect*, 10 June 1910, 9. Correspondence to be addressed to J. F. Karaka, Bombay.

[24] 'Kinemacolour in Bombay', *The Times of India*, 8 July 1911, 7.

[25] 'Theatrical Enterprise. Coming Bombay Season', *The Times of India*, 29 September 1911, 8.

and by the end of the year it was being used intermittently by touring companies, mainly Bandmann's own. After the season was complete, the theatre would close and building or decoration work would continue. By 1912, it was certainly functioning as a theatre when it hosted the legendary Lang-Holloway Shakespeare season, with its sold-out performances (see Chapter 4). By 1915, it had reached a more-or-less final state of completion when it had 'its permanent opening' as a cinema.[26] This did not mean that it no longer functioned as a theatre, but rather that the owner, J. F. Karaka, was trying to better capitalize on the building, as theatrical performances alone did not bring in sufficient revenue.

The completed theatre was documented in a publication entitled *From the Territorials in India: From the Royal Opera House* (1916).[27] This lavishly illustrated volume by J. F. Karaka to commemorate the arrival of the Territorial Army in India – troops who replaced the regular Indian army serving in the war – contains a detailed description of the theatre in its finished state. It provides ample illustration of the theatre's baroque opulence. From its classical Greek foyer guarded by statues of the muses to its gilded boxes in the interior, the theatre put a premium on luxury and European cultural achievement (Fig. 7.4). Karaka presented the theatre as a 'home of Art, Music, and Science', a place where the cultural elite could and should gather. On the more material level, it contained, like the Empire in Calcutta, up-to-date ventilation and cooling by means of fans and 'cold-air pipes' which sucked in air from the outside that passed over blocks of ice before rising up through iron gratings in the floor.

While the side boxes, with their 'beautifully designed dadoes', looked back to the eighteenth century (but could also be found in most 'modern' Frank Matcham theatres in England), the ceiling design attempted to accommodate up-to-date acoustic properties: 'By a scheme based on the principle of the horn of a gramophone, the ceilings are so devised that they form a long sounding-board high up over the stage.'[28]

The publication also contains detailed information on hiring the theatre by stressing its selectivity ('reserved for Artistes of reputed ability'),

---

[26] 'Bombay Amusements: Opera House Opens as a Cinema', *The Times of India*, 13 December 1915, 11.
[27] The full title reads *Territorials in India: A Souvenir of Their Historic Arrival for Military Duty in the 'Land of the Rupee'. From the Royal Opera House, Bombay. Prepared in Accordance with the Instructions of the Proprietor, J. F. Karaka*. Edited by J. J. Sheppard. Bombay: J. J. Sheppard, 1916.
[28] Ibid., 120.

VIEW FROM FLOOR TO CEILING OF THE RIGHT PORTION OF THE INTERIOR OF THE THEATRE (FROM THE STAGE).
[*Photo, by Vernon & Co.*]

Figure 7.4 Auditorium of the Royal Opera House, Bombay, 1916.
(*Territorials in India: A Souvenir of Their Historic Arrival... From the Royal Opera House, Bombay.* Bombay: J. J. Sheppard 1916, p. 123. Author's collection.)

its track record (Matheson Lang, Bandman Opera Company, Maud Allan) and the provision of 'high class stock scenery'. A special feature were the twenty-four dressing rooms equipped with electric fans and hot and cold shower-baths.[29] The Royal Opera House was certainly in its day the 'premier theatre in the East', superseding the Empire and rivalled only by the Imperial Theatre in Tokyo (where Bandmann regularly performed). Although Bandmann was intimately involved in the

---

[29] Ibid., 124.

planning and execution of the edifice, his connection with it was largely over by 1914. The reasons for the break with Karaka were never made public, but by the end of 1914 he had relinquished his share in the building and was performing in the newer and somewhat smaller Excelsior Theatre owned by J. F. Madan. There is good reason to suspect that Karaka was not prepared to host Bandmann's variety companies, which came to dominate his repertoire after 1914 (see Chapter 4). Karaka's emphasis on the elite of Bombay and artistic edification appear ill suited to the rough and tumble, to say nothing of the risqué nature, of variety. Despite this break, Bandmann is still remembered as the spiritus rector of the Royal Opera House, one of the few remaining (and most recently restored) colonial-period theatres in India (see Chapter 8).

Bandmann's various schemes to improve theatrical infrastructure run parallel to a wider, even global debate on the provision of public institutions for theatre, music and art. An example of this can be found in an article entitled 'The Theatre in Bombay', published in 1905 in the *Times of India*. The article was occasioned by a highly successful season by the Bandmann Opera Company, which played for two weeks 'in the torrid month of May' in the decrepit Novelty theatre.[30] While praising the quality of the performances, the author deplored the conditions of the wood and corrugated-iron venue, complaining that the provision of theatre was not regarded as a 'legitimate object of official or public enterprise':

There is much talk just now of schemes for new public halls and museums and art galleries: but we are inclined to think that a good many people would frankly own to a preference for a new and commodious and well-equipped theatre and opera-house. The citizen who supplies this real want will deserve to take rank as a public benefactor. Unfortunately for some occult reason, the provision of a theatre is not regarded by English opinion as a legitimate object of official or public enterprise, or as a suitable purpose to which to devote funds raised for commemorative reasons. That is one of the things they order better in France.[31]

---

[30] The Novelty Theatre was built in 1887 by the Parsi-owned Victoria Theatre Company. It was an exceptionally large theatre with a stage measuring 90' by 65' and could seat 1,400. It was demolished and replaced by the Excelsior Theatre in 1909 at the same location. See Hansen, 'Parsi Theatre and the City', 44.

[31] 'The Theatre in Bombay', *The Times of India*, 23 May 1905, 4. Indeed, the French colonial authorities supported opera in its colonies directly through subventions. See Michael E. McClellan, 'Performing Empire: Opera in Colonial Hanoi', *Journal of Musicological Research* 22 (2003): 135–66.

We find here an echo of similar discussions taking place in England and other countries, arguing for more public investment in the arts. The touchstone is usually the call for a national theatre or its equivalent for music. We can here observe the seeds of a global debate that begins in the nineteenth century, focused on classical music and the visual arts, which sociologist and neo-institutional theorist Paul DiMaggio, looking at the United States, has termed the 'sacrilization of the high culture model'. But as he notes, theatre did not lend itself to the 'transcendent, quasi-religious discourse employed to sacralize classical music or the visual arts…Of all the art forms to which the high culture models extended, the stage was the most improbable; the most commercially successful; the one least in need, as it was organised during the 19th century, of elite patronage.'[32] Indeed, Bandmann as a commercial entrepreneur was to some extent the exact antithesis of the high-culture model, yet his regular provision of high-quality professional entertainment, including Shakespeare, may have sown the seeds for later developments towards some kind of publically funded theatre, which in most colonies only came to fruition after decolonization.

The Last Empire

On 13 November 1920, Bandmann wrote to J. R. Crook, government engineer of Gibraltar, announcing his intention to apply for a two-year lease (with an option for renewal) of the Empire Theatre in order to convert it into a 'Cinema Theatre' for the 'exhibition of the very best and up to date English picture productions'.[33] On a recent visit, he had noted the lack of such films. He claimed to have a virtual monopoly on the distribution of English films in Egypt and Palestine, and enclosed a garish red and yellow letterhead of his Bandman Film Control company printed in pseudo-Egyptian style with pyramids and palm trees in the background.[34] Bandmann had indeed begun to extend his theatrical and cinematic empire into the Middle East in the wake of the

[32] Paul DiMaggio, 'Cultural Boundaries and Structural Change: The Extension of the High Culture Model to Theater, Opera, and the Dance, 1900–1940', in Michèle Lamont and Marcel Fournier, eds., *Cultivating Differences: Symbolic Boundaries and the Making of Inequality* (Chicago, 1992), 21–67, here 23.
[33] Unless otherwise indicated all quotations in this section are taken from a file kept at the Gibraltar Government Archives, Special File No. 24: Empire Theatre, Public Visitors and Brothels. It is abbreviated as GGA.
[34] The letterhead is reproduced in my blog entry on https://gth.hypotheses.org/285 (last accessed 2 April 2019).

First World War and the British presence in the region following the collapse of the Ottoman Empire. *The Era* reported in 1919 that he was expanding his 'Oriental Operations', which meant 'playhouses at Port Said, Beyrouth, Jaffa, Aleppo, Damascus and Jerusalem'.[35] These centres were now effectively under British and French control following the Sykes-Picot Agreement of 1916 and the end of the Ottoman Empire. The fact that he now claimed to 'rule the big Indian theatres from my headquarters in Cairo' suggests that he saw the Middle East as a new area for theatre-building.[36] He co-managed, in fact, three theatres in Cairo – the Empire, the Kursaal and the Piccadilly (a variety theatre), plus the Alhambra in Alexandria.

Crook noted in a memorandum to Colonial Secretary C. W. J. Orr that there were plans to demolish the theatre – which was in a bad state of repair and had been unoccupied for some years – in order to erect forty tenements in the chronically constricted fortress town.[37] Orr, however, proved to be very receptive to the idea of a cinema, and a correspondence with Bandmann ensued in which the latter extended his offer from two to three years and from cinema to light opera and variety. Initially, Bandmann seems to have planned to build a new cinema rather than convert an old one, because he inquired about the availability of a centrally located section: 'would you very kindly let me know whether any ground could be obtained for this purpose, and if so, in what locality. The minimum area required would be 100 × 80 ft.'[38] Although aware of the availability of the vacant Empire, he was reluctant to take it on, because of its location outside the town centre on Rosia Road. His main place of performance had been the Theatre Royal (1847), centrally located at the north end of Governor's Way, which had closed and, after a major re-fit, reopened in 1914.

On 19 December 1921, an agreement was signed between the Colonial Office and Bandmann, including a detailed 'Schedule of proposed repairs and renovations'. The lease was for three years at a nominal rent of £2 per month in light of the substantial investment required. Renovations included the installation of flush toilets on all floors, tiled urinals, a corrugated-iron roof, concrete steps and new floorboards for the veranda, plus major rebuilding inside and out. Two days before

[35] 'Theatrical Gossip: Bandmann's Oriental Operations', *The Era*, 27 August 1919, 8.
[36] 'Mr. Bandman's Plans – The Theatre in the East', *The Times of India*, 30 September 1919, 11.
[37] GGA 19.11.20.
[38] Bandmann to Orr, Colonial Secretary, 12 August 1921. GGA.

the scheduled opening, an advertisement in the *Gibraltar Chronicle* announced with typical Bandmann puff: 'New Empire Theatre. Licencee Maurice E. Bandman. Grand Opening This Saturday 4 Feb., 1922. NOTE. – This Theatre has been re-modelled, re-furnished, re-seated, re-decorated and re-lighted throughout at enormous cost.'[39] The costs had indeed been substantial, as a colonial official later admitted, and amounted to about £4,000.[40]

The final result was deemed impressive. A preview article, published a day after the self-advertisement, confirmed that

the building has received a complete renovation inside and out, most comfortable cane arm chairs have been installed, refreshment bars arranged for different parts of the house, cloakrooms and all modern conveniences... One is particularly struck by the excellent view of the stage obtainable from the whole of the seats. An orchestra has been engaged which will perform the music specially arranged for each film. The pictures screened will be sixteen by twenty feet and the fire proof operator's box is a novelty in Gibraltar, equipped with dual projection, thus obviating waiting between the parts or in case of a breakdown. At the back of the circle is a commodious lounge with liquor and coffee bars.[41]

At the actual the opening, the *Gibraltar Chronicle* enthused:

Wonders have been worked with the building since Mr. Bandman took it in hand, the seating arrangements could not be more comfortable, without a suspicion of crowding in spite of the fact that the big auditorium has accommodation for a thousand people. A very well got up programme giving all essential information was not the least welcome of the many provisions made for the convenience of the public.[42]

Unfortunately, the city council also had a say in the matter. In 1921, the first city council had been elected and had begun to flex its political muscles against the colonial administration.[43] In a long report, the council engineer outlined a list of additional repairs and alterations required. The building was not particularly solid, as it was constructed of wood, steel framing and corrugated iron and quite literally built on sand. One of the stanchions had even dropped about six inches, but the steel frame still provided enough flexibility. The engineer even

---

[39] *Gibraltar Chronicle*, 2 February 1922, n.p.
[40] Letter from J. Rowen to the Colonial Secretary, 18 February 1922. GGA.
[41] 'Opening of New Empire Theatre', *Gibraltar Chronicle*, 3 February 1922, n.p.
[42] *Gibraltar Chronicle*, 6 February 1922, n.p.
[43] The historian Stephen Constantine argues that 'the City Council became... not just a passive agent of government but an alternative interest group and actor', *Community and Identity: The Making of Modern Gibraltar since 1704* (Manchester: Manchester University Press, 2009), 332.

recommended the installation of dust extraction by vacuum cleansers. The involvement of the city council, often at odds with the colonial secretary, deepened and led to the issue of a license for 'cinema purposes only'. For live performances, the council insisted that Bandmann install a fire curtain between the stage and the auditorium, a major additional expense. Although the license was issued by Orr on 24 February 1922 and the cinema opened on 4 March, on 9 March, the day Bandmann died, the city council reiterated its opposition to a license for 'plays or other performances necessitating the use of scenery'. The council admitted, however, that in a wooden building, a fire curtain only provided a marginal improvement and that asbestos lining or even fire-proof paint might be acceptable.[44]

The first test case came in April 1922, with the impending arrival of The Scamps, a variety company that had been touring the Bandmann Circuit in the east and was now on its way back to England. The new manager of the New Empire, Charles Lewis (actually Lewinstein), the younger brother of Bandmann's secretary and main heir, Nancy Lewis, wrote to the colonial secretary on 19 and 20 April 1922 requesting permission in reference to a decision by the city council, pointing out that the company did not carry any scenery and that provision would be made to ensure fire safety: 'in the way of having a fireman in continuous attendance on the stage throughout each performance as also a goodly supply of water and sand fire buckets'. Exceptional permission was granted, but no further licenses would be entertained until the necessary requirements of the council were complied with.

This restriction was a major blow for the enterprise, because Bandmann had planned the New Empire as a stopping-off point for his companies on the way to his main circuit. It meant that the company was now operating an expensively renovated cinema for which high ticket prices could not be demanded. Charles Lewis cancelled the lease on 31 May 1924, and the building was returned to the Colonial Office or, more precisely, to J. R. Crook, the government engineer, who was once again saddled with the building. In a memorandum to the colonial secretary, he stated that no new tenders had been forthcoming and expressed his despair over its possible use: 'The building has since it was erected 20 years ago proved a "white elephant" and failing a satisfactory offer...should be pulled down.' This is indeed what happened – at a cost of £1,000.00 to the government of Gibraltar.[45]

[44] Letter to Orr by Chairman of the City Council, 9 March 1922. GGA.
[45] GGA, 25 July 1924.

From Theatre to Cinema

The New Empire in Gibraltar was designed as a cinema, and in fact Bandmann would have preferred to construct a purpose-built cinema if the colonial government could have provided a location. His plans to build a cinema rather than a theatre after the end of the war suggest that he was already shifting his operations towards the new medium. This was not just a sign of business acumen or opportunism, but rather an extension of a parallel track in his career as a theatrical impresario.

As early as 1897, Bandmann, together with his partner Malcolm Wallace, had begun to exhibit 'cinématographe' films both as a prelude to the main theatrical bill and in the context of variety performances.[46] As well as exhibiting the films themselves, they also hired out the new visual technology to eager theatre managers looking for variety in their variety shows. This consisted of sending a man, a machine and a selection of short films to the venue. That the 'product' was still beset with teething problems became evident in March 1897, when an irate theatre manager from Chester sued Bandmann and his partner for not providing what he had contracted to do. In his evidence, the manager claimed that 'the frame for the pictures was of a paltry character, and the screen itself a dirty rag. The performance was a wretched affair, and could easily have been beaten by an ordinary magic lantern... One scene depicted a horse race...The horses started at the winning post and ran in the wrong direction, to the amusement of the audience.'[47] Although the Lumière Brothers only exhibited their short films in 1895, by 1897 trade newspapers were already advertising the new medium under various names such as 'films', 'cinematographic machines', 'moto-photoscope', 'cinematograph' and 'kinematograph'. These offerings still shared the same page space with 'Wrestling Lions' and 'Captain Val's Theatrical Baboons'.[48] They were competing technologies that were gradually superseded by the bioscope, the forerunner of modern cinematic projection. Together, they can be regarded as a form of travelling cinema that was usually integrated into variety shows.

Once Bandmann established himself in Calcutta around 1907, he quickly entered the film business, although it remained very much a side-line compared to the theatrical tours. During a brief tenure as

[46] For example, a performance of his *Manxman* company on 23 February 1897 in Folkestone was preceded by '"Birt Acres" Royal Cinématographe, a Decided Attraction', *The Era*, 27 February 1897, 23.
[47] 'The Cinematographe at Chester Pantomime', *Cheshire Observer*, 20 March 1897, 8.
[48] *The Era*, 3 April 1897, 30.

sub-lessee and manager of the Lily Theatre in 1908 and before he
opened his new Empire Theatre in December of that year, Bandmann
combined live performances with offerings from the London Bioscope,
'with the actual films from the Alhambra Theatre, London, using projected electric light of 10.000 candle power'.[49] Film showings also
became a feature of the programmes at both the Empire and the Theatre
Royal in Calcutta when his companies were out of town. Competition
had already emerged in the form of Madan's Elphinstone Bioscope
Co., which began to develop the film business in Calcutta and elsewhere. This was the period of tent cinemas, which were often erected
on the Maidan in various Indian cities, particularly in Calcutta and
Bombay. As Kaushik Bhaumik has shown, by 1910 authorities were
worried about the safety aspects and 'the Government of Bombay
decided to phase out tent-shows in the Maidan amid growing worries
about fire hazards posed by cinematograph exhibitions'.[50] Bandmann
was directly involved, because his corrugated-iron Bandmann Theatre
had also been erected on the Maidan, and he too was asked to move.
He was informed that 'the maidan is now used for tent-shows that look
very disreputable'.[51] The Parsi businessman and entertainment entrepreneur A. J. Bilimoria, head of the Tata Bombay office, complained about
tent cinemas in a lengthy letter to the *Times of India*. As chairman of
the City of Bombay Building Co., Bilimoria was owner of the Novelty
Theatre and later the Excelsior and an important Bandmann partner
after the latter shifted his operations from the Royal Opera House to the
Excelsior.[52] As the owner-manager of significant theatrical and cinematic
real estate, he pointed out the unfair competition posed by the largely
unregulated tents.

When Bandmann finally opened the Royal Opera House in 1911,
although it was by no means complete, the attraction was cinematic, not
theatrical, with the introduction of Kinemacolor, 'a new system of colour
cinematography whereby the actual colours are photographed instead of
the films being painted'. He claimed to have secured 'the sole far Eastern
rights for the Kinemacolor process of animated photography by special

---

[49] 'Advertisement', *The Amrita Bazar Patrika*, 27 February 1908, 3.
[50] Kaushik Bhaumik, 'Cinematograph to Cinema: Bombay 1896–1928', *BioScope: South Asian Screen Studies* 2 (January 2011): 41–67, here 47.
[51] Proceedings of the Public Works Department, Bombay, 1909, 4. Cited in Bhaumik, 'Cinematograph to Cinema', 47.
[52] A. J. Bilimoria, 'The Bombay Theatres: Unfair Competition', *The Times of India*, 31 March 1910, 8. His company merged with Madan's operations, and he thus became by default a partner with Bandmann.

arrangement with Urban'.[53] The reference here is to American Charles Urban, who, together with his British partner, G. Albert Smith, developed a colour film process based on Edward R. Turner's earlier patent for a three-colour motion-picture system. This process was first shown to the general public in 1909 and 1911 (the latter being the same year as the preliminary opening of the Royal Opera House). Significantly, perhaps, one of the most famous Kinemacolor productions was of the Royal Durbar of that year to commemorate the royal visit of the new emperor and empress of India, George V and Mary.

Bandmann's interest in cinema was given a more secure business footing with the establishment of the Bandmann Variety and Asiatic Cinema Company in 1914 (see also Chapter 2). With a registered capital of Rs. 600.000, Bandmann was not just investing in the variety business but also in film production. In addition to setting up a film studio in Chowringhee Place (the location of the Empire Theatre), he also began to make films. *The Leader* published in Allahabad carried a report in 1914 about 'improvements' in the 'cinema business' in which 'the actual filming of plays' was beginning in India after having overcome technical problems of a chemical nature owing to the hot climate:

It was only a few weeks ago that the Botanical Gardens at Sibhur were used as a setting for a humorous Bandmann film and the jungle around Calcutta has often of late been used for the purpose of lending colour to various dramas and Indian plays. Yesterday morning, writes the *Englishman*, the Elphinstone Bioscope Company took our lawn at Eden Gardens for this purpose and the stage management of a gathering of gaudily-clad Indian actors and actresses provided a rare treat for those who know so little of the ways of the cinematographer.[54]

There is no record of this 'humorous Bandmann film' being completed, let alone shown. More productive was definitely J. F. Madan's Elphinstone Bioscope Company, which is generally acknowledged to be one of the earliest producers of Indian films. It is clear that Bandmann and Madan were rubbing shoulders by this time through their involvement in the entertainment business. However, two years later, they found themselves in direct competition, as both tendered for the British government's lucrative war propaganda films contract.

[53] 'Handsome Theatre for Bombay. New Building Being Erected by the Head of the Bandmann Companies', *The New York Clipper*, 2 September 1911, 8.
[54] 'Cinematograph in India: Probable Improvements', *The Leader* (Allahabad), 12 May 1914, 5.

The War Films War

In 1915, the war was not going well for Britain: troops were bogged down in France and Gallipoli. It was decided to open a new front – propaganda, also by cinematic means.[55] The office in charge of overseas propaganda situated at Wellington House was a covert operation run by Charles Masterman, aided by Ernest Gowers, who ran the cinematic division. In 1915, the decision was taken to produce a propaganda film entitled *Britain Prepared*. Sponsored openly by the Admiralty and the War Office and covertly by Wellington House, production was entrusted to Jury's Imperial Pictures and Kineto, under the supervision of Charles Urban. The film was exhibited widely, including the Indian subcontinent and the Far East. Gowers was entrusted with the task of finding a suitable distributor in the region and soon turned to Bandmann. Before he received a reply from Bandmann, however, he was contacted by J. F. Madan, who, via an agent in England, had already applied for permission to exhibit the film. Thus began a bidding war for the rights to distribute the first British propaganda film.

Paradoxically, Wellington House, which, being a secret operation, did not 'exist', was entrusted with the task of organizing highly public events for the cinematic exhibition of war propaganda. Over a period of about a year, Bandmann and Madan lobbied for what was obviously a lucrative contract in a monopolistic market. In a letter dated 26 May 1916, Gowers 'clarified' an extremely 'abstruse' situation, as he had to admit, and reported that the contract had been awarded to Bandmann: 'Mr. Bandman will have the exclusive right of showing the film "Britain Prepared" in India. It cannot be placed or effectively shown on any other terms than exclusive terms.'[56]

As it transpired, Bandmann obtained a virtual monopoly not just for *Britain Prepared* but subsequently for all films produced under the supervision of Wellington House. While it was acknowledged that Madan had the larger distribution network on the Indian subcontinent, Bandmann's operations extended all the way to Japan. It became clear that the exhibition of *Britain Prepared* – as well as other films, such as *The Battle of the Somme* – should have as wide a distribution as possible, and the Bandmann theatrical circuit ensured this. In the official

---

[55] For a discussion of the use of cinema for propaganda in India, see Philip Woods, 'Film Propaganda in India, 1914–23', *Historical Journal of Film, Radio and Television* 15(4) (1995): 543–53.

[56] Letter from Gowers to India Office, National Archives of India (NAI), Home Department 1916. Part B. nos. 416–420, 12.

agreement between the Cinema Committee and Bandmann, the question of distribution was an integral part of the contract. It laid out an exact itinerary of exhibition, stipulating wherever possible the actual theatres and cinemas to be used. The financial conditions were also extremely advantageous for Bandmann, but more importantly, the contract contained a provision that 'new films shall thereupon be included in the program and shall be in substitution for such films of the original programme as may be agreed'.[57] These so-called 'new films' meant in effect a monopoly on other propaganda films still to be produced. The agreement also allowed Bandmann to retain almost 70 per cent of total gross receipts. The Cinema Committee was extremely anxious that the film *Britain Prepared* receive maximum publicity, and for this reason, its premiere in Simla was timed so that the viceroy was present. Official correspondence with the British Embassy in Tokyo ensured a command performance at the Imperial Opera House in front of the emperor.

To manage this new lucrative business in war propaganda, Bandmann – who had by now dropped the second 'n' in his name – set up a new company dedicated to marketing and distributing the official war films. The letterhead declares him to be 'sole director for India in the East'. Indeed, the Maurice E. Bandman War Films became a well-known fixture on the theatrical circuit of India and the Far East. The exhibition was accompanied by generous advertising space in the local papers – much greater then he usually employed for his theatrical tours. An advertisement for the *The Battle of the Somme* (Fig. 7.5), the next film and, historically speaking, the most famous of the war films, conveys an accurate idea of the discursive strategies at work towards marketing this highly lucrative commodity.

This 'great War sermon' employs the common euphemistic term 'the big push' to characterize what is now considered to be the greatest disaster in British military history, with the loss of 20,000 men on the first day and over half a million total casualties on the Allied side alone. This film has been much analysed in recent years, especially in terms of its problematic authenticity in depicting battle scenes (mentioned explicitly in the advertisement). It is now accepted that some of these scenes were staged and filmed well away from the battlefield, although

---

[57] Agreement as to the exhibition of 'BRITAIN PREPARED' and 'OFFICIAL WAR FILMS' in India and the Far East between W. F. Jury, Esquire, and Others and M. E. Bandmann, Esquire, 23 June 1916. Vizard, Oldham, Crowder, & Cash, 51 Lincoln's Inn Fields. W.C. London. NAI, Home Department 1916. Part B. nos. 416–420.

Figure 7.5 Advertisement for *The Battle of the Somme*, in the *Amrita Bazar Patrika*, Calcutta, 8 November 1916, 8. (Newsbank – Readex.)

in the immediate vicinity of the Somme.[58] The advertisement is also a rich text in its own right, containing a plethora of information and rhetorical devices, including options in terms of reception: 'war in all its heroism, all its hideous ruin, or all its glory'.

Advertising for the next film to be exhibited, *The Battle of the Ancre: The Advance of the Tanks,* superseded the *Battle of the Somme* in terms of its pictorial and textual richness. The text accompanying the images was clearly written by the propaganda department and engages with the previous film's reception: it had been too graphic in its depiction of war, and evidently questions had been raised about its 'authentic'

---

[58] Roger Smither, '"A Wonderful Idea of the Fighting": The Question of Fakes in "The Battle of the Somme"', *Historical Journal of Film, Radio and Television* 13(2) (1993): 149–69.

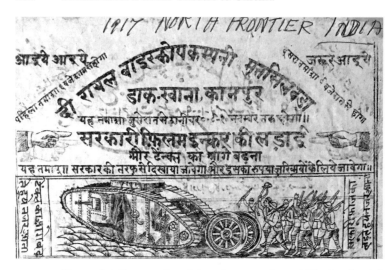

Figure 7.6 Poster advertising the screening of *The Battle of the Ancre* in Kanpur (Cawnpore), northern India, 1917. (Vanessa Lopez Family Archive.)

depiction of battle. It includes a note that reads, 'The British General headquarters is responsible for the censorship of these films and allows nothing in the nature of a "fake" to be shown. The pictures are authentic and taken on the battlefield.' The film depicted a later phase of the Battle of the Somme, which lasted until November 1916. A review in *The Statesman*, the Calcutta-based national daily, praised the relative restraint – 'there is less evidence of the horrors of the grim struggle now in progress' – and highlighted the 'appearance of the "tanks," these wonderful engines of destruction which … are leading our troops to victory and mowing down the German defences'.[59]

The distribution was not just limited to the Anglophone realm. Bandmann or the propaganda department also produced advertising in local languages. A poster from 1917 preserved by Bandmann's manager Stephen Lopez (Fig. 7.6) shows advertising in Hindustani for *The Battle of the Ancre*. Like the English version, it contains a relatively detailed synopsis of the action and reference to proceeds being donated to war charities.

---

[59] For a reproduction of the images, see Christopher Balme, 'Managing Theatre and Cinema in Colonial India: Maurice E. Bandmann, J. F. Madan and the War Films' Controversy', *Popular Entertainment Studies* 6(2) (2015): 6–21.

The triumphant and no doubt commercially lucrative progress of the Bandmann War Films did not pass without critical notice along the itinerary of his tours between Bombay and Tokyo. On 9 January 1917, *The Straits Times* in Singapore carried a report outlining not only Bandmann's newest theatrical offerings – his acquisition of 'the exclusive rights of a large and wonderful repertoire of the latest London successes with which to enliven theatre-goers in 1917' – but also a new undertaking:

Another enterprise is connected with films, and the Bandmann Film Control is being formed to supply picture theatre managers throughout India and the Far East with all British films. This is in addition to the Government pictures Britain Prepared and The Battle of the Somme, practically the whole profits of which go to military charities.[60]

The key word here is 'practically', because almost 70 per cent of gross receipts went to Bandmann, while 33 per cent went to the Cinema Committee, which did indeed donate its profit to war charities. This somewhat murky financial arrangement did not go unnoticed. A month later, the same paper reproduced an article from *The Peking and Tientsin Times* in which the whole question of distribution of propaganda for personal profit was criticized. The author compares the German practice of actually paying for their war films to be exhibited: 'They did not bargain for ninety percent of the receipts wherever their films were shown. In Tientsin they were willing to pay $2,000 for the use of a theatre in the Chinese City for two weeks, besides allowing the proprietor the benefit of all receipts at the door.' He complains that the British war films have not been shown in Tientsin or anywhere in north China. The reason for this neglect is, he argues, obvious:

The exclusive rights of exhibiting each series have been granted, upon what terms, we are not in a position to state, to Mr. Maurice E. Bandmann, who is following the natural course of a man enjoying so valuable a concession, of showing them where and when he can obtain the best financial results... [W]e are constrained to ask whether it was wise of the British authorities, in any case, to part with the exclusive rights in such valuable and inspiring films to an individual in the theatrical business.[61]

The contrast between a profit-driven English theatrical business model and 'stupid German money', i.e. state-supported distribution, could not be clearer and marks a fundamental difference between the two

---

[60] 'Untitled', *The Straits Times*, 9 January 1917, 6.
[61] 'Propaganda by Films', *The Straits Times*, 7 February 1917, 10.

countries, even allowing for the special case of propaganda which is exhibited in the first instance to 'produce the most moral effect'.[62] In fact, Tsientin and Peking were expressly included in the original agreement for *Britain Prepares,* and as Bandmann frequently visited these cities with his theatre companies, there was no reason not to include them. The criticism may have simply been premature. Bandmann responded to these criticisms by announcing to the press later in 1917 that he had remitted 'the magnificent total of £7,333 for distribution amongst charitable societies', adding with characteristic modesty 'that by no other single unaided effort has any such sum ever before been raised'.[63]

Towards the end of the war, Bandmann even began to entertain the idea of producing films himself for the War Office. A part of the propaganda effort involved demonstrating the commitment of imperial troops towards the war effort. In October 1918, Lew Marks, Bandmann's Calcutta-based manager, wrote to the Central Publicity Board of the Indian government informing them of a film entitled *Life of a Recruit.*[64] It is not entirely clear whether the work was fictional or documentary in nature, but probably the latter, as filming in Delhi was planned over a four-day period. There is no record of the film being completed or exhibited, no doubt because a few weeks later the war was over.

After the end of the First World War, the equilibrium of theatrical and cinematic entertainment shifted significantly as the business of touring live theatre became less profitable. A report in the *Times of India* published in 1920 confirmed the difficult business climate for itinerant troupes in Bombay. The rising transportation and rental costs of venues had not been matched by an increase in ticket prices, which had remained largely unchanged for a decade. The article compares the less than two hundred spectators at the 1,200-seat Royal Opera House to the full houses at the smaller but more expensive Excelsior Theatre. The latter (described as a 'bright little theatre') was owned by J. F. Madan and became Bandmann's preferred venue in Bombay, because patronage was better and 'a tolerably good company' could expect to attract good houses. Located opposite the Victoria Terminus, the Excelsior was more centrally located than the Royal Opera House, but the downside for companies was the high rental cost, which could not be easily recouped: 'The travelling expenses of a theatrical company are twice as high today as they were before the war, and there has been no compensating increase of revenue, for the theatre

---

[62] Ibid.
[63] 'Gossip and Opinions', *The Bioscope,* 20 September 1914, 9.
[64] Lew Marks to Sir Stanley Reid, Central Publicity Board, Simla, 8 October 1918. India Office L/PJ/6 1493.

going public in India is still small.'[65] Advertisements on the amusements pages of the Bombay and Calcutta newspapers show an overwhelming preponderance of films, while a Bandmann troupe often provided the only professional theatrical shows on offer. A year later, the *Times of India* reported that Madan & Sons 'had entered into a fresh agreement with Mr ME Bandman for the presentation of all Bandman Theatrical Companies exclusively at our theatres in towns where one exists, except in Calcutta, and also with Messrs Pathe Cinema of India for the exclusive rights throughout our territory for all Pathe films including the famous series'.[66] This notice marks the beginning of what was to become a veritable cinematic and theatrical empire in South Asia as the Madan company achieved in some places monopolistic control.

Due to its rapid spread, cinema was becoming a 'problem' in the eyes of colonial authorities and certain morally righteous sections of the Western population, owing to the importation of cheap American product, especially Westerns, and their problematic representation of race. The English trade paper *The Bioscope* carried an article in 1920 entitled 'Films in India', which adumbrated the problem: 'It must be obvious that films showing acts of violence on white women by Mexicans and such-like films are highly dangerous.'[67] The article reprised what was an ongoing public debate in India on the dangers of cinema (see also Chapter 4) and the need for censorship, which resulted in the implementation of a committee of inquiry whose report, published in 1928, ran to six volumes.

In an era predating state subsidy, theatre and cinema needed to be traded for a profit, and they could be highly profitable. The War Films were for Madan an opportunity lost, for Bandmann a lucrative one gained. This case provides insight into the mechanics and dynamics of theatrical entrepreneurship under the special circumstances of wartime propaganda. In the context of imperial politics, theatrical management needs to be understood not as a mere administrative task but as perhaps the most important activity in a complex actor network linking covert wartime propaganda, entrepreneurial vision, existing distribution networks, marketing strategies and fundamental unease about 'theatrical business' in a time of war. As demonstrated in Chapter 2, the theatre business was inherently pluralistic and diversified: outside the

---

[65] 'Bombay Theatre Prices – The Touring Company', *The Times of India*, 7 October 1920, 11.

[66] 'Trade and Finance', *The Times of India*, 14 May 1921, 6.

[67] 'Films in India', *The Bioscope* (1920), 18d–18e, here 18e.

metropolitan centres, managers such as Bandmann traded in spectacle ranging from puppet shows to cinema. Bandmann's success in obtaining the war film contract was determined largely by his pre-existing theatrical circuit, on which he showed almost anything. The monopolistic tendencies of his war film operation, aptly named the Bandman Film Control, was not of his own devising although certainly in his interest, but its operation went directly against the principles of free trade and competition. Yet all the large-scale theatre managers operating 'abroad' attempted to establish monopolies, and they were often successful. Bandmann's operations shifted slowly towards cinema, and after his death, his company, Bandmann Varieties Ltd., became associated exclusively with cinematic distribution in India before being absorbed by the Indian film company Humayan Properties Ltd. in 1936, which turned Bandmann's first purpose-built theatre, the Empire, into the Roxy. Fittingly enough, Humayan Properties is still the proprietor of cinemas in Kolkata.

8   Legacies

The Bandmann Circuit is an example of the globalization of theatre. Maurice Bandmann moved theatre companies around the globe in a carefully calibrated rotation system based on a constant supply of theatrical entertainment. When there was no theatre, then he offered cinema to fill in the gaps. His companies covered most major and minor genres except grand opera. The Bandmann Circuit is an example of a theatrical network, and I have used certain concepts from historical network theory to propose how we might explain the strengths of the heterophilic network model Bandmann employed. Heterophilic networks are usually contrasted with homophilic ones such as family and kinship, which are marked by strong ties and reveal relatively stable connections yet often lack the openness necessary to form links with other networks. Such alliances can be better effected by networks with weak ties which for all their instability lend themselves well for strategic alliances, however short-lived. Multiple ties were a precondition for the Bandmann Circuit to function. These were lateral, not hierarchical, but their very laterality or low homophilic connectivity meant that they could be quickly formed and detached as the situation required. The rapid economic and political globalization of the period 1870–1914 was predicated on the spread of horizontal networks that could operate largely without regulation. And despite the hierarchical structures of colonial administration, itinerant theatre could operate with little regulation.

Maurice Bandmann inherited a model of theatrical production based around the touring family, involving mainly a husband-and-wife double act and sometimes including the children. His innovation was to recognize that this model, so dependent on kinship and affective affinities, was not able to provide the necessary stability for the large-scale, multi-company touring that he envisaged. The actor-managerial model offers essentially a limited product range focused on one or two persons; the network model, on the other hand, enables any kind of theatrical material to be distributed: comedy, musical comedy, variety, cinema and dance. It can also survive its progenitor. Once the nodes and edges are in place, they can be reactivated and reused.

Bandmann's reliance on heterophilic networks had, however, a detrimental effect on his long-term legacy and place in theatre-historical memory. In the field of memory studies, there exists an important distinction between 'communicative' and 'cultural' memory. The former refers to memory reliant on direct, usually verbal, transmission and seldom lasts more than three generations. Cultural memory, in contrast, is anchored in monuments and institutions and can therefore endure much longer.[1] The communicative memory of Bandmann has all but disappeared. The last of his children, Millicent Joan, passed away in 2000, and she was still a young girl when Bandmann died in 1922. The only existing testimony to his cultural memory is the Royal Opera House in Mumbai, which, because of its recent renovation, has led to a resurgence of interest in the building, and by association in Bandmann in India. The Empire Theatre in Kolkata, now the Roxy cinema, still exists, but there is no communicative or cultural memory of its progenitor. Like most people of the theatre who were not writers or extremely prominent performers, Bandmann has been consigned to archival oblivion. Very few stage actors predating the screen age have any purchase on the cultural memory of the present; Sarah Bernhardt is one, Eleonora Duse another. Some exceptional dancers, such as Anna Pavlova or Nijinsky, have managed to remain 'household names' and enter our cultural memory. Theatre managers have even less claim to the scarce space in the archive, unless they were able to establish robust companies, such as J. C. Williamson in Australia, which survived until the 1970s, or the Shubert Brothers in New York, which still owns valuable theatrical real estate and maintains its own archive.

Bandmann's rapid disappearance was in part due to the nature of his profession, but also to the networked nature of his operations. We began by establishing an opposition between hierarchies and networks, with the former producing by definition the archives that historians are reliant on. Although Bandmann was no doubt a brand in his own right on his circuit – his name 'a guinea stamp' among itinerant theatre circles[2] – the circuit did not remain a 'monument to his memory' for very long, as the Singapore *Straits Times* incorrectly predicted in

---

[1] For this distinction, see Jan Assmann, 'Communicative and Cultural Memory', in Astrid Erll and Ansgar Nünning, eds., *Cultural Memory Studies: An International and Interdisciplinary Handbook* (Berlin: De Gruyter, 2008), 109–18.

[2] *Eastern Daily Mail and Straits Morning Advertiser*, 16 February 1906, 2.

its obituary.[3] On the contrary, his network survived little more than a decade. While some of his employees, such as Warwick Major, James McGrath, David Forbes Russell and Stephen Lopez, made use of the established infrastructure to pursue their own touring enterprises, the absence of Bandmann himself as the central hub removed the key node. In the language of formal network analysis, the network had reduced degree centrality, in the sense that Bandmann had provided numerous edges to other nodes. His betweenness centrality, i.e. the importance of the connections he enabled, was so pronounced that his absence deprived the circuit of its main relay station for information in both quantitative and qualitative terms. There were other reasons beyond Bandmann's premature death that resulted in the network's disappearance: most prominently the altered marketplace for itinerant commercial entertainment caused by the emergence of the film industry and rising transportation costs.

Preservation in cultural or communicative memory can function through association with prominent people. The example of Anna Pavlova in India illustrates the efficacy of the network beyond Bandmann's death. In late 1922 and early 1923, the star ballerina toured India as part of a world tour. The Indian section was promoted by J. J. Madan (J. F. Madan's son) in conjunction with Bandman's Eastern Circuit. In Calcutta, she performed at the Empire Theatre (Fig. 8.1) and only had a guest performance at the Madan-owned Corinthian Theatre, where – to her dismay – she witnessed a crude version of *nautch* dancing.[4] The distribution network was Bandman's Eastern Circuit Ltd., and the Calcutta performances took place at the Empire Theatre, leased by Bandman Varieties Ltd. In this combination of intersecting interests, we can see heterophilic ties at work. Although Madan actually bankrolled the tour, he permitted Pavlova to perform in Bandmann's Empire, as it was the more luxurious venue.

The Bandmann connection can also be traced in the subsequent careers of numerous performers and other employees. Perhaps the most prominent in terms of pure stardom on the Indian subcontinent was the Anglo-Indian actress Patience Cooper (1905–1983), who began her career as a chorus girl and dancer with Bandmann before switching to Madan's Corinthian Theatre and then to films, many of

---

[3] 'The Late Mr. M. E. Bandman: India's Greatest Amusement Provider', *The Straits Times*, 23 March 1922, 11.

[4] This distinctly underwhelming performance has almost legendary status in Pavlova folklore and in Indian dance history. For a detailed description and an attempt at explanation (the British were to blame), see Keith Money, *Anna Pavlova: Her Life and Art* (London: Collins, 1982), 313.

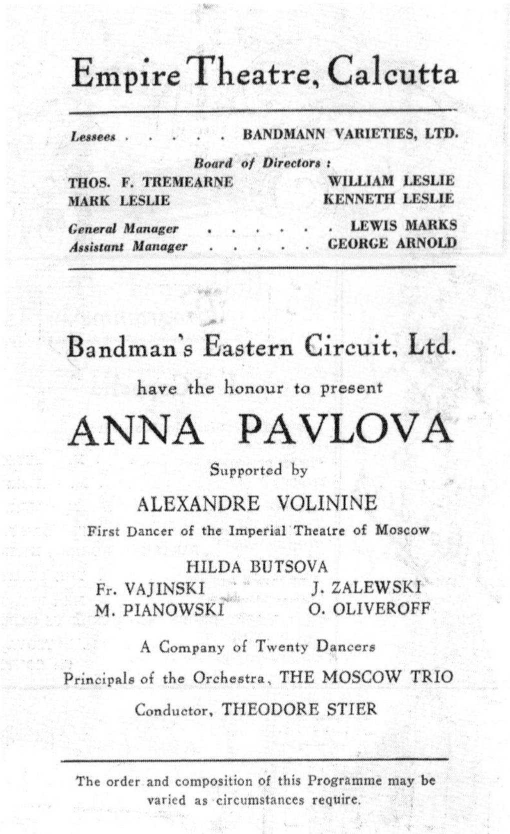

Empire Theatre, Calcutta

Lessees . . . . . BANDMANN VARIETIES, LTD.

Board of Directors :
THOS. F. TREMEARNE   WILLIAM LESLIE
MARK LESLIE   KENNETH LESLIE

General Manager . . . . . . LEWIS MARKS
Assistant Manager . . . . . GEORGE ARNOLD

Bandman's Eastern Circuit, Ltd.

have the honour to present

ANNA PAVLOVA

Supported by

ALEXANDRE VOLININE

First Dancer of the Imperial Theatre of Moscow

HILDA BUTSOVA
Fr. VAJINSKI   J. ZALEWSKI
M. PIANOWSKI   O. OLIVEROFF

A Company of Twenty Dancers

Principals of the Orchestra, THE MOSCOW TRIO

Conductor, THEODORE STIER

The order and composition of this Programme may be
varied as circumstances require.

Figure 8.1 Programme of Anna Pavlova at the Empire Theatre, Calcutta, December 1922. (Laurence Senelick Collection.)

which were directed by J. J. Madan. Although her collaboration with Bandmann was brief, it was significant in the sense that it provided a stepping stone or connection to the Parsi theatre and film industry, which was still in its infancy. According to Kathleen Hansen, Anglo-Indian or Eurasian actresses such as Cooper filled an ambivalent role in the burgeoning Indian cinema, which offered the Indian male spectator the fantasy of being able to 'possess the "English" beauty, and in so doing enact a reversal of the power relations that prevailed in British-dominated colonial society'.[5] Cooper looked European, which

[5] Kathryn Hansen, 'Stri Bhumika: Female Impersonators and Actresses on the Parsi Stage', *Economic and Political Weekly* 33 (1998): 2291–2300, here 2297.

enabled to her perform in musical comedies, but she could also 'pass' as a desirable Indian heroine in a long career that spanned both silent films and talkies.

Cooper was something of an exception, as most of Bandmann's performers were pukka English, an identity they could use later to good effect. British actor Leyland Hodgson became a Hollywood actor of the 1930s and 1940s, playing quintessentially English roles: officers, butlers and 'gentlemen'. From 1915 to 1919, Hodgson toured with the Bandmann Opera Company and was considered a main attraction as the romantic male lead.[6] Another British-born Hollywood actor was Reginald Denny, who toured the East with Bandmann for a number of years before the First World War. A handsome character actor, his good looks made him a star in the silent and talkie era, and he featured in films such as Hitchcock's *Rebecca*.

Interestingly, dance rather than musical comedy became the medium through which the Bandmann network continued to function and which, indirectly at least, kept the name alive. The activities and involvement of Stephen Lopez with new Indian dance illustrate how distributional networks could still function even though the progenitor, Bandmann, was no longer alive. Stephan Lopez, one of Bandmann's managers, continued to work as an agent and impresario along the established trade routes of the Bandmann Circuit. Lopez, who came from a Gibraltese family, joined the company around 1900 in Gibraltar as a stage carpenter, and from there he worked his way up to the positions of advance manager and then company manager. In the latter capacity he managed the Comedy Company and other troupes. After Bandmann's death, he stayed on in India with his wife, Bessie Webb (also a performer), and remained involved with Bandmann Varieties Ltd. until the late 1920s before working as an independent tour manager based in Calcutta. He retired to the UK at the beginning of the Second World War.

Lopez worked actively on behalf of Uday Shankar and Menaka, two Indian dancers who pioneered hybrid forms that found enthusiastic responses at home and abroad. They were, in turn, influenced by Anna Pavlova's two Indian tours (1922–1923 and 1928), which are generally acknowledged to have had a galvanizing effect on Indian dancers looking for new idioms.[7] Pavlova's world tours led to a profound interest in

---

[6] Philip Greave, 'Theatre Gossip and Sketches', *The Empire* (Calcutta), 14 June 1919, 9.

[7] See, for example, Janet O'Shea, *At Home in the World: Bharata Natyam on the Global Stage* (Middletown: Wesleyan University Press, 2007); and Jennifer Fisher, 'The Swan Brand: Reframing the Legacy of Anna Pavlova', *Dance Research Journal* 44(1) (2012): 51–67.

HAREN GHOSH

presents

"He is endowed with one of the finest and most perfect bodies I have even seen in men in any country."
— *Pavlova.*

UDAY SHANKAR

&

his company of

HINDU DANCERS AND MUSICIANS

SEASON — 1935 — INDIA.

Calcutta Shows open on 26th January, 1935
NEW EMPIRE THEATRE.

Figure 8.2 Programme of Uday Shankar's Indian season, Calcutta, New Empire Theatre, 1935.

Indian culture on the part of the Russian prima ballerina. In 1926, she encountered at a private soirée in Paris a young Indian art student, Uday Shankar (the older brother of Ravi Shankar), who was performing Indian dance (Fig. 8.2). She was looking for artists to collaborate with on India-based themes, and he joined her company. When she returned to India in 1929, she included two 'Indian ballets' in her programme: *Radha and Krishna* and *Hindu Wedding*. Uday Shankar went on to become a pioneer of modern dance in India and is best known for creating a fusion style of dance that adapted European theatrical techniques to Indian classical dance forms, imbuing them with elements of Indian classical, folk and tribal dance – a style he later popularized in India, Europe and the United States in the 1920s and 1930s. When Shankar embarked on tours to India and the Far East, he travelled through the Bombay-based Showtrust theatrical agency, whose business manager and representative was Stephen Lopez, Bandmann's company manager. Showtrust were the sole booking agents in India for Uday Shankar's Hindu Dancers & Musicians.

Figure 8.3 Programme of Menaka, 1935. (Vanessa Lopez Family Archive.)

As mentioned earlier, Lopez also represented Menaka (Fig. 8.3). Born Leila Sokhey, she was an instrumental figure in the transformation of the maligned North Indian *nautch* dance to the respectable *kathak* in the 1930s. Not only was she among the first Brahmin women to perform *kathak* on the public stage at a time when public female performance was stigmatized due to its association with prostitution, but she was also a pioneer in refashioning the form as modern dance-drama. She introduced *kathak* technique to the international community for the first time through her troupe's tours of Europe and Southeast Asia. She had a close working relationship with Lopez, whom she entreated to act as her tour manager.[8]

---

[8] Undated note from Menaka to Lopez, ca. 1935, Vanessa Lopez Collection. Menaka was particularly popular in Germany, where she performed at the international dance competitions during the 1936 Berlin Olympics and was awarded – together with her orchestra – an honorary certificate signed by Rudolf von Laban. A copy of this award is contained in the Lopez collection.

If there is any memory of Bandmann in India today, his main theatre of operations, then it is due to the Royal Opera House (ROH) in Mumbai. An iconic building that gives its name to the eponymous precinct known as Opera House, it had fallen into disrepair and was closed in 1992 for safety reasons. As we have seen in Chapters 3 and 7, Bandmann severed his connection with the building soon after its completion, possibly due to disagreements with J. F. Karaka, the co-owner and main investor. Although a number of illustrious artists appeared there, in 1927 ownership passed to the Bank of Baroda, which in turn leased it to Madan Theatres Ltd. In 1932, it was resold to The Ideal Pictures, Ltd., which resolved to renovate the building. In 1936, the opera house/cinema was subjected to a major overhaul, especially in the interior, to make it more suitable for cinematic projection.[9] Although it continued to host plays, political meetings and even fashion shows, the Royal Opera House figured in the city's communicative memory as a cinema that showcased Bollywood movies.

The status of the theatre changed in the late 1990s, when the building and the whole precinct were identified as a cultural heritage site by local historian and tireless advocate for Mumbai's historical buildings, Sharada Dwivedi (1942–2012). The Royal Opera House was placed on the Mumbai cultural heritage watch list as a Grade 2 heritage building. In 2002, the Mumbai Heritage Conservation Society published detailed conservation guidelines for the building and other Edwardian structures in the precinct.[10] The publication described the theatre as a landmark building situated at the conjunction of three busy arteries: Mama Paramanand Road (formerly New Queens Road), Ram Mohan Roy Road and Sardar Vallabhbhai Road. Together, they form an important architectural ensemble built around 1900 as part of efforts by the Bombay Improvement Trust to 'modernize' the neighbourhood. One hundred years later, the surviving buildings represent three distinct styles: Edwardian, Indo-Edwardian and Vernacular. Many, if not most of them, were listed as Grade 2 (buildings of regional or local importance possessing special architectural or aesthetic merit or cultural or historical value) or Grade 3 (buildings evoking architectural, aesthetic or sociological interest which determine the character of the locality).[11]

---

[9] See two articles in the *The Times of India*: 'The Royal Opera House: Renovated Royal Opera House Reopens Today – the Story of the City's Chief Theatre', 6 February 1936, 5–6; and 'From Opera to Talkies – Transformation of Bombay Theatre', 6 February 1936, 8.

[10] *Conservation Guidelines for Opera House Precinct* (Mumbai: MMR-Heritage Conservation Society, 2002).

[11] Ibid., 11.

Of the twenty-six buildings listed, the Royal Opera House was by far the most important. The guidelines stipulate in considerable detail how buildings should be conserved in order to retain the architectural character of the area and, by extension, to prevent the precinct from falling victim to the indiscriminate development typical of Mumbai in recent times.

The Royal Opera House had been purchased by the Maharaja of Gondal Shri Vikramsinhji in 1952 and had remained in possession of the family ever since, despite its closure in 1992. In 2008, conservation plans were announced. The new Maharaja of Gondal commissioned the prize-winning conservation architect Abha Narain Lambah with the task of restoring the building according to the stringent specifications of the Mumbai Heritage Conservation Society and with a view to not just returning the Royal Opera House to its original state but making it a working theatre and a cultural space for the city.[12] By 2011, the building's structural stability had been ensured and work on the dilapidated façade had begun. This led, in turn, to renewed public interest in the derelict structure.[13]

I first visited the site in 2013, by which time the exterior work had been completed but work on the interior had still to begin. I met with Abha Narain Lambah, and she explained that the team still had little knowledge of the original interior. I was able to contribute to the restoration effort by providing the conservation team with rare written and visual material describing the interior of the building anno 1916.[14] In an interview, Lambah acknowledged this help.[15]

On 20 October 2016, the historic Royal Opera House in Mumbai reopened after extensive restoration (Fig. 8.4), which had been a huge job, as Lambah acknowledged on the eve of the opening:

[12] Shweta Desai, 'Glorious Days Set to Return for Royal Opera House', *The Indian Express*, 23 May 2008.
[13] Supriya Nair, 'Opera around the Corner', www.livemint.com/Leisure/ VHH6Mo35YzYkGI1YooU57J/Opera-around-the-corner.html (last accessed 31 March 2019).
[14] While researching a term paper for an MA seminar, a student research assistant, David Berger, located an extremely rare publication in the Bavarian State Library: J. J. Sheppard, ed., *Territorials in India: A Souvenir of Their Historic Arrival for Military Duty in the 'Land of the Rupee'. From the Royal Opera House, Bombay. Prepared in Accordance with the Instructions of the Proprietor, J. F. Karaka* (1916). This publication (World Cat lists only two extant copies) contains a detailed description with photographs of the interior.
[15] Reema Gehi, 'After a Gap of 23 Years, Opera House Will Reopen in October', 17 September 2016, *Mumbai Mirror*, www.mumbaimirror.indiatimes.com/ mumbai/cover-story/Mumbais-Opera-House-to-finally-reopen-in-October/ articleshow/54373881.cms (last accessed 31 March 2019).

Figure 8.4 View of the Royal Opera House, Mumbai, after exterior renovation, March 2015. (Author's collection.)

More than 54,000 days of manpower, skilled craftsmanship, stone sculptors, stain glass conservators, art restorators and technical engineers have gone into recreating this piece of history. About 100 years ago the Opera House was India's most stunning cultural venue. We hope with this restoration it would open its doors once again to some of the finest live performances in music, dance, theatre, fashion and opera.[16]

The opening attracted a great deal of media attention in India and beyond. I was interviewed for one of India's leading online cultural publications, *scroll.in*, to provide more information about Bandmann and his largely forgotten role in India's theatre history.[17] Since its reopening, the Royal Opera House has developed into a performance venue hosting a wide range of performance genres from operatic recitals to comedy.

---

[16] Ibid.
[17] Arkash Kikare, 'Remembering the 20th Century Theatre Impresario Who Built Mumbai's Iconic Opera House', scroll.in/article/818739/remembering-the-20th-century-theatre-impresario-who-built-mumbais-iconic-opera-house (last accessed 31 March 2019).

With its restoration as a cultural heritage building and reopening as a working performance venue, the Royal Opera House has come full circle. Under Bandmann, the theatre was inaugurated, in a semi-completed state, in 1911 with a demonstration of Kinemacolor, followed by the master magician the Great Raymond, before successful seasons by Shakespearean actors such as Allan Wilkie (April 1912) and Matheson Lang (May 1912) provided an artistic seal of approval. Its long inter-regnum as a cinema gave way to the twin pressures of video rentals and multiplex cinemas, and it thus reached a provisional endpoint in 1992. Now the new old theatre has been revived under the twin impera-tives of cultural heritage preservation on the one hand and sustainable commercial rentals on the other. Although heralded as India's 'only surviving Opera House', its current use has as little connection with the Italian performance genre as it did in Bandmann's day (unless one were to extend the term 'opera' to include musical comedy). 'Opera House' functions instead as a marker of social and artistic refinement, and its self-proclaimed status as the city's 'Cultural Crown' would seem to hark back directly and without remorse to a bygone age.

Looking for Bandmann

As noted in the Introduction, there has been, apart from fleeting refer-ences in a few scattered footnotes, no scholarly interest in Bandmann amongst theatre historians. I first came across his name in a brief para-graph in Tracy C. Davis's book *The Economics of the British Stage*, where she notes that he remitted royalties to George Edwardes' Gaiety Theatre Co. On the basis of the stationery, Davis reconstructed the extent of his circuit, which 'extended from Calcutta, Colombo, Bangalore, Bombay, Amballa, Lahore, Quetta, and Karachi to Alexandria and Cairo in the west and Rangoon, Kuala Lumpur, Singapore, Manila, Hong Kong, Shanghai, Tiensin, Osaka, Kobe, Kyoto, and Yokohama in the east'.[18] Further research drew a blank, because he did not feature in library catalogues or bibliographical databases: he neither produced texts, nor had texts been written about him. A first breakthrough was the dis-covery of a superb private website devoted to one of Bandmann's man-agers, Stephen Lopez. He kept extensive scrapbooks of his time with Bandmann, which extended from 1900 to 1922 and after. His grand-daughter, Vanessa Lopez, had painstakingly reconstructed her grandfa-ther's career on a website which provides still the most detailed record of Bandmann's activities, including a touring diary, posters, programs,

---

[18] Davis, *Economics of the British Stage*, 351.

photographs and even receipts.[19] A second breakthrough came when I discovered that the Singapore National Library had digitalized all its newspapers from the mid-nineteenth century onwards. The name 'Maurice E. Bandmann' generated over 1,500 hits. It quickly became apparent that he visited Singapore on a regular basis with his companies, and the local newspapers carried not only numerous advertisements but also articles and interviews. The next stage of research, which continues until the present, involved locating digitalized newspapers along the circuit. This became a waiting game as ever more material became available. It also became a negotiation between publicly accessible material available through the national libraries of Singapore, Australia or Hong Kong and the increasingly proprietary world of large-scale digitalization projects of ProQuest, newspaperarchive.com and Readex.com. Access to these invaluable resources requires, unfortunately, memberships or friendly cooperation with colleagues at well-financed US universities. Knowledge we can gain is dependent on the limits of the archive, which in this case is expanding all the time in quantity but also, regrettably, in cost.

Bandmann's family history could be reconstructed with the help of genealogy websites such as ancestry.com and findmypast.co.uk. The former includes a rich trove of ancillary documents such as passport applications, including photographs and shipping timetables, so that the exact movements of Bandmann and his company members could be traced. I also employed a professional genealogist to reconstruct the unspectacular fortunes of Bandmann's estranged wife, Moyna, and their daughters, in the vain hope that some personal papers might have survived.

Old-style archival research was also necessary. Many days were spent in the less-than-salubrious environment of the national newspaper archive in Kolkata (when it was still housed at Esplanade) and the Maharashtra State Archives in Mumbai, where I consulted physical copies of newspapers. Handling such source material became a highly ambivalent experience as pages crumbled under the touch. Additional newspapers were consulted on microfilm at the British Library. Fortunately, however, most of the sources for this study were available in digital form. Indeed, there is no doubt that Bandmann is a product of the digital age. Without digital resources, mainly newspapers, itinerant theatre of his kind cannot be reconstructed: it could be argued that, historiographically speaking, Maurice E. Bandmann and

---

[19] See www.joydiv.org/familygoingback/career.htm (last accessed 30 August 2018).

his companies did not exist prior to the technical possibilities that make this activity accessible. Since most archives and libraries are founded on local and national imperatives but hardly ever on transnational ones, global theatre research requires tools and methods that transcend such spatial constraints.

Archival research, both digital and physical, confirmed the underlying thesis of this study – that Bandmann's operations were founded on the principle of heterophilic networks. As Niall Ferguson notes, archives are produced and maintained within hierarchical structures such as nation states or large corporations, whereas networks by definition leave behind few traces.[20] Bandmann features almost nowhere in national archives, because colonial administrations did not regard itinerant theatre as part of their administrative responsibility. The new nation states which maintain most of the archival resources along the circuit have little interest in their colonial 'prehistory', preferring instead to start with a clean slate after independence.

The final stage was Gibraltar, which I visited to consult the government archives there (which did have material located in a file entitled 'Empire Theatre, Public Visitors and Brothels') and in an attempt to locate Bandmann's gravestone. He was buried in the North Front Cemetery next to the airport.[21] Although there was a record of a plot number, the area was extensive and overgrown with grass, weeds and flowers. Quite apart from the vegetation, many gravestones had been polished clean by the corrosive salt air, which rendered many inscriptions illegible. As I could be fairly sure that nobody had tended the grave for ninety years, and the cemetery's own records were imprecise, it became clear, sadly, that even this small monument to Bandmann's cultural memory had disappeared forever.

---

[20] See Ferguson, *The Square and the Tower*, xx, and the Introduction to this book.
[21] For an anecdotal account of researching in Gibraltar, see my article 'Looking for Maurice E. Bandmann in Gibraltar', https://gth.hypotheses.org/277 (last accessed 2 April 2019).

Bibliography

Published Sources

Abu-Lughod, Janet L. *Cairo: 1001 Years of the City Victorious*. Princeton, NJ: Princeton University Press, 1971.

Acemoglu, Daron and James Robinson. *Why Nations Fail: The Origins of Power, Prosperity, and Poverty*. New York: Crown, 2012.

Anae, Nicole. "'The Majestic Hebrew Racial Ideal": Herr Daniel E. Bandmann's Shylock on the Australian Stage, 1880–1883'. *Shakespeare Jahrbuch* (2014): 128–45.

Anderson, G. M. *Tivoli King: Life of Harry Rickards, Vaudeville Showman*. Kensington, NSW: Allambie, 2009.

Appadurai, Arjun. *Modernity at Large: Cultural Dimensions of Globalization*. Minneapolis, MN: University of Minnesota Press, 1996.

Assmann, Jan. 'Communicative and Cultural Memory'. *Cultural Memory Studies: An International and Interdisciplinary Handbook*. Eds. Astrid Erll and Ansgar Nünning. Berlin: De Gruyter, 2008, pp. 109–18.

Badawi, Muhammed. *Modern Arabic Drama in Egypt*. Cambridge: Cambridge University Press, 1987.

Balme, Christopher. *The Theatrical Public Sphere*. Cambridge: Cambridge University Press, 2014.

'The Bandmann Circuit: Theatrical Networks in the First Age of Globalization'. *Theatre Research International* 40 (2015): 19–36.

'Managing Theatre and Cinema in Colonial India: Maurice E. Bandmann, J. F. Madan and the War Films' Controversy'. *Popular Entertainment Studies* 6(2) (2015): 6–21.

'Repertoire and Genre'. *A Cultural History of Theatre in the Age of Empire*. Ed. Peter W. Marx. London: Bloomsbury, 2017, pp. 181–201.

Balme, Henry. 'Between Modernism and Japonism: The Mousmé and the Cultural Mobility of Musical Comedy'. *Popular Entertainment Studies* 7(1–2) (2016): 6–20.

Bandmann, Daniel E. *An Actor's Tour; or, Seventy Thousand Miles with Shakespeare*. Boston, MA: Cupples, Upham and Co., 1885.

Barraclough, Geoffrey, ed. *Times Atlas of World History*. 3rd ed. London: HarperCollins, 1989.

Becker, Tobias. 'Entertaining the Empire: Theatrical Touring Companies and Amateur Dramatics in Colonial India'. *The Historical Journal* 57 (2014): 699–725.

Benton, Lauren. 'Law and Empire in Global Perspective: Introduction'. *American Historical Review* 117 (2012): 1092–1100.

Bhaumik, Kaushik. 'Cinematograph to Cinema: Bombay 1896–1928'. *BioScope: South Asian Screen Studies* 2(1) (2011): 41–67.

Birla, Ritu. *Law, Culture, and Market Governance in Late Colonial India.* Durham, NC: Duke University Press, 2009.

Bratton, Jacky. *New Readings in Theatre History.* Cambridge: Cambridge University Press, 2003.

The Making of the West End Stage: Marriage, Management and the Mapping of Gender in London, 1830–1870. Cambridge: Cambridge University Press, 2011.

Brett, Henry, Sir and T. C. Tilly. *Brett's New Zealand and South Pacific Pilot.* Auckland: Henry Brett, 1881.

Burt, Ronald S. *Brokerage and Closure: An Introduction to Social Capital.* Oxford: Oxford University Press, 2005.

Cabranes-Grant, Leo. *From Scenarios to Networks: Performing the Intercultural in Colonial Mexico.* Evanston, IL: Northwestern University Press, 2016.

Campbell, Patrick. *My Life and Some Letters.* New York: Dodd, Mead and Co., 1922.

Chandler, Alfred D. *The Visible Hand: The Managerial Revolution in American Business.* Cambridge, MA: Harvard University Press, 1977.

Choudhury, Ranabir Ray (ed.). *Early Calcutta Advertisements, 1875–1925: A Selection from* The Statesman. Calcutta: Nachiketa Publications, 1992.

Cochrane, Claire. *Twentieth-Century British Theatre: Industry, Art and Empire.* Cambridge: Cambridge University Press, 2011.

Cohen, Matthew Isaac. *The Komedie Stamboel: Popular Theater in Colonial Indonesia, 1891–1903.* Athens, OH: Ohio University Press and KITLV Press, 2006.

Performing Otherness: Java and Bali on International Stages, 1905–1952. Basingstoke: Palgrave Macmillan, 2010.

Cohen, Matthew Isaac and Laura Noszlopy. 'Introduction'. *Contemporary Southeast Asian Performance: Transnational Perspectives.* Newcastle upon Tyne: Cambridge Scholars Publishing, 2010, 7.

Constantine, Stephen. *Community and Identity: The Making of Modern Gibraltar since 1704.* Manchester: Manchester University Press, 2009.

Danahay, Martin A. and Alex Chisholm. *Jekyll and Hyde Dramatized.* Jefferson, NC: McFarland, 2005.

Darwin, John. *Unfinished Empire: The Global Expansion of Britain.* London: Penguin Press, 2012.

Das Gupta, Hemendra Nath. *The Indian Stage.* Vol. 4. Calcutta: Metropolitan Printing & Publishing House, 1944.

Davis, Tracy C. *Actresses as Working Women: Their Social Identity in Victorian Culture.* London: Routledge, 1991.

The Economics of the British Stage, 1800–1914. Cambridge: Cambridge University Press, 2000.

'Female Managers, Lessees and Proprietors of the British Stage (to 1914), a Database Collected and Introduced by Tracy C Davis'. *Nineteenth Century Theatre* 28(2) (2000): 115–44.

The Broadview Anthology of Nineteenth-Century British Performance. Peterborough, ON: Broadview Press, 2012.

Deleuze, Gilles and Félix Guattari. *Anti-Oedipus: Capitalism and Schizophrenia.* Trans. R. Hurley, M. Seem and H. R. Lane. London: Athlone Press, 1984. *A Thousand Plateaus.* Trans. Brian Massumi. Minneapolis, MN: University of Minnesota Press, 1987.

Den Otter, Sandra. 'Law, Authority, and Colonial Rule'. *India and the British Empire.* Eds. Douglas M. Peers and Nandini Gooptu. Oxford: Oxford University Press, 2012.

DiMaggio, Paul. 'Cultural Boundaries and Structural Change: The Extension of the High Culture Model to Theater, Opera, and the Dance, 1900–1940'. *Cultivating Differences: Symbolic Boundaries and the Making of Inequality.* Eds. Michèle Lamont and Marcel Fournier. Chicago, IL: University of Chicago Press, 1992, 21–67.

The Directory & Chronicle for China, Japan, Corea, Indo-China, Straits Settlements, Malay States, Siam, Netherlands India, Borneo, the Philippines, and etc. Hong Kong: Hong Kong Daily Press Office, 1910, 1920.

Dossal, Miriam. *Theatre of Conflict, City of Hope.* New Delhi: Oxford University Press, 2010.

Dwivedi, Sharada and Mehrotra Rahul. *Bombay: The Cities Within.* Bombay: India Book House, 1995.

Egypt: Karl Baedeker. Leipzig: Rpt. Elibron Classics, 1898.

Emirbayer, Mustafa and Jeff Goodwin. 'Network Analysis, Culture, and the Problem of Agency'. *American Journal of Sociology* 99(6) (1994): 1411–54.

Ewick, Patricia and Susan S. Silbey. *The Common Place of Law: Stories from Everyday Life, Language and Legal Discourse.* Chicago, IL: University of Chicago Press, 1998.

Ferguson, Niall. *The War of the World: Twentieth-Century Conflict and the Descent of the West.* New York: Penguin Press, 2006.

The Square and the Tower: Networks and Power, from the Freemasons to Facebook. New York: Penguin, 2018.

Fisher, Jennifer. 'The Swan Brand: Reframing the Legacy of Anna Pavlova'. *Dance Research Journal* 44(1) (2012): 51–67.

Freeman, Linton C. 'A Set of Measures of Centrality Based on Betweenness'. *Sociometry* 40 (1977): 35–41
'Centrality in Social Networks: Conceptual Clarification'. *Social Networks* 1 (1978/79): 215–39.

Frost, Mark Ravinder. 'Maritime Networks and the Colonial Public Sphere, 1840–1920'. *New Zealand Journal of Asian Studies* 6(2) (2004): 63–94.

Frost, Mark Ravinder and Yu-Mei Balasingamchow. *Singapore: A Biography.* Singapore: Editions Didier Millet, 2009.

Gänzl, Kurt. *The British Musical Theatre.* Vol. 1. Basingstoke: Macmillan, 1986.

Geyer, Michael and Charles Bright. 'World History in a Global Age'. *American Historical Review* 100 (1995): 1034–60.

Gooptu, Sharmistha. *Bengali Cinema: 'An Other Nation'.* London: Routledge, 2011.

Granovetter, Mark. 'The Strength of Weak Ties: A Network Theory Revisited'. *Sociological Theory* 1 (1983): 201–33.

Greenblatt, Stephen. *Cultural Mobility: A Manifesto*. Cambridge: Cambridge University Press, 2010.

Gupta, Somanatha. *The Parsi Theatre: Its Origins and Development*. Trans. Kathryn Hansen. Calcutta: Seagull Books, 2005.

Hall, N. John. *Max Beerbohm Caricatures*. New Haven, CT: Yale University Press, 1997.

Hammond, Mary. 'Hall Caine and the Melodrama on Page, Stage and Screen'. *Nineteenth Century Theatre and Film* 31 (2004): 39–57.

Hansard. (30 July 1925). Vol. 187, cc671 for a list of average earnings in 1920 and 1925.

Hansen, Kathryn. 'Stri Bhumika: Female Impersonators and Actresses on the Parsi Stage'. *Economic and Political Weekly* 33 (1998): 2291–300.

   'Parsi Theatre and the City: Locations, Patrons, Audiences'. *Sarai Reader 2002: The Cities of Everyday Life*. New Delhi: Centre for the Study of Developing Societies, 2002.

Haynes, Douglas E. *Rhetoric and Ritual in Colonial India: The Shaping of a Public Culture in Surat City, 1852–1928*. Berkeley, CA: University of California Press, 1991.

Hinckley, F. E. 'Extraterritoriality in China'. *The Annals of the American Academy of Political and Social Science*. Vol. 39, China: Social and Economic Conditions (1912), pp. 97–108.

Holloway, David. *Playing the Empire: The Acts of the Holloway Touring Theatre Company*. London: Harrap, 1979.

Howard, Tony. *Women as Hamlet: Performance and Interpretation in Theatre, Film and Literature*. Cambridge: Cambridge University Press, 2007.

Kelly, Veronica. *The Empire Actors: Stars of Australasian Costume Drama 1890s–1920s*. Sydney: Currency House, 2010.

Kendal, Felicity. *White Cargo*. London: Michael Joseph, 1998.

Kendal, Geoffrey. *The Shakespeare Wallah: The Autobiography of Geoffrey Kendal with Clare Colvin*. London: Sidgwick and Jackson, 1986.

Lang, Matheson. *Mr Wu Looks Back: Thoughts and Memories*. London: Stanley Paul, 1940.

Latour, Bruno. 'On Recalling ANT'. *Actor-Network Theory and After*. Eds. John Law and J. Hassard. Oxford: Blackwell, 1999, 15–26.

   Reassembling the Social: An Introduction to Actor-Network-Theory. Oxford: Oxford University Press, 2005.

Law, John. 'Actor Network Theory and Material Semiotics'. *The New Blackwell Companion to Social Theory*. Ed. Bryan S. Turner. Oxford: Blackwell, 2009, 141–58.

Leavitt, M. B. *Fifty Years in Theatrical Management*. New York: Broadway Publishing Co., 1912.

Lei, Daphne P. *Operatic China: Staging Chinese Identity across the Pacific*. New York: Palgrave Macmillan, 2006.

Leonhardt, Nic. '"From the Land of the White Elephant through the Gay Cities of Europe and America": Re-routing the World Tour of the Boosra Mahin Siamese Theatre Troupe (1900).' *Theatre Research International* 40(2) (2015): 140–55.

Liu, Siyuan. *Performing Hybridity in Colonial-Modern China, Palgrave Studies in Theatre and Performance History*. New York: Palgrave Macmillan, 2013.

Macpherson, Ben. *Cultural Identity in British Musical Theatre, 1890–1939: Knowing One's Place*. London: Palgrave Macmillan, 2018.

Masahiko, Masumoto. *Yokohama Geite-za*, 2nd ed. Yokohama: Iwasaki Hakubustukan Gēteza Kinen Shuppankyoku, 1986.

Mayer, David and Katherine K. Preston. *Playing Out the Empire: Ben-Hur and Other Toga Plays and Films, 1883–1908: A Critical Anthology*. Oxford: Clarendon Press, 1994.

McClellan, Michael E. 'Performing Empire: Opera in Colonial Hanoi'. *Journal of Musicological Research* 22 (2003): 135–66.

McKeown, Adam. 'Global Migration, 1846–1940'. *Journal of World History* 15 (2004): 155–89.

Money, Keith. *Anna Pavlova: Her Life and Art*. London: Collins, 1982.

Newey, Katherine. 'Feminist Historiography and Ethics: A Case Study from Victorian Britain'. *Theatre History and Historiography: Ethics, Evidence and Truth*. Ed. Claire Cochrane and Jo Robinson. Basingstoke: Palgrave, 2016, 85–102.

Nightbirds: A Musical Comedy in Three Acts. Libretto by Gladys Unger, lyrics by Arthur Anderson. Composed by Johann Strauss. London: Cranz & Co, n.d.

Nijhar, Preeti. *Law and Imperialism: Criminality and Constitution in Colonial India and Victorian England*. Vol. 10, Empires in Perspective. London: Pickering & Chatto, 2009.

Ocean Highways: Illustrated Souvenir of Elder, Dempster & Co. Liverpool: Shipping Gazette and Lloyd's List, 1902.

Osanai Kaoru, Osanai. 'Bandoman no tsuioku to inshô'. *Engekironshû* 4 (1914): 407–11. Translation by Stanca Scholz-Cionca.

O'Shea, Janet. *At Home in the World: Bharata Natyam on the Global Stage*. Middletown, CT: Wesleyan University Press, 2007.

'Peggy': New Musical Play in Two Acts. Book by George Grossmith Jr. (founded on Xanroff and Guerin's 'L'Amorcage'). Lyrics by C. H. Bovill. Music by Leslie Stuart. Vocal Score. London: Chappell & Co., 1911.

Pemberton, Edgar T. *The Birmingham Theatres: A Local Retrospect*. Birmingham: Cornish Brothers, 1890.

Phillips, Levi Damon. 'Uses of the Term "Manager" in 19th Century U.S. Theatre'. *Theatre Survey* 20(2) (1979): 62–3.

Platt, Len. *Musical Comedy on the West End Stage, 1890–1939*. Houndmills: Palgrave Macmillan, 2004.

Postlewait, Thomas. 'George Edwardes and Musical Comedy: The Transformation of London Theatre and Society, 1878–1914'. *The Performing Century: Nineteenth-Century Theatre's History*. Eds. Tracy C. Davis and Peter Holland. Basingstoke: Palgrave Macmillan, 2007, 80–102.

Pratt, Mary Louise. 'Arts of the Contact Zone'. *Profession 91*. New York: MLA, 1991, 33–40.

Reith, G. M. *Handbook to Singapore*. 2nd ed. [1907]. Reprint. Singapore: Oxford University Press, 1985.

Roberts, David. 'Writing the Ethical Life: Theatrical Biography and the Case of Thomas Betterton'. *Theatre History and Historiography: Ethics, Evidence and Truth*. Eds. Claire Cochrane and Jo Robinson. Basingstoke: Palgrave Macmillan, 2016, 33–47.

Roms, Heike. 'Mind the Gaps: Evidencing Performance and Performing Evidence in Performance Art History'. *Theatre History and Historiography: Ethics, Evidence and Truth*. Eds. Claire Cochrane and Jo Robinson. Basingstoke: Palgrave Macmillan, 2016, 163–81.

Rosen, Sherwin. 'The Economics of Superstars'. *American Economic Review* 71(5) (1981): 845–58.

Savran, David. 'Trafficking in Transnational Brands: The New "Broadway-Style" Musical'. *Theatre Survey* 55(3) (2014): 318–42.

Scholz-Cionca, Stanca and Nic Leonhardt. 'Circulation: Theatrical Mobility and its Professionalization in the Nineteenth Century'. *A Cultural History of Theatre in the Age of Empire*. Vol. 5. Ed. Peter W. Marx. London: Bloomsbury, 2017, 113–33.

Schweitzer, Marlis. *When Broadway Was the Runway: Theater, Fashion, and American Culture*. Philadelphia, PA: University of Pennsylvania Press, 2009.

Transatlantic Broadway: The Infrastructural Politics of Global Performance. Basingstoke: Palgrave Macmillan, 2015.

Sheppard, J. J. (ed.). *Territorials in India: A Souvenir of Their Historic Arrival for Military Duty in the 'Land of the Rupee'. From the Royal Opera House, Bombay. Prepared in Accordance with the Instructions of the Proprietor, J. F. Karaka.* Bombay: J. J. Sheppard, 1916.

Shope, Bradley G. *American Popular Music in Britain's Raj*. Rochester, NY: University of Rochester Press, 2016.

Silver, Christopher. *Planning the Megacity: Jakarta in the Twentieth Century*. London: Routledge, 2008.

Smith-Doerr, Laurel and Walter W. Powell. 'Networks and Economic Life'. *The Handbook of Economic Sociology*. Eds. Neil Smelser and Richard Swedberg. Princeton, NJ: Princeton University Press Russell Sage Foundation, 2005, 379–402.

Smither, Roger. '"A Wonderful Idea of the Fighting": The Question of Fakes in "The Battle of the Somme"'. *Historical Journal of Film, Radio and Television* 13(2) (1993): 149–69.

Taylor, Frederick Winslow. *Principles of Scientific Management*. New York: Harper & Brothers, [1911] 1919.

'Theatre and Music Hall Companies'. *The Stage Yearbook*. Ed. Lionel Carson. London: The Stage, 1917.

'Theatrical Touring in the Far East by One Who Has Tried It'. *The Stage Yearbook*. London: The Stage, 1917.

Tilly, Charles. 'Migration in Modern European History'. *Human Migration: Patterns and Policies*. Eds. W. H. McNeill and R. S. Adams. Bloomington, IN: Indiana University Press, 1978, 48–72.

Titmuss, R. M. 'Health'. *Law and Opinion in England in the 20th Century*. Ed. Morris Ginsberg. Berkeley, CA: University of California Press, 1959, 299–318.

Tögl, Gero. *The Bayreuth Enterprise 1848–1914*. Würzburg: Königshausen & Neumann, 2017.

Trocki, C. A. *Opium and Empire: Chinese Society in Colonial Singapore, 1800–1910*. New York: Cornell University Press, 1990.

Voicu, Ştefan-Valentin. 'Making the Family: Actors, Networks and the State'. *Journal of Comparative Research in Anthropology and Sociology* 3 (2012): 117–27.

Warnk, Holger. 'Faust Does Nusantara'. *Lost Times and Untold Tales from the Malay World*. Eds. Jan van der Putten and Mary Kilcline Cody. Singapore: NUS Press, 2009, 227–40.

Weller, Bernard. 'How to Protect a Play'. *The Stage Yearbook*. London: "The Stage" Offices, 1908, pp. 35–44.

Wells, Stanley and Gary Taylor (eds.). *The Complete Oxford Shakespeare*. Vol. 2. Oxford: Oxford University Press, 1987.

Wenzlhuemer, Roland. *Connecting the Nineteenth-Century World: The Telegraph and Globalization*. Cambridge: Cambridge University Press, 2013.

Wetherell, Charles. 'Historical Social Network Analysis'. *International Review of Social History* 43 (1998): 125–44.

Who Was Who in the Theatre: 1912–1976. A Biographical Dictionary of Actors, Actresses, Directors, Playwrights, and Producers of the English-Speaking Theatre. Detroit, MI: Gale Research, 1978.

Winder, G. M. 'Imagining Geography and Citizenship in the Networked Newspaper: "La Nación" Reports the Assassination at Sarajevo, 1914'. *Historical Social Research/Historische Sozialforschung*, Special Issue, 35(1) (2010): 140–66.

Woods, Philip. 'Film Propaganda in India, 1914–23'. *Historical Journal of Film, Radio and Television* 15(4) (1995): 543–53.

Yamomo, MeLê. *Theatre and Music in Manila and the Asia Pacific, 1869–1946: Sounding Modernities*. London: Palgrave Macmillan, 2018.

Yeh, Catherine Vance. *Shanghai Love: Courtesans, Intellectuals, and Entertainment Culture, 1850–1910*. Seattle, WA: University of Washington Press, 2006.

Newspapers and Serials

The Amrita Bazar Patrika, Calcutta
The Anaconda Standard
The Anglo-Argentine: An Illustrated Weekly, Buenos Aires
The Argus, Melbourne
Australian Town and Country Journal, Sydney
Bataviaasch nieuwsblad, Batavia, Dutch East Indies
Bell's Life in London and Sporting Chronicle
Berliner Tageblatt
The Bioscope
Bombay Gazette
Border Watch, Mount Gambier, Australia
The British Architect, London
The Bulletin
Burnley News, Burnley, Padiham

Ceylon Observer, Colombo
Cheshire Observer, Chester
Cheshire Observer and Chester, Birkenhead, Crewe and North Wales Times, Chester
The China Mail, Hong Kong
The Chronicle, Leigh
The Cobargo Chronicle
Daily Mail, London
The Daily Malta Chronicle
The Daily News, New York City
Dundee Advertiser
Dundee Evening Telegraph
Eastern Daily Mail and Straits Morning Advertiser, Singapore
Egyptian Gazette
The Empire, Calcutta
The Englishman, Calcutta
The Era, London
The Evening Telegraph and Post, Dundee
The Far East, Shanghai
The Friend of India, Calcutta
Gibraltar Chronicle
The Helena Independent, Helena, Montana
Homeward Mail from India, China and the East, London
Hong Kong Daily Press
Hull Daily Mail
The Indian Daily News, Mumbai
The Indian Express, Madras
The Japan Weekly Chronicle, Kobe
The Leader, Allahabad
Le Gaulois, Paris
Liverpool Daily Post
London and China Telegraph
London Evening Standard
Malaya Tribune, Kuala Lumpur
The Malta Times and the United Service Gazette
Manawatu Standard, Palmerston North
Manchester Courier and Lancashire General Advertizer
Mexican Herald, Mexico City
Mumbai Mirror
The New York Clipper
The New York Dramatic Mirror
New York Herald
The New York Times
The North-China Herald, Shanghai
The Nottingham Argus
Nottingham Evening Post
The Observer, London
Pall Mall Gazette, London

Play Pictorial, London
The Playgoer: An Illustrated Magazine of Dramatic Art, London
The Referee, London
The Referee, Sydney
Sheffield Daily Telegraph
Sheffield Independent
The Singapore Free Press and Mercantile Advertiser
The Sketch, London
Soerabaijasch handelsblad, Surabaya
South Australian Register, Adelaide
South China Morning Post, Hong Kong
The Stage Archive, London
The Statesman, Calcutta, Delhi
The Straits Times, Singapore
The Sydney Morning Herald
The Times, London
The Times of India, Mumbai
Weekly Sun, Singapore
The Westminster Budget, London
The Worcester Chronicle

Websites

Ancestry.com. www.ancestry.com. Last accessed 21 August 2018.
Colligan, Mimi. 'Tallis, Sir George (1869–1948)'. *Australian Dictionary of Biography*. National Centre of Biography, Australian National University. http://adb.anu.edu.au/biography/tallis-sir-george-8744/text15313. Last accessed 1 May 2018.
Collins Dictionary of Law. S.v. *Lex loci and lex fori*. https://legal-dictionary.thefreedictionary.com/lex+fori. Last accessed 22 August 2018.
Cressman, Darryl. *A Brief Overview of Actor-Network Theory: Punctualization, Heterogeneous Engineering & Translation*. www.sfu.ca/content/dam/sfu/cmns/research/centres/cprost/recentpapers/2009/0901.pdf. Last accessed 22 August 2018.
Famiglia Dalbagni. http://xoomer.virgilio.it/nuovopapiro/in_egitto_file/dalbagni_famiglia.htm. Last accessed 22 August 2018.
FamilySearch. www.familysearch.org. Last accessed 21 August 2018.
Findmypast.co.uk. www.findmypast.co.uk. Last accessed 21 August 2018.
Fletcher, Justice. *E. M. D. Cohen vs Allan Wilkie on 11 March, 1912*. Calcutta High Court. http://indiankanoon.org/doc/1026435/. Last accessed 6 November 2013.
Gehi, Reema. 'After a Gap of 23 Years, Opera House Will Reopen in October', *Mumbai Mirror*, 17 September 2016. www.mumbaimirror.indiatimes.com/mumbai/cover-story/Mumbais-Opera-House-to-finally-reopen-in-October/articleshow/54373881.cms. Last accessed 31 July 2018.
George, Muriel. www.murielgeorge.info/index/view/story/memoirs/id/13. Last accessed 22 August 2018.

Kikare, Arkash. *Remembering the 20th Century Theatre Impresario Who Built Mumbai's Iconic Opera House.* http://scroll.in/article/818739/remembering-the-20th-century-theatre-impresario-who-built-mumbais-iconic-opera-house. Last accessed 21 August 2018.

Madan Theatres Research Group. https://madantheatres.com. Last accessed 21 August 2018.

Nair, Supriva. *Opera around the Corner.* www.livemint.com/Leisure/VHH6Mo35YzYkGI1YooU57J/Opera-around-the-corner.html. Last accessed 31 July 2018.

Screening the Past. http://tlweb.latrobe.edu.au/humanities/screeningthepast/25/rose-of-rhodesia/parsons-1.html. Last accessed 21 August 2018.

Springfield, Maurice. *Hunting Opium and Other Scents.* Suffolk: Norfolk and Suffolk Publicity Services, 1966. www.earnshaw.com/sites/earnshaw.com/files/shanghai-ed-india/tales/library/opium/opium03.htm. Last accessed 21 August 2018.

Stagebeauty. www.stagebeauty.net/th-main.html. Last accessed 22 August 2018.

Stephen Lopez Career (with Maurice E. Bandmann). www.joydiv.org/familygoingback/career.htm.

Thulaja, Naidu Ratnala. *Opium and Its History in Singapore.* http://eresources.nlb.gov.sg/infopedia/articles/SIP_622_2004-12-16.html. Last accessed 21 August 2018.

Vanessa Lopez Family Archive. www.familygoingback.co.uk. Last accessed 30 August 2018.

Wood, Paul. *The History of Elder Dempster.* www.rakaia.co.uk/assets/elder-dempster-history-summary.pdf. Last accessed 21 August 2018.

Manuscripts

British Library Manuscripts
  Add MS 56627
  British India Office Wills & Probate L-AG-34-29-167
  India Office L/PJ/6 1424, 1465, 1493
  Letter to G. Herbert Thring, 16 May, 1912. Add 56627
  Lord Chamberlain's Collection, Add MS 53584, number 261, Add. MS. 65917 N, LC Plays 1911/7, No. 998
Gibraltar Government Archives (GGA)
  The Empire Theatre 1903–1918
  Special File, No. 24: Empire Theatre, Public Visitors and Brothels
Harvard Theatre Collection
HM Courts & Tribunals Service, Probate Search Service
Laurence Senelick Collection
Municipal City Council, Kolkata
  'Proposed additions to No.4, Chowringhee Place (Empire Theatre)'
National Archives of India (NAI)
  Commerce and Industry Department 1905–1920, Companies 1912–1916.
  Home Department 1916. Part B. nos. 416–420.

The National Archives, London (NAL)
  Board of Trade, BT 31/8984/66396
  Divorce Court Files J 77/570/17428, J 77/1832/7170
National Archives, Singapore (NAS)
  Singapore: Govt Printer, 1908), 10. National Archives of Singapore
  Singapore: Govt Printer, 1916), 74. National Archives of Singapore
  Singapore: Govt Printer, 1917), 5. National Archives of Singapore
  Singapore Municipal Reports
V&A Theatre & Performance Collections (V&ATP)
  D'Oyly Carte Archive, GB 71 THM/73/4/1
  Gaiety Theatre Co. Royalties Book
Vanessa Lopez Family Archive
University of Liverpool, Library
  D42/PR3/7/38
  D42/PR3/9/46/1

Index